Psychotherapy Research and Behavior Change

Master Lecturers

Annette M. Brodsky
Jerome D. Frank
Alan E. Kazdin
Michael J. Mahoney
Hans H. Strupp

Edited by
John H. Harvey
and Marjorie M. Parks

THE MASTER LECTURES

AMERICAN PSYCHOLOGICAL ASSOCIATION
WASHINGTON, D.C. 20036

Library of Congress Cataloguing in Publication Data
Main entry under title:
Psychotherapy research and behavior change
(Master lecture series; v.1)
1. Psychotherapy—Research—Congresses. 2. Behavior modification—Congresses.
I. Harvey, John H., 1943-. II. Parks, Marjorie M.
III. American Psychological Association. IV. Series.
RC 337.P77 616.89'14 82-1668

Copies may be ordered from:
Order Department
American Psychological Association
1200 Seventeenth Street, N.W.
Washington, D.C. 20036

Published by the American Psychological Association, Inc.,
1200 Seventeenth Street, N.W., Washington, D,C, 20036
 Reprinted February, 1989.

Printed in the United States of America.

CONTENTS

PREFACE

At its annual convention in 1974, the American Psychological Association introduced the Master Lecture Series, a series of lectures by outstanding scholars of psychology designed to provide a forum for the presentation of theory and research in basic scientific psychology. Each year five renowned scholars present lectures on topics of social and ethical importance and of broad interest to the profession. At the presentation, the audience is invited to participate in a discussion of these issues.

As one of the Association's most prestigious and significant activities, the series of lectures attracts large audiences. Indirectly the series reaches an even broader audience through the distribution of tapes of all lectures and of paper copies of selected presentations. This volume, *Psychotherapy Research and Behavior Change,* is the first in a series of bound volumes derived from the Master Lecture presentations.

The Master Lecture Series was initiated and organized by the Committee on Program Innovations of the Board of Convention Affairs. This committee sponsored the series from 1974 through 1976. When the Continuing Education Committee of the Education and Training Board was established in 1976, it was given responsibility for administering the Master Lecture Series beginning in 1977.

Titles for the Master Lecture Series have included the following:

Physiological Psychology (1974)
Developmental Psychology (1975)
Behavioral Control (1976)
Brain-Behavior Relationships (1977)
Psychology of Aging (1978)
Sex and Gender in Psychology (1979)
Cognitive Psychology (1980)
Psychotherapy Research and Behavior Change (1981)

In 1982, the title will be *Psychology and the Law,* and, in 1983, *Psychology and Health.*

Psychotherapy Research and Behavior Change

Presented at the 1981 APA Convention in Los Angeles, the lectures in this volume are the work of five leading scholars in clinical psychology—Jerome D. Frank, Hans H. Strupp, Michael J. Mahoney, Annette M. Brodsky, and Alan E. Kazdin. Each lecture probes the art and science of contemporary psychotherapy.

In the first three lectures, Frank, Strupp, and Mahoney provide general analyses of major issues involved in psychotherapy theory, research, and practice. More specific discussions by Brodsky and Kazdin follow. Brodsky discusses sex, race, and class issues in psychotherapy research; Kazdin discusses recent developments and limitations in the methodology of psychotherapy outcome research.

Two major themes are present in these lectures. The first is a recognition of major problems facing practitioners because of the diverse conceptual and methodological approaches that compose modern psychotherapeutic practice and research. Frank suggests that the present "bewildering array" of theories and techniques of psychotherapy may be viewed as variations of age-old procedures in psychological healing. Strupp contends that persistent misunderstandings in this field derive from a failure to appreciate psychotherapy as both a personal (involving a unique human relationship) and a technical (involving a particular therapeutic approach) enterprise. Mahoney argues for a broader conceptualization of psychotherapy with an emphasis upon its place in the fundamental processes of personal development and change. Brodsky focuses on the evidence about racism, sexism, and classism in psychotherapeutic practice and advocates a continued exploration of positive approaches in training therapists to deal with their biases. Kazdin analyzes some of the limits associated with existing psychotherapy research strategies and concludes that the field is on the right track to achieve significant methodological advances but that "the journey will be longer than originally thought."

The second major theme is an emphasis upon the human qualities of the interaction between therapist and patient. Frank stresses the healing nature of the "emotionally-charged, confiding relationship with a helping person" in the context of a healing setting, rationale, and script for change. Relatedly, Strupp reminds us of Harry Stack Sullivan's famous postulate that we are all much more simply human than otherwise. He also discusses Sigmund Freud's view that psychotherapy bears a closer relationship to the teacher-student model than it does to the therapist-patient model and that, within this tutorial model, an active collaborative interaction is most conducive to healing. From philosophical and logical positivist perspectives, Mahoney emphasizes the active participation of humans in the creation or change of meaning in their lives in general, not merely in the context of therapy. Brodsky focuses on the often-neglected but potent variables of sex, race, and class as determinants of the success of psychotherapy. While Kazdin's methodological analysis does not specifically treat these substantive issues surrounding the therapist-patient relationship, it deals extensively with issues of the ways investigators can take a more finely grained, long-term approach in examining components of that relationship.

There is a definite critical thrust to these analyses, and the authors do not hesitate to question those elements in research and practice that they feel are problems in and disservices to the field. Mixed with this questioning attitude, however, is a note of optimism about what can be done to address and possibly to solve the problems. Moreover, each lecture itself is an expression of faith in the capacity of psychotherapy to advance through an uncompromising examination of its most deep-seated values and shibboleths.

Psychotherapy Research and Behavior Change represents a unique contribution to the field because of the authors' insightful analyses of central problems that require attention if psychotherapy theory, research, and practice are to continue to develop and prosper. The volume should appeal to all of those—scholars, professional practitioners, beginning students, and nonpsychologists—who wish to stay informed about current issues in psychotherapy.

We are indebted to the Continuing Education Committee, which included Leonard Bickman, Ursula Delworth, Cynthia Deutsch, Irene Goldenberg, Joseph Hasazi, Beth Sulzer-Azaroff, and Carl Thoresen, for the careful planning that led to the development of this volume. Furthermore, we thank our contributors whose diligence in submitting virtually finished first drafts allowed timely publication. Their cooperation and thoughtfulness is much appreciated. Finally, we are grateful to Rosemary Beiermann and Eleanor Fuller of the staff of the Educational Affairs office who provided major assistance in preparing this volume and to Brenda Bryant, APA's Manager of Special Publications, who provided valuable editorial commentary.

John H. Harvey
Marjorie M. Parks

JEROME D. FRANK

THERAPEUTIC COMPONENTS SHARED BY ALL PSYCHOTHERAPIES

JEROME D. FRANK

Udel & Solomon

Jerome D. Frank, professor emeritus of psychiatry at Johns Hopkins School of Medicine, received his doctorates in psychology (1934) and in medicine (1939) from Harvard University and his psychiatric training at the Henry Phipps Psychiatric Clinic of the Johns Hopkins Hospital. He has held faculty positions at Johns Hopkins University School of Medicine since 1949 and has devoted his professional career to the practice, teaching, and study of psychotherapy.

Frank has authored or coauthored over 200 journal articles and five books including *Persuasion and Healing: A Comparative Study of Psychotherapy* (1973), *Effective Ingredients of Successful Psychotherapy* (1978), and *Psychotherapy and the Human Predicament* (1978). The first is one of the best known works in the field of clinical psychology.

Frank is a fellow of many professional organizations, including the American Psychological Association, the American Psychiatric Association, and the American College of Psychiatrists, and is an active member of others. He is past president of the Society for the Psychological Study of Social Issues and of the American Psychopathological Association.

Frank has received honorary lectureships and professorships in universities throughout the world. His many honors and awards include the 1972 Kurt Lewin Memorial Award of the Society for the Psychological Study of Social Issues, the Special Research Award of the Society for Psychotherapy Research in 1981, and the McAlpin Research Achievement Award of the National Mental Health Association in 1981.

JEROME D. FRANK

THERAPEUTIC COMPONENTS SHARED BY ALL PSYCHOTHERAPIES

The field of psychotherapy in the United States has presented a bewildering array of theories and techniques, accompanied by a deafening cacophony of rival claims. A recent comprehensive review of the field requires over 250 pages simply to describe extant approaches (Wolberg, 1977). Now, however, observers are beginning to detect increasing signs that representatives of different schools are willing to acknowledge the potential value of a range of techniques and to show increasing flexibility in applying them (Goldfried & Padawer, in press).

These stirrings of rapprochement reflect a growing recognition that all psychotherapeutic procedures share certain healing components which account for a considerable proportion of their effectiveness, so that practitioners of different schools may usefully learn from each other. In order to contribute to this welcome development, in this paper I shall consider healing components mobilized by all forms of psychotherapy and the ways these components may work.

All psychotherapeutic methods are elaborations and variations of age-old procedures of psychological healing. These include confession, atonement and absolution, encouragement, positive and negative reinforcements, modeling, and promulgation of a particular set of values. These methods become embedded in theories as to the causes and cures of various conditions which often become highly elaborated.

In view of their use of time-tested healing procedures, it is not surprising that all psychotherapies have many features in common. Those features which distinguish them from each other, however, receive special emphasis in the pluralistic, competitive American society. Since the prestige and the financial security of psychotherapists depend to a considerable extent on their being able to show that their particular theory and method is more successful than that of their rivals, they inevitably emphasize their differences; and each therapist attributes his or her successes to those conceptual and procedural features that distinguish that theory and method from its competitors rather than to the features that all share.

Let me now offer a definition of psychotherapy that is sufficiently broad to include everything that goes by that term but excludes informal help from relatives, friends, and bartenders. Psychotherapy is a planned, emotionally charged, confiding interaction between a trained, socially sanctioned healer and a sufferer. During this interaction the healer seeks to relieve the sufferer's distress and disability through symbolic communications, primarily words but also sometimes bodily activities. The healer may or may not involve the patient's relatives and others in the healing rituals. Psychotherapy also often includes helping the patient to accept and endure suffering as an inevitable aspect of life that can be used as an opportunity for personal growth.

Distinguishing Features of Psychotherapy

Before proceeding further, let us pause briefly to consider the features that distinguish psychotherapy thus defined from other forms of giving and receiving help. The psychotherapist has credentials as a healer. These are provided by society at large in the form of licensure or other official recognition. The therapist has earned this recognition by having undergone special training, usually prolonged, which entitles him or her to the status symbol of an academic degree. Therapists lacking such generally recognized credentials are sanctioned by the particular sect or cult they represent. Persons who go to them thereby imply that they accept the validity of these sanctions.

It is assumed that, whatever his or her credentials, the therapist is not attempting to gratify any personal needs or make any personal emotional demands on the patient. Nor need the patient guard his own responses for fear of hurting the therapist. In these respects the therapist differs fundamentally from family members or friends. Finally, psychotherapeutic procedures, in contrast to informal help, are guided by conceptual schemes which prescribe specific rituals.

In different societies, psychotherapy reflects not only a society's conceptualizations of illness and health but also its values. In American psychotherapy, for example, patient and therapist are generally required to work at some form of mutual activity to justify their spending time together, and increased autonomy is regarded as an important feature of mental health. Hindus find these attitudes astonishing. For them, simply being together is a worthwhile end in itself, and dependency on others is a valued feature of life (Pande, 1968; Neki, 1973).

An aspect of the American world view shared by most psychotherapists is the high prestige accorded to science. As a result, psychotherapists of most schools, from psychoanalysis to behavior modification, claim that their procedures are grounded on scientific evidence. The extent to which psychotherapists view themselves as applied scientists, or at least wish to be seen as such, was brought home to me many years ago at a conference attended by leading exponents of different psychotherapeutic schools. Each speaker introduced his or her presentation by a genuflection toward science. One showed kymographic tracings, another referred to work on rats, and a third displayed anatomical charts—all of which had only tenuous relevance to the therapies they were presenting.

The scientific world view assumes that man is part of the animal kingdom which, like all of nature, is ruled by natural laws. Human behavior, thinking, and feeling are determined and constrained by genetic endowment, biologically based needs, and the effects of beneficial and harmful environmental influences. Therapy consists of the application of special techniques to combat maladaptive patterns and encourage more appropriate ones.

The American psychotherapeutic scene also includes a minority but influential viewpoint, termed humanist or existential, that rejects the scientific view of man. According to this view, the essence of being human is the right and the capacity for self-determination, guided by purposes, values, and options. Out of our free will we can give our lives meaning even in the face of inevitable death. The essence of therapy is a particular kind of relationship, the "encounter," which cannot be objectively described. Existential-humanist therapists describe what they do in such terms as "relating to the patient as one existence communicating with another," or "entering the world of the patient with reverent love," or "merging with the patient." Through this total acceptance, the patient comes to value his or her own uniqueness, becomes free to exert choice, to make commitments, and to find a meaning in life (Seguin, 1965).

A basic assumption of all psychotherapies is that humans react to their interpretation of events, which may not correspond to events as they are in reality. All psychotherapies, therefore, try to alter favorably patients' views of themselves, their relations with others, and their system of values. To this extent psychotherapies resemble both religion (Szasz, 1978) and rhetoric. To enhance their credibility, psychotherapists try to project the same personal qualities as rhetoricians, such as perceived expertness, trustworthiness and attractiveness; and they use many of the same rhetorical devices, such as metaphors and sensory images, to focus the patients' attention "on ideas central to the therapeutic message and . . . [make them] appear more . . . believable" (Glaser, 1980, p. 331; see also Frank, 1980).

Psychotherapy also has analogies to other arts, music, for example. Like the practitioner of any art, the psychotherapist must master a certain amount of scientific and technical information, but this mastery takes one only so far. For example, a composer or performer must know something of the rules of harmony and of the physical principles of pitch and volume, but the application of scientific method will never be able to explain a Mozart or to determine whether the music of Cole Porter is better than that of Richard Rodgers. To be sure, one can analyze their songs in terms of patterns of harmony, pitch, and volume and administer any number of rating scales to cohorts of listeners; but this information casts little, if any, light on the nature of their aesthetic impact. To the extent that the analogy is valid, determining scientifically whether, let us say, Gestalt therapy is preferable to Transactional Analysis should prove equally futile.

Limitations of Research

A brief consideration of the limitations of research in psychotherapy may not be inappropriate as a general introduction in the first of a lecture series entitled "Psychotherapy Research and Behavior Change." An authority on research in psychology has recently concluded that "psychology is . . . a collectivity of studies of various cast, some few of which may qualify as science, while most do not. . . . Extensive and important sectors of psychological study require modes of inquiry rather more like those of the humanities than the sciences" (Koch, 1981, pp. 268–269).

One of these important sectors is psychotherapy, which presents special difficulties to the researcher. These difficulties permit only modest hopes as to the extent to which application of the scientific method will lead to insights that will improve psychotherapies.

As mentioned earlier, a general problem which plagues all psychological experiments is that humans respond to their interpretations of situations and the subject's interpretation of the experimental situation may differ strikingly from the one that the experimenter thinks has been created (Orne, 1969). Thus the experimental findings may reflect the subject's efforts to comply with what he or she thinks the experimenter wants rather than reflecting a response to the experimental conditions. In psychotherapy this problem is aggravated because the patient typically experiences strong "evaluation apprehension," which has been shown to increase a psychological subject's susceptibility to influence by the experimenter's unspoken expectations (Rosenberg, 1969). In psychotherapy, the patient depends on the therapist for relief, which would be expected to enhance this susceptibility. Therefore, it is particularly difficult to disentangle how much of a patient's apparent response to psychotherapy is an effort to meet the therapist's expectations.

Psychotherapy is just one more influence operating briefly and intermittently on the patient in the context of his ongoing life experiences. At best psychotherapeutic interviews represent only infrequent, intermittent, brief personal contacts wedged in among innumerable others. What goes on between sessions may be more important in determining outcome than what occurs during sessions. Also psychotherapy and ongoing life experiences may interact in complex ways because a change in the patient's outlook or behavior brought about by psychotherapy inevitably affects the attitudes of others toward him and these attitudes may reinforce or counteract the changes induced by therapy. Mere acceptance of the patient for psychiatric treatment, for example, may lead family members to change their view of the individual from a person who is lazy or bad to one who is sick, with corresponding favorable changes in their attitudes toward the patient. Conversely, if the patient's symptoms or deviant behaviors contribute to the equilibrium of the family, losing these symptoms or behaviors might lead other family members to sabotage treatment. Thus it may be difficult to assess the relative extent to which patients' changes during psychotherapy are attributable to the treatment itself, to factors outside it, and to the interaction between treatment and outside factors.

At a more fundamental level, some important experiences in psychotherapy may in principle be unamenable to scientific study because they occur in altered states of consciousness, in ways not accessible to the senses, and in levels of reality differing from the everyday one (Smith, 1977; LeShan, 1974).

When we return from this uncomfortable line of thought to more familiar ground, we find that psychotherapy research bristles with practical difficulties such as the dearth of suitable patients and experienced therapists, inadequate ways of classifying patients and describing therapies, and problems of measuring outcome. These difficulties create an often irresistible temptation to choose research problems on the basis of methodological simplicity rather than on that of intrinsic interest.

Finally, motivational problems, especially in therapists, create difficulties. Not only are therapists' personal and financial security and status wrapped up in the success of their methods, but much of their success may depend on personal qualities. So therapists are understandably reluctant to submit themselves to investigations which could reveal that they have attributes which militate against therapeutic success. Such a finding could be devastating not only to their pocketbooks but also to their self-esteem.

All in all, it is no wonder that, despite the outstanding ability of many researchers in psychotherapy, findings by and large have been tentative and disappointing. Reviews of psychotherapy research studies characteristically bemoan their lack of impact on practice and conclude with comments on their inadequacies and the need for further research.

Actually, my impression is that most innovative psychotherapeutic procedures are really derived from clinical experience and the discoverer then seeks to support them by laboratory analogies. The great 19th-century German psychiatrist, Emil Kraepelin, for example, described his treatment for "dread neurosis"—what we would call "generalized anxiety disorder"—in terms that could easily be translated into a combination of reciprocal inhibition and operant conditioning (Diefendorf, 1915, p. 400).

Perhaps the greatest contribution of the scientific method is that it requires the experimenter to take negative findings seriously. As a result, the scientific study of psychotherapy has performed a useful function by rescuing common sense from the clutches of dogmatic theories. A good example of such a rescue has been the overemphasis on unconscious processes by certain schools and the insistence by others that subjective symbolic processes are irrelevant, both of which have had to yield to scientific evidence that conscious cognitive processes are important features of human functioning—a blatant truism, one might say, but one that certain people have been reluctant to accept.

The preceding discussion is by way of justifying that in this presentation, although I shall cite research findings as far as possible, I shamelessly admit that my conclusions are based at least as much on reflection about my own and others' clinical experience as they are on experiments. Research findings are offered as illustrations of points rather than as proofs of their validity.

Generalizations About Outcomes of Psychotherapies

To open the discussion of therapeutic features common to all types of psychotherapy, let me briefly state four generalizations that are relatively firmly established. The first is that patients who receive any form of psychotherapy do somewhat better than controls observed over the same period of time who have received no formal psychotherapy, which does not, of course, exclude their having benefited from informal helping contacts with others (Smith, Glass, & Miller, 1980; Sloane, Staples, Cristol, Yorkston, & Whipple, 1975). Second, follow-up studies seem to show consistently that, whatever the form of therapy, most patients who show initial improvement maintain it (Liberman, B. L., 1978b). Moreover, when two therapies yield differences in outcome at the close of treatment, with rare exceptions these differences disappear over time, and the closing of the gap seems to depend more on patients who receive the less successful therapy catching up than on both groups regressing equally toward the mean (Gelder, Marks, & Wolff, 1967; Liberman, B. L., 1978b). This result suggests that the main beneficial effect of psychotherapy with many patients may be to accelerate improvement that would have occurred eventually in any case. Third, more of the determinants of therapeutic success lie in the personal qualities of and the interaction between patient and therapist than in the particular therapeutic method used. Finally, there are a few conditions in which the therapeutic method does make a significant difference in outcome. Behavior therapies seem to be somewhat more effective for phobias, compulsions, and obesity and sexual problems than are less focused therapies.

Of particular interest from the standpoint of the hypothesis to be offered presently is that cognitive therapy, which seeks to combat negative cognitions about oneself, the future, and one's relationships with other people, seems particularly effective with depressed patients (Rush, Beck, Kovacs, & Hollon, 1977). The efficacy of all procedures, however, depends on the establishment of a good therapeutic relationship between the patient and the therapist. No method works in the absence of this relationship.

With increasing refinement of categorization of patients and their symptom pictures, more precise delineation of therapies, and more differentiated measures of outcome, further advantages of specific therapies for specific conditions may yet be found. It does seem safe to conclude, however, that features shared by all therapies account for an appreciable amount of the improvement observed in most psychiatric patients who respond at all (Frank, 1973).

Demoralization Hypothesis

If the preceding conclusion is so, patients, whatever their symptoms, must share a type of distress that responds to the components common to all schools of psychotherapy. A plausible hypothesis is that patients seek psychotherapy not for symptoms alone, but for symptoms coupled with demoralization, a state of mind characterized by one or more of the following: subjective incompetence, loss of self-esteem, alienation, hopelessness (feeling that no one can help), or helplessness (feeling that other people could help but will not). These states of mind are often aggravated by cognitive unclarity as to the meaning and seriousness of the symptoms, not uncommonly accompanied by a sense of loss of control, leading to a fear of going crazy.

Demoralization occurs when, because of lack of certain skills or confusion of goals, an individual becomes persistently unable to master situations which both the individual and others expect him or her to handle or when the individual experiences continued distress which he or she cannot adequately explain or alleviate. Demoralization may be summed up as a feeling of subjective incompetence, coupled with distress (Frank, 1974; deFigueiredo & Frank, Note 1).

One must add that not all demoralized people get into treatment and not all patients in psychotherapy are demoralized. Sometimes patients are brought to treatment not because they are demoralized, but because people around them are: for example, the parents of sociopaths or the spouses of alcoholics. This mention of alcoholics is a reminder that some people, such as skid row alcoholics, are too demoralized even to seek help. Finally, of course, a small proportion of patients seek treatment for specific symptoms without otherwise being demoralized because they have heard that behavior therapy will cure their phobia of heights.

The most common symptoms of demoralization presented by patients in psychotherapy are subjective or behavioral manifestations, such as, on the one hand, anxiety, depression, loneliness, or, on the other, conflict with significant persons, such as spouse, boss, or children. Anxiety and depression or loss of self-esteem are the symptoms most common among psychiatric outpatients and most responsive to treatment (Smith, Glass, & Miller, 1980).

Whatever their source or nature, all symptoms interact with demoralization in various ways. They reduce a person's coping capacity, predisposing the individual to demoralizing failures. Whether the symptom be schizophrenic thought disorder, reactive depression, or obsessional ritual, it may cause the patient to be defeated by problems of living that asymptomatic persons handle with ease. Furthermore, to the extent that the patient believes them to be unique, psychiatric symptoms contribute to demoralization by heightening feelings of alienation. Finally, symptoms wax and wane with the degree of demoralization; thus schizophrenics' thinking becomes more disorganized when they are anxious, and obsessions and compulsions become worse when the patients are depressed.

Most patients present themselves with specific symptoms, and both they and their therapists assume that psychotherapy is aimed primarily at relieving these. Such patients do indeed exist, but for the great bulk, I suggest, much of the improvement resulting from any form of psychotherapy lies in its ability to restore the patient's morale, with the resulting diminution or disappearance of symptoms. One must add, of course, that alleviation of the patient's symptoms may be the best way to restore morale.

Indirect evidence for the demoralization hypothesis comes from several sources. One source consists of studies comparing cohorts of persons who seek or have sought psychotherapy with those who have not. Studies of college students (Galassi & Galassi, 1973), alumni out of college for 25 years (Vaillant, 1972), and ordinary citizens in England and America (Kellner & Sheffield, 1973) showed that the treated had a higher incidence or greater severity of social isolation, helplessness, or sense of failure or unworthiness—all symptoms of demoralization—than the untreated.

The strongest empirical support has been supplied by the surveys of Bruce and Barbara Dohrenwend, who have devised a set of scales to determine the extent of psychiatric symptoms and clinical impairment in the general population (Dohrenwend, Shrout, Egri, & Mendlsohn, 1980). To their surprise, they found that eight of their scales correlated as highly with each other as their internal reliabilities would permit; that is, they all seemed to measure a single dimension. These scales included features of demoralization such as anxiety, sadness, hopelessness, and low self-esteem (Dohrenwend, Oksenberg, Shrout, Dohrenwend, & Cook, in press). About one fourth of the persons in the population they surveyed were estimated to be demoralized according to this criterion. Of these about one half were also clinically impaired (Link & Dohrenwend, 1980). The finding most supportive of the hypothesis was that about four fifths of clinically impaired outpatients scored above the cut-off point on a scale that later was found to correlate above 0.90 with the demoralization scales (Dohrenwend & Crandall, 1970).

Surveys of reported emotional distress and presence or absence of supportive social networks provide further indirect evidence for the demoralization hypothesis. A general population survey found that persons who possess such a network are much less likely to be distressed by severe environmental stresses than those who are not so supported (Henderson, Byrne, & Duncan-Jones, 1981). In response to a similar survey, members who had joined a religious cult reported a sharp decline in anxiety, depression, and general emotional problems and attributed this decline primarily to emotional support from all the group members (Galanter, 1978). Apparently emotional support from others protects individuals from demoralization.

Quite different indirect support for the demoralization hypothesis is that many patients come to psychotherapy only after other forms of relief have failed. At least this inference seems justified by the finding in one setting that patients did not appear until 6 months to 2 years after their symptoms first appeared (Karasu, Note 2). A study of college students' use of a university's psychological services similarly found that "the decision to actually use psychotherapy was likely to come only after ineffective attempts to cope with the problem one's self or with the help of a close friend or relative" (Farber & Geller, 1977, p. 306).

That demoralization may account for the emergence of specific symptoms in the course of psychoanalysis is suggested by a detailed content analysis of psychoanalytic sessions which showed that complaints of migraine headaches were reported in a context of lack of self-control, hopelessness, and helplessness, and stomach pains in a context of helplessness and anxiety (Luborsky & Auerbach, 1969).

Further indirect support for the demoralization hypothesis is that many patients improve very quickly in therapy, suggesting that their favorable response is to the reassuring aspects of the therapeutic situation itself rather than to the particular procedure. In clinic settings the mean number of therapeutic interviews is between five and six (Garfield, 1978, pp. 195–197). This finding is usually interpreted to mean that many patients who are in need of psychotherapy reject it. Undoubtedly this interpretation is true of some. Others, however, probably stop because they have obtained sufficient symptom relief and no longer feel the need to continue. Unfortunately, patients who drop out of therapy early are not usually called back for reassessment. In one study which did call them back, the average symptomatic relief was found to be just as great in those who dropped out before their fourth session as in those who had received 6 months of therapy (Frank, Gliedman, Imber, Stone, & Nash, 1959).

A finding with the same implications is that about three fourths of psychiatric outpatients on a waiting list for 4 months were rated as improved. During this period, their only contact was an occasional telephone call from a research associate to ensure that they would wait for the assigned treatment (Sloane et al, 1975). Apparently some patients gain relief from any contact in a therapeutic setting, probably because they perceive the contact as therapy.

Shared Therapeutic Components

Turning at last to the shared therapeutic components of all forms of psychotherapy, we find that most forms can be viewed as means of directly or indirectly combating demoralization. The list which follows, with minor variations, is similar to those components propounded by many therapists (Goldfried & Padawer, in press; Marmor, 1976; Rosenzweig, 1936).

1. *An emotionally charged, confiding relationship with a helping person,* often with the participation of a group. With some possible minor exceptions, the relationship with the therapist is a necessary, and perhaps often a sufficient, condition for improvement in any kind of psychotherapy (Rogers, 1957). As Sloane et al. (1975, p. 225) found, "Successful patients rated the personal interaction with the therapist as the single most important part of their treatment."

Especially thought provoking in this connection is the finding that male college students in time-limited psychotherapy experienced as much improvement, on the average, when treated by college professors chosen for their ability to form understanding relationships as when treated by highly experienced psychotherapists (Strupp & Hadley, 1979).

Patients let themselves become dependent on the therapist for help because of their confidence in the therapist's competence and good will. This dependence is reinforced by the patient's knowledge of the therapist's training, by the setting of treatment, and by the congruence of the therapist's approach with the patient's expectations. While the therapist's status or reputation in the patient's eyes may initially determine the therapist's ascendency, success of therapy depends on the therapist's ability to convey to the patient that the therapist cares about the patient, is competent to help, and has no ulterior motives (Gurman, 1977)—an attitude summed up by one eminent psychotherapist by the term "therapeutic Eros" (Seguin, 1965).

2. *A healing setting,* which has at least two therapeutic functions in itself. First, it heightens the therapist's prestige and strengthens the patient's expectation of help by symbolizing the therapist's role as a healer, whether the setting is a clinic in a prestigious hospital or a private office complete with bookshelves, impressive desk, couch, and easy chair. Often the setting also contains evidences of the therapist's train-

ing, such as diplomas and pictures of his or her teachers. Second, the setting provides safety. Surrounded by its walls, patients know they can let themselves go within wide limits, dare to reveal aspects of themselves that they have concealed from others, and discuss various alternatives for future behavior without commitment and without any consequences outside the office.

3. *A rationale, conceptual scheme, or myth* that provides a plausible explanation for the patient's symptoms and prescribes a ritual or procedure for resolving them.

4. *A ritual* that requires active participation of both patient and therapist and that is believed by both to be the means of restoring the patient's health.

The words "myth" and "ritual" are used advisedly to emphasize that, although typically expressed in scientific terms, therapeutic rationales and procedures cannot be disproved. Successes are taken as proof of their validity, often erroneously, while failures are explained away. "No form of therapy has ever been initiated without a claim that it had unique therapeutic advantages. And no form of therapy has ever been abandoned because of its failure to live up to these claims" (M. B. Parloff quoted in Hilts, 1980). To my knowledge, no therapeutic school has ever disbanded because it concluded that another's doctrine and method was superior.

An often overlooked function of therapeutic rituals is to provide a face-saving excuse for the patient to abandon a symptom or complaint when ready to do so. To relinquish a symptom without an adequate external reason would carry the implication that it was trivial or that the patient had produced it for some ulterior motive. The more spectacular the ritual, the greater its usefulness from the individual's standpoint. This circumstance necessitates caution in attributing remission of a symptom to a particular maneuver. The patient might have been ready to relinquish the symptom for other reasons, and the role of the procedure may simply have been to serve as the occasion for doing so.

Functions of Myth and Ritual

All therapeutic myths and rituals, irrespective of differences in specific content, have in common functions that combat demoralization by strengthening the therapeutic relationship, inspiring expectations of help, providing new learning experiences, arousing the patient emotionally, enhancing sense of mastery or self-efficacy, and affording opportunities for rehearsal and practice. Let us consider each of these briefly in turn.

1. *Strengthening the therapeutic relationship, thereby combating the patient's sense of alienation.* A shared belief system is essential to the formation and maintenance of groups, so the adherence of therapist and patient to the same therapeutic myth creates a powerful bond between them. Within this context, the therapist's continued acceptance of the patient after the patient has "confessed" combats the latter's demoralizing feelings of alienation, especially if, as is usually the case, the therapist represents a group. The ritual serves to maintain the patient-therapist bond, especially over stretches when nothing much seems to be happening. By giving patient and therapist something to do together, the ritual sustains mutual interest. The chief problem of Strupp's kindly college professors (Strupp & Hadley, 1979) was that they sometimes ran out of things to talk about, a predicament never reported by the experienced therapists.

2. *Inspiring and maintaining the patient's expectation of help.* By inspiring expectations of help, myths and rituals not only keep the patient coming to treatment but also may be powerful morale builders and symptom relievers in themselves (Friedman, 1963; Jacobson, 1968; Uhlenhuth & Duncan, 1968). The arousal of hope may also account for the findings in several studies that "the best predictor of later benefits is . . . expectations of early benefits expressed in the early sessions" (Luborsky, 1976, p. 107).

Several colleagues and I were put on the track of the importance of positive expectations in the relief of symptoms by the results of our first study of psychotherapy. In this study we compared the effects on symptoms and social behavior of 6 months of one of three forms of psychotherapy: group therapy, individual therapy once a week, or minimal contact treatment not more than one-half hour every 2 weeks. We found that patients in all three therapies showed equal symptom reduction on the average, but so did those who had dropped out of treatment within the first four interviews (Frank et al, 1959). Symptom reduction, therefore, seemed in large part a response to the hope of relief engendered by being offered treatment. We decided to explore this theory by studying the effects of placebos on psychiatric symptoms, since this effect must depend solely on arousing the patient's positive expectations through administering an inert medication which symbolizes the physician's role (Frank, Nash, Stone, & Imber, 1963).

The experiment called for research personnel to administer a discomfort scale, followed by a half-hour series of tests aimed at discovering personality attributes related to placebo responsiveness. Then the discomfort scale was readministered, and it was followed by an administration of the placebo. After another half hour, during which the placebo was given time to "work" and the patient received additional tests, the discomfort scale was again administered. The patients were kept on the placebo for 2 weeks, the discomfort scale being administered at the end of each week, and then the placebo was discontinued. Figure 1 illustrates the findings. We can see that the biggest drop in discomfort occurred before the administration of the placebo, that the reduction in discomfort was largely maintained at 1 and 2 weeks and, for those patients whom we were able to recall after 3 years, the average discomfort was still lower than it was at the time of admission to treatment.

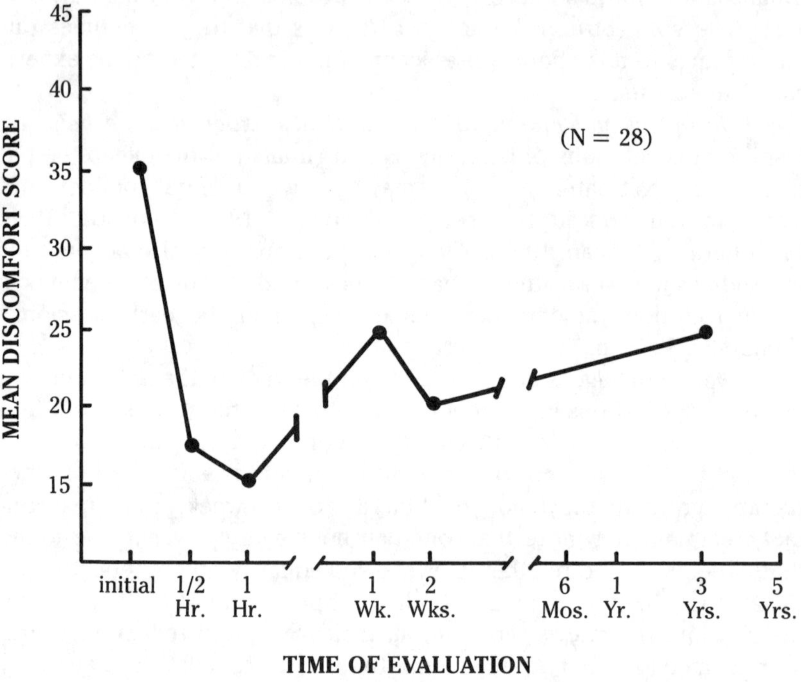

Figure 1. Changes in mean discomfort over time following administration of placebo. Placebo administered at the half hour. From *Effective Ingredients of Successful Psychotherapy* by J. D. Frank, R. Hoehn-Saric, S. D. Imber, B. L. Liberman, and A. R. Stone. Reprinted by permission.

A comparison of symptom reduction by psychotherapy and by placebo is illustrated in Figure 2, which portrays the findings from two groups of patients, one of which had initially received a placebo and the other 6 months of psychotherapy, who were recalled after 3 years because of some recurrence of symptoms. At this point, both groups received a placebo and their discomfort level was checked 1 or 2 weeks later. You will note that the initial average drop in discomfort was virtually identical after 6 months of psychotherapy and after the administration of a placebo for a week. On being given a placebo 3 years later,

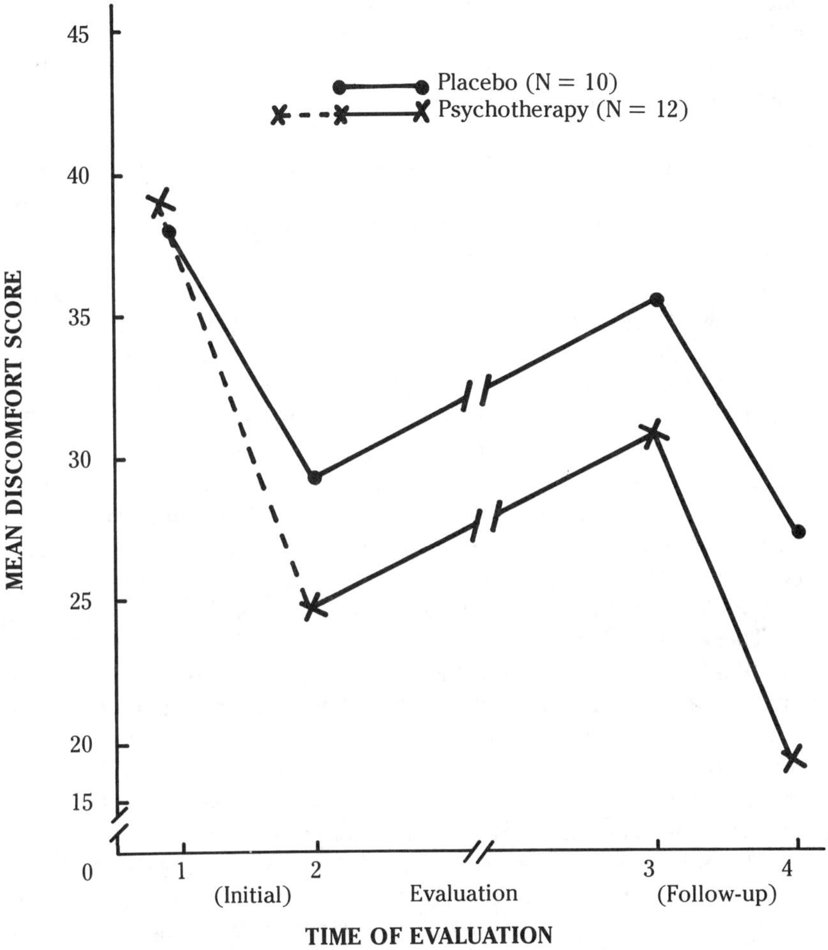

Figure 2. Reduction in mean discomfort following placebo and psychotherapy. Interval between 1 and 2 is one week in the placebo study, 6 months in the psychotherapy study. Interval between 2 and 3 is 3 years in both studies. Interval between 3 and 4 is one week in the placebo study, 2 weeks in the psychotherapy study. From *Effective Ingredients of Successful Psychotherapy* by J. D. Frank, R. Hoehn-Saric, S. D. Imber, B. L. Liberman, and A. R. Stone. Reprinted by permission.

both groups showed the same average drop, which was the same as the initial drop in discomfort with 6 months of psychotherapy.

An important point is that, although the mean drop in discomfort was the same after 3 years as it was initially, the responses of individual patients on the two occasions were widely different. Some responded the first time and not the second, and vice versa. This finding is evidence that responsiveness to placebos depends not so much on a personal trait as on the interaction of the immediate state of the patient with factors in the environment, an observation that has been confirmed by other studies (Liberman, R., 1964).

The response after 3 years also rules out a possible interpretation of the very rapid relief of discomfort with the initial placebo group, namely that their initial mean discomfort score was artificially heightened by their apprehension as to what was to transpire. Although this apprehension may have had some effect, it could not explain all of the drop, since it would not operate with patients who 3 years previously had received, and therefore were familiar with, psychotherapy.

To be therapeutically effective, hope for improvement must be linked in the patient's mind to specific processes of therapy as well as outcome (Imber, Pande, Frank, Hoehn-Saric, Stone, & Wargo, 1970; Wilkins, 1979). This link could be taken for granted by purveyors of traditional therapies like psychoanalysis because most patients came to them already familiarized with their procedures (Kadushin, 1969). Introducers of new or unfamiliar therapies regularly spend considerable time and effort at the start teaching the patient their particular therapeutic game and shaping the patient's expectations accordingly.

These considerations led me and several colleagues to devise a controlled experiment comparing the results of 4 months of therapy between patients who first received a preliminary "role induction interview" designed to coordinate their expectations with what they would receive and patients who were treated identically but did not have the preparatory interview (Hoehn-Saric, Frank, Imber, Nash, & Battle, 1964; Nash, Hoehn-Saric, Battle, Stone, Imber, & Frank, 1965).

The purposes of the role-induction interview were (1) to clarify the processes of treatment; (2) to assure the patient that treatment would be helpful; (3) to dispel unrealistic hopes (thereby guarding against disillusionment); and (4) to help the patient behave in a way that accorded with the therapist's image of a good patient, thereby indirectly heightening the latter's interest and optimism.

As a group, patients receiving the role-induction interview showed more appropriate behavior in therapy and had a better outcome than the controls. This finding has been replicated in another setting (Sloane, Cristol, Pepernick, & Staples, 1970). It should be emphasized that by leading the patients to behave better in therapy, the role-induction interview made them more attractive to the therapists, thereby improving the patient-therapist relationship.

3. *Providing new learning experiences.* These new learning experiences can enhance morale by enabling patients to discover potentially helpful alternate ways of looking at themselves and their problems and to develop alternate values. In this connection, improvement in therapy seems to go along with movement of the patient's values toward those of the therapist (Pande & Gart, 1968; Parloff, Goldstein, & Iflund, 1960; Rosenthal, 1955).

Learning may occur in several ways, including instruction, modeling (Bandura, 1969), operant conditioning (in which the therapist's responses serve as positive or negative reinforcers), and exposure to new emotionally charged experiences, including transference reactions and emotional arousal by attempts to change contingencies governing behavior.

The more numerous and more intense the experiential, as opposed to the purely cognitive, components of learning, the more likely they are to be followed by changes in the patient's attitudes or behavior. It is a truism that intellectual insight alone is essentially powerless to effect change. This brings us to the fourth therapeutic ingredient common to all therapeutic conceptualizations and rituals, emotional arousal.

4. *Arousing emotions.* Such arousal is essential to therapeutic change in at least three ways. It supplies the motive power to undertake the effort and to undergo the suffering usually involved in attempts to change one's attitudes and behavior, facilitates attitude change, and enhances sensitivity to environmental influences. If the emotional arousal is unpleasant, it leads the patient to search actively for relief. When this occurs in therapy, the patient naturally turns to the therapist. Arousal intense enough to be disorganizing further increases this dependence and, in addition, may facilitate the achievement of a better personality integration by breaking up old patterns.

Eliciting intense emotions characterizes almost all healing rituals in nonindustrialized societies. In the West, the popularity of such approaches waxes and wanes. In the recent past these approaches emerged in Mesmerism and Freudian abreaction, and currently they are flourishing under various labels such as implosive therapy (Stampfl, 1976); primal therapy (Janov, 1970), reevaluation counseling (Jackins, 1965), bioenergetics (Lowen, 1975), and many, many more.

Influenced by the *Zeitgeist,* my colleagues and I conducted a series of experiments on emotional arousal and susceptibility to attitude change (Hoehn-Saric, 1978). To produce arousal we first used small doses of ether given by drip inhalation, because of the preanesthesia excitatory stage it produces in most persons. The semantic differential (Osgood, Suci, & Tannenbaum, 1957), which permits the ratings of meanings of a given concept on a set of bipolar scales, was used as the measure of attitude change. In consultation with their therapists during interview therapy, patients selected a "focal" concept that the therapist would try to shift and others that the therapist would not try to change. (The patients were not told which concepts the therapist would try to shift.) Examples of focal concepts were "my mother's influence on me" and "my tolerance of imperfections in persons close to me." In a preliminary uncontrolled experiment, patients received three interviews under slow-drip administration of ether a week and a half apart, and the therapist tried to shift only the focal concept during or immediately after the excitatory phase. The focal concept shifted cumulatively in the predicted direction, and the shift achieved statistical significance after the third interview, as compared to the shift in the initial session without ether. The other concepts remained unchanged throughout.

We next devised a controlled experiment in which the purpose and those patients who received ether were unknown to the therapists. The experimental room smelled of ether for all patients. The results, although less striking than in the preliminary study, confirmed it.

Since ether produces confusion, which might account for the patients' increased susceptibility to influence, we repeated the experiment using inhalation of vapor containing adrenalin (which stimulates the sympathetic nervous system without clouding consciousness), with essentially the same result.

In all these studies the effects on patients' attitudes were transitory; that is, the concepts soon reverted to their original positions. Perhaps this reversion is related to the repeated decline of interest in abreactive techniques after a wave of popularity. Although emotional arousal may facilitate attitude change, something else seems to be needed to maintain the change. If one may generalize from this observation, which is consistent with others, it may be important to distinguish factors that produce therapeutic change from those that sustain it (Liberman, B. L., 1978a).

From the perspective of the demoralization hypothesis, the therapeutic effect of intense emotional arousal may be in its demonstration to patients that they can stand, at high intensity, emotions which they feared and which therefore caused them to avoid or escape from situations that threatened to arouse them. Surviving such an experience would strengthen self-confidence directly and also encourage a patient to enter and cope successfully with these feared situations, thereby indirectly further bolstering morale.

Thus the maintenance of improvement following emotional flooding may depend on the ability of this procedure to enhance the patient's sense of mastery (Liberman, B. L., 1978a) or self-efficacy (Bandura, 1977), to which I now turn.

5. *Enhancing the patient's sense of mastery or self-efficacy.* Self-esteem and personal security depend to a considerable degree on a sense of being able to exert some control over the reactions of others toward oneself as well as over one's own inner states. Inability to control feelings, thoughts, and impulses not only is demoralizing in itself but also impedes one's ability to control others by preempting too much attention and distorting one's perceptions and behavior. The feeling of loss of control gives rise to emotions such as anxiety which aggravate and are aggravated by the specific symptoms or problems for which the person ostensibly seeks psychotherapy. All schools of psychotherapy seek to bolster the patient's sense of mastery in at least two ways: (1) by providing the patient with a conceptual scheme that labels and explains symptoms and supplies the rationale for the treatment program and (2) by giving the individual experiences of success.

Since the verbal apparatus is a human being's chief tool for analyzing and organizing experience, the conceptual scheme increases the patient's sense of control by making sense out of experiences that had seemed haphazard, confusing, or inexplicable and giving names to them. This effect has been termed the principle of Rumpelstiltskin (Torrey, 1972) after the fairy tale in which the queen broke the wicked dwarf's power over her by guessing his name.

To have this effect, interpretations, which are the primary means of transmitting the conceptual framework, need not necessarily be correct, but may merely be plausible. One therapist demonstrated this concept by offering six "all-purpose" interpretations to four patients in intensive psychotherapy. An example of such an interpretation is "You seem to live your life as though you are apologizing all the time." The same series of interpretations, spaced about a month apart, was given to all four patients. In 20 of these 24 instances, the patients responded with a drop in anxiety level. All patients experienced this move from the "preinterpreted" to the "postinterpreted" state at least once (Mendel, 1964).

Experiences of success, a major source of enhanced self-efficacy, are implicit in all psychotherapeutic procedures. Verbally adept patients get them from achieving new insights; behaviorally oriented patients from carrying out increasingly anxiety-laden behaviors. As already mentioned, by demonstrating to the patient that he or she can withstand at their maximal intensity the emotions he or she fears, emotional flooding techniques yield powerful experiences of success.

Furthermore, performances which the patient regards as due to his or her own efforts would be expected to reflect more strongly on an individual's self-esteem than those which the patient attributes to factors beyond his or her control, such as a medication or the help of someone else. In recognition of this expectation, psychotherapists of all persuasions convey to the patient that progress is the result of the individual's own efforts. Nondirective therapists disclaim any credit for the patient's acquiring new insights, and directive ones stress that the patient's gains depend on his or her ability to carry out the prescribed procedures.

6. *Providing opportunities for practice.* A final morale-enhancing feature of all psychotherapies is that they provide opportunities and incentives for internalizing and reinforcing therapeutic gains through repeated testing both within and outside the therapeutic session.

For completeness, it should be mentioned that group therapies involve the same morale-building principles as individual ones, often to a greater degree. The presence of other patients and the emergence of processes specific to groups introduce additional ways of combating the alienation that accompanies demoralization and provide different opportunities for cognitive and experiential learning and for practicing what has been learned. They also provide more occasions for emotional arousal and more opportunities to achieve a sense of mastery through weathering the stresses of group interactions. Finally, as social microcosms more closely resembling real life than individual interview situations, groups facilitate transfer of what has been learned to daily living.

Determinants of Therapeutic Success

The most powerful determinants of the success of any therapeutic encounter probably lie in properties of the patient, the therapist, and the particular patient-therapist pair rather than in the therapeutic procedure. Despite its importance, this area presents particular problems for research, as already indicated, so research findings are scanty and, for the most part, simply confirm clinical impressions. This situation enables me to be mercifully brief.

There is general agreement that the good patient is characterized by sufficient distress to be motivated for treatment and by the capacity to profit from a helping relationship. Strupp (1976) suggests that to be able to so profit, the patient must have had sufficiently rewarding experiences with his or her own parents so that the patient has developed "the capacity to profit from and change as a result of the forces operating in a 'good' human relationship" (p. 99).

Patients with a good prognosis are characterized, in addition, by such terms as good ego strength, coping capacity, or personality assets. An illuminating approach to therapeutically favorable personal qualities is provided by Harrower (1965). On the basis of a follow-up study of 622 patients in psychoanalysis or analytically oriented therapy, she was able to devise an index of mental-health potential based on score patterns on projective tests that correlated highly with improvement as judged retrospectively by the patients' therapists. Mental-health potential included capacity for emotional warmth and friendliness, adequate intellectual control combined with freedom and spontaneity, inner resources, and intuitive empathy for others. In short, the psychologically healthier the patient is at the start, the better the prognosis for response to treatment.

One would like to know much more about factors determining ability to profit from specific therapeutic procedures. For example, Malan (1976) presents evidence that "motivation for insight" may be important for the success of brief psychoanalytically oriented psychotherapy. A promising lead is classification of patients in terms of locus of control—that is, whether the person sees control of his or her life as lying primarily within or outside of self (Rotter, 1966; Seeman & Evans, 1962). In one study, my colleagues and I stumbled on an interesting interaction between locus of control, therapeutic improvement, and the source to which patients were led to attribute their improved performance in therapy-linked tasks (that is, whether their improvement in therapy was attributed to their own efforts or to the effect of taking a placebo pill). The internally controlled patients did significantly better than the externally controlled in the first condition, while the results were reversed in the second (Liberman, B. L., 1978a; see Figure 3). Studies of the relation between locus of control and responses to a variety of therapies are accumulating (Friedman & Dies, 1975; Ollendick & Murphy, 1977).

In examining the therapeutic qualities of therapists, we find that the success rate of therapists varies widely, even within the same therapeutic school. For example, in a study of encounter groups that used at least two therapists from each of several therapeutic schools, Lieberman, Yalom, & Miles (1973) found that the best and the worst outcomes were in groups conducted by therapists belonging to the same school. Participants in encounter groups are sufficiently similar to those in therapy groups to justify applying this finding to them. In a retrospective analysis of 150 women treated by 16 male and 10 female therapists, Orlinsky & Howard (1980) found that two thirds of the patients of the most successful therapists were much improved and none were worse, while for the least successful only one third were much improved and one third were worse. As to what qualities of therapists account for differences in

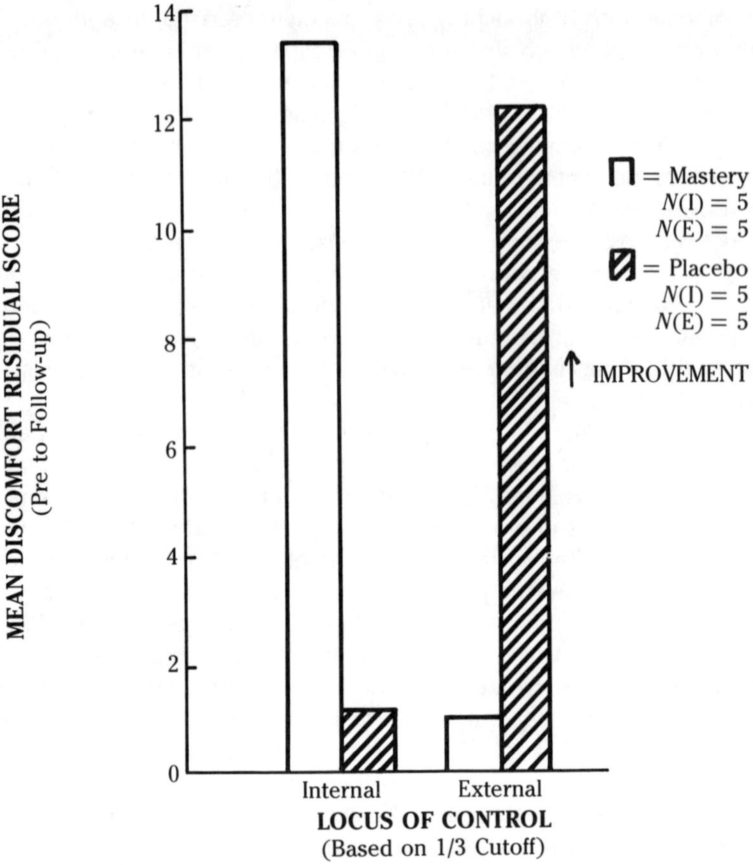

Figure 3. HSCL residual scores for mastery and placebo conditions with reference to initial mastery orientation (high residual scores reflect greater maintenance of improvement). From *Effective Ingredients of Successful Psychotherapy* by J. D. Frank, R. Hoehn-Saric, S. D. Imber, B. L. Liberman, and A. R. Stone. Reprinted by permission.

therapeutic success, however, our understanding has not progressed beyond the empathy, warmth, and genuineness found by Rogers and his school (1957) to be helpful with neurotics and the active personal participation perhaps related to success with schizophrenics (Dent, 1978; Whitehorn & Betz, 1975); and the ability to generalize about these findings remains questionable (Parloff, Waskow, & Wolfe, 1978).

To return to our analogy of psychotherapy with music, we find that psychotherapists, like musical performers, seem to vary in innate talent, which in most can be enhanced by training. Almost anyone can learn to play the piano; but no amount of training can produce a Horowitz or a

Rubinstein, nor can it turn someone who is tone deaf into a piano player. Analogously, some therapists seem to obtain extraordinary results while the patients of a few do no better, or even fare worse, than if they had received no treatment at all. It would be highly desirable to weed out these "tone-deaf" therapists early in training, thereby preventing harm to patients and sparing the therapists from misery; but, unfortunately, adequate screening methods for this purpose do not yet exist.

My own hunch, which I mention with some trepidation, is that the most gifted therapists may have telepathic, clairvoyant, or other parapsychological abilities (Ehrenwald, 1966, 1978; Freud, 1964; Jung, 1963). They may, in addition, possess something that is similar to the ability to speed plant growth (Grad, 1967) or to produce spectacular auras on Kirlian photographs (Krippner & Rubin, 1973) and that can only be termed "healing power." Any researcher who attempts to study such phenomena risks his reputation as a reliable scientist, so their pursuit can be recommended only to the most intrepid. The rewards, however, might be great.

Descending to more solid ground, we see that the therapeutic relationship is, of course, a two-way street; so efforts to determine aspects of patients and therapists which make good or poor therapeutic matches should be promising. Again, information about this is very scanty, but thought provoking. For example, it appears that with hospitalized chronic schizophrenics, composed therapists work best with anxious patients, therapists comfortable with aggression work well with hostile patients, grandparental therapists do well with seductive patients, and therapists comfortable with depression do well with depressed schizophrenics (Gunderson, 1978). Hardly a world-shaking finding, you will say, but it is a beginning.

The study of women in therapy mentioned earlier (Orlinsky & Howard, 1980) unearthed some interesting leads. The differential success rate of therapists appeared to be due primarily to interaction of patient-therapist pairs rather than to properties of the therapist alone, except that experience seemed to operate across the board. Therapists with less than 6 years' experience, compared with those with more, had twice as many patients who were unchanged or worse and only half as many who were considerably improved. The role of experience in therapeutic success, however, remains moot (Parloff et al, 1978). Of more interest is that although the sex of the therapist made no difference overall, young single women benefited more from women therapists, suggesting that men may have been somewhat threatening to them. Conversely, the only female patients who did better with the men were parents without partners. Could it be that the therapists represented to them a potential new partner?

Finally, the level of conceptualization may prove highly relevant to the matching of patients with therapists (Carr, 1970). Although no conclusive findings have emerged, it seems probable that persons who conceptualize at relatively concrete levels respond best with structured therapies in a structured environment. Furthermore, studies of smokers (Best, 1975), psychiatric outpatients treated by medical students, alcoholics, college students, and delinquents all found that patients whose conceptual level was similar to that of their therapist did better than those in which there was a mismatch (Posthuma & Carr, 1975).

Conclusion

In concluding, let me attempt to correct a common misunderstanding of the demoralization hypothesis, namely that, since features shared by all therapies that combat demoralization account for much of their effectiveness, training is unnecessary. The point I have sought to make is that healing factors mobilized by all techniques contribute significantly to the outcome of any specific one.

Through personal characteristics and past experiences, however, some patients may be more attuned to behavioral, cognitive, abreactive, hypnotic, or other procedures. Thus it remains probable that certain specific techniques are more effective for some patients, or even for some symptoms, than others.

But even in the unlikely eventuality that all therapeutic techniques prove to be fully interchangeable, this substitutability would not mean that mastery of one or more is unnecessary. Such an unwarranted conclusion confuses the content of therapeutic conceptualizations and procedures with their function. Some therapeutically gifted persons, to be sure, can be effective with very little formal training, but most of us need to master at least one therapeutic rationale and ritual. Because the techniques are irrefutable and are supported by a like-minded group to which the therapist belongs (Festinger, 1957), they maintain the therapist's sense of competence, especially in the face of inevitable therapeutic failures. As one young adherent of a psychotherapeutic school remarked, "Even if the patient doesn't get better, you know you are doing the right thing." This attitude indirectly strengthens the patient's confidence in the therapist as a person who knows what he or she is doing.

If any moral can be drawn from this presentation, it is that the choice of procedures should be guided by the therapist's personal predilections. Some therapists are effective hypnotists; others are not. Some welcome emotional displays; others shy away from them. Some work best with groups; others in the privacy of the dyad. Some enjoy exploring psyches; others prefer to try to change behavior. Ideally, from this standpoint, training programs should expose trainees to a range of rationales and procedures and encourage them to select those which are most congenial to their own personalities. The greater the number of approaches that the therapist can handle, the wider the range of patients he or she will be able to help.

Summary

Whatever their specific symptoms, patients coming to psychotherapy are also demoralized; and much of patients' disability and distress is caused by this demoralization. The sources of demoralization, whether a general response or a response to specific stress situations, insofar as it is amenable to psychotherapy, spring from warping experiences in the patients' past histories. These experiences result in three interacting, mutually reinforcing components: intrapsychic conflicts coupled with low self-esteem, distorted perception of others, and deficient coping skills. In conjunction, these components engender failure experiences or other distressing emotions that further undermine morale.

All psychotherapies aim to break the resulting vicious circle and to restore morale by providing experiences with a helping person that offer general encouragement and support, in addition to sometimes combating specific perceptual distortions and maladaptive behaviors.

The effectiveness of any psychotherapy with a specific patient depends on the morale-building features it shares with all other psychotherapies as well as its specific rationale and procedures. The relative contribution of these depends on the role of demoralization in the production or exacerbation of the patient's symptoms. Selection of technique is usually best guided less by the symptoms than by the personal characteristics and predilections of therapist and patient. The more closely these accord with each other and with the type of therapy, the better the prospects for a successful outcome.

Reference Notes

1. deFigueiredo, J., & Frank, J. D. Subjective incompetence, the clinical hallmark of demoralization. Unpublished manuscript, 1981.
2. Karasu, T. B. Personal communication, July 24, 1981.

References

Bandura, A. *Principles of behavior modification.* New York: Holt, Rinehart & Winston, 1969.

Bandura, A. Self-efficacy: Toward a unifying theory of behavioral change. *Psychological Review,* 1977, *84,* 191–215.

Best, J. A. Tailoring smoking withdrawal procedures to personality and motivational differences. *Journal of Consulting and Clinical Psychology,* 1975, *43,* 1–8.

Carr, J. E. Differentiation similarity of patient and therapist and the outcome of psychotherapy. *Journal of Abnormal Psychology,* 1970, *76,* 361–369.

Dent, J. K. *Exploring the psychosocial therapies through the personalities of effective therapists.* Publication No. ADM 77–527. Washington, D.C.: U.S. Government Printing Office, 1978.

Diefendorf, A. R. *Clinical psychiatry: A textbook for students and physicians abstracted and adapted from the 7th German edition of Kraepelin's "Lehrbuch der Psychiatrie."* New York: Macmillan, 1915.

Dohrenwend, B. P., & Crandall, D. L. Psychiatric symptoms in community, clinic and mental hospital groups. *American Journal of Psychiatry,* 1970, *126,* 1611–1621.

Dohrenwend, B. P., Oksenberg, L., Shrout, P. E., Dohrenwend, B. S., & Cook, D. What brief psychiatric screening scales measure. In S. Sudman (Ed.), *Proceedings of the 3rd biennial conference on health survey research methods, May, 1979.* Washington, D.C.: National Center for Health Services Statistics and National Center for Health Services Statistics, in press.

Dohrenwend, B. P., Shrout, P. E., Egri, G., & Mendlsohn, F. S. Nonspecific psychological distress and other dimensions of psychopathology, measures for use in the general population. *Archives of General Psychiatry,* 1980, *37,* 1229–1236.

Ehrenwald, J. *Psychotherapy: Myth and method.* New York: Grune & Stratton, 1966.

Ehrenwald, J. *The ESP experience: A psychiatric validation.* New York: Basic Books, 1978.

Farber, B. A., & Geller, J. D. Student attitudes toward psychotherapy. *Journal of the American College Health Association,* 1977, *25,* 301–307.

Festinger, L. *A theory of cognitive dissonance.* Evanston, Ill.: Row, Peterson, 1957.

Frank, J. D. *Persuasion & healing* (2nd ed.). Baltimore: Johns Hopkins University Press, 1973.

Frank, J. D. Psychotherapy: The restoration of morale. *American Journal of Psychiatry,* 1974, *131,* 271–274.

Frank, J. D. Aristotle as psychotherapist. In M. J. Mahoney (Ed.), *Psychotherapy process: Current issues and future directions.* New York: Plenum, 1980.

Frank, J. D., Gliedman, L. H., Imber, S. D., Stone, A. R., & Nash, E. H. Patients' expectancies and relearning as factors determining improvement in psychotherapy. *American Journal of Psychiatry,* 1959, *115,* 961–968.

Frank, J. D., Nash, E. H., Stone, A. R., & Imber, S. D. Immediate and long-term symptomatic course of psychiatric outpatients. *American Journal of Psychiatry,* 1963, *120,* 429–439.

Freud, S. Dreams and occultism. In J. Strachey (Ed.), *The complete psychological works of Sigmund Freud.* London: Hogarth, 1964.

Friedman, H. J. Patient expectancy and symptom reduction. *Archives of General Psychiatry,* 1963, *8,* 61–67.

Friedman, M. L., & Dies, R. R. Reactions of internal and external test-anxious students to counseling and behavior therapies. *Journal of Consulting and Clinical Psychology,* 1975, *42,* 921.

Galanter, M. The "relief effect": A sociobiological model for neurotic distress and large-group therapy. *American Journal of Psychiatry,* 1978, *135,* 588–591.

Galassi, J. P., & Galassi, M. D. Alienation in college students: A comparison of counseling seekers and nonseekers. *Journal of Counseling Psychology,* 1973, *20,* 44–49.

Garfield, S. L. Research on client variables in psychotherapy. In S. L. Garfield & A. E. Bergin (Eds.), *Handbook of psychotherapy and behavior change: An empirical analysis* (2nd ed.). New York: Wiley, 1978.

Gelder, M. G., Marks, I. M., & Wolff, H. H. Desensitization and psychotherapy in phobic states: A controlled inquiry. *British Journal of Psychiatry,* 1967, *113,* 53–73.

Glaser, S. R. Rhetoric and psychotherapy. In M. J. Mahoney (Ed.), *Psychotherapy process: Current issues and future directions.* New York: Plenum, 1980.

Goldfried, M. R., & Padawer, W. Current status and future directions in psychotherapy. In M. R. Goldfried (Ed.), *Converging themes in the practice of psychotherapy.* New York: Springer, in press.

Grad, B. The "laying on of hands": Implications for psychotherapy, gentling, and the placebo effect. *Journal of the American Society for Psychical Research,* 1967, *61,* 286–305.

Gunderson, J. C. Patient-therapist matching: A research evaluation. *American Journal of Psychiatry,* 1978, *135,* 1193–1197.

Gurman, A. S. The patient's perception of the therapeutic relationship. In A. S. Gurman & A. M. Razin (Eds.), *Effective psychotherapy: A handbook of research.* New York: Pergamon, 1977.

Harrower, M. *Psychodiagnostic testing: An empirical approach.* Springfield, Ill.: Thomas, 1965.

Henderson, S., Byrne, D. G., & Duncan-Jones, P. *Neurosis and the social environment.* New York: Academic Press, 1981.

Hilts, P. J. Psychotherapy put on couch by government. *Washington Post,* September 14, 1980.

Hoehn-Saric, R. Emotional arousal, attitude change, and psychotherapy. In J. D. Frank, R. Hoehn-Saric, S. D. Imber, & A. R. Stone, *Effective ingredients of successful psychotherapy.* New York: Brunner/Mazel, 1978.

Hoehn-Saric, R., Frank, J. D., Imber, S. D., Nash, E. H., & Battle, C. C. Systematic preparation of patients for psychotherapy. I. Effects on therapy behavior and outcome. *Journal of Psychiatric Research,* 1964, *2,* 267–281.

Imber, S. D., Pande, S. K., Frank, J. D., Hoehn-Saric, R., Stone, A. R., & Wargo, D. G. Time-focused role induction: Report of an instructive failure. *Journal of Nervous and Mental Disease,* 1970, *150,* 27–30.

Jackins, H. *The human side of human beings.* Seattle: Rational Island Publishers, 1965.

Jacobson, G. The briefest psychiatric encounter. *Archives of General Psychiatry,* 1968, *18,* 718–724.

Janov, A. *The primal scream: Primal therapy, the cure for neurosis.* New York: Putnam, 1970.

Jung, C. G. *Memories, dreams and reflections.* New York: Vintage, 1963.

Kadushin, K. *Why people go to psychiatrists.* New York: Atherton, 1969.

Kellner, R., & Sheffield, B. F. The one-week prevalence of symptoms in neurotic patients and normals. *American Journal of Psychiatry,* 1973, *130,* 102–105.

Koch, S. The nature and limits of psychological knowledge: Lessons of a century qua "science." *American Psychologist,* 1981, *36,* 257–269.

Krippner, S., & Rubin, D. (Eds.). *Galaxies of life: The human aura in acupuncture and Kirlian photography.* New York: Gordon & Breach, 1973.

LeShan, L. *The medium, the mystic, and the physicist: Toward a general theory of the paranormal.* New York: Viking, 1974.

Liberman, B. L. The role of mastery in psychotherapy: Maintenance of improvement and prescriptive change. In J. D. Frank, R. Hoehn-Saric, S. D. Imber, B. L. Liberman, & A. R. Stone, *Effective ingredients of successful psychotherapy.* New York: Brunner/Mazel, 1978. (a)

Liberman, B. L. The maintenance and persistence of change: Long-term follow-up investigations of psychotherapy. In J. D. Frank, R. Hoehn-Saric, S. D. Imber, B. L. Liberman, &

A. R. Stone, *Effective ingredients of successful psychotherapy.* New York: Brunner/Mazel, 1978. (b)

Liberman, R. An experimental study of the placebo response under three different situations of pain. *Journal of Psychiatric Research,* 1964, *2,* 233–246.

Lieberman, M. A., Yalom, I. D., & Miles, M. B. *Encounter groups: First facts.* New York: Basic Books, 1973.

Link, B., & Dohrenwend, B. P. Formulation of hypotheses about the true prevalence of demoralization in the United States. In B. P. Dohrenwend, B. S. Dohrenwend, M. S. Gould, B. Link, R. Neugebauer, & R. Wunsch-Hitzig (Eds.), *Mental illness in the United States: Epidemiological estimates.* New York: Praeger, 1980.

Lowen, A. *Bioenergetics.* New York: Coward, McCann, & Geoghegan, 1975.

Luborsky, L. Helping alliances in psychotherapy. In J. L. Claghorn (Ed.), *Successful psychotherapy.* New York: Brunner/Mazel, 1976.

Luborsky, L., & Auerbach, A. H. The symptom-context method: Quantitative studies of symptom formation in psychotherapy. *Journal of the American Psychoanalytical Association,* 1969, *17,* 68–99.

Malan, D. H. *Toward the validation of dynamic psychotherapy: A replication.* New York: Plenum, 1976.

Marmor, J. Common operational factors in diverse approaches to behavior change. In A. Burton (Ed.), *What makes behavior change possible?* New York: Brunner/Mazel, 1976.

Mendel, W. M. The phenomenon of interpretation. *American Journal of Psychoanalysis,* 1964, *24,* 184–189.

Nash, E. H., Hoehn-Saric, R., Battle, C. C., Stone, A. R., Imber, S. D., & Frank, J. D. Systematic preparation of patients for short-term psychotherapy. II. Relation to characteristics of patient, therapist and the psychotherapeutic process. *Journal of Nervous and Mental Disease,* 1965, *140,* 374–383.

Neki, J. S. Gurú-chelá relationship: The possibility of a therapeutic paradigm. *American Journal of Orthopsychiatry,* 1973, *43,* 755–766.

Ollendick, T. H., & Murphy, M. J. Differential effectiveness of muscular and cognitive relaxation as a function of locus of control. *Journal of Behavioral Therapy and Experimental Psychiatry,* 1977, *8,* 223–228.

Orlinsky, D. E., & Howard, K. I. Gender and psychotherapeutic outcome. In A. Brodsky & R. T. Hare-Mustin (Eds.), *Women and psychotherapy.* New York: Guilford Press, 1980.

Orne, M. T. Demand characteristics and the concept of quasi-controls. In R. Rosenthal & R. L. Rosnow (Eds.), *Artifact in behavioral research.* New York: Academic Press, 1969.

Osgood, C. E., Suci, G. J., & Tannenbaum, P. H. *The measurement of meaning.* Urbana: University of Illinois Press, 1957.

Pande, S. K. The mystique of "Western" psychotherapy: An Eastern view. *Journal of Nervous and Mental Disease,* 1968, 146, 425–432.

Pande, S. K., & Gart, J. J. A method to quantify reciprocal influence between therapist and patient in psychotherapy. In J. Shlien, H. F. Hunt, J. D. Matarazzo, & C. Savage (Eds.), *Research in psychotherapy.* Washington, D.C.: American Psychological Association, 1968.

Parloff, M. B., Waskow, I. E., & Wolfe, B. E. Research on therapist variables in relation to process and outcome. In S. L. Garfield & A. E. Bergin (Eds.), *Handbook of Psychotherapy and behavior change.* New York: Wiley, 1978.

Parloff, M. B., Goldstein, N., & Iflund, B. Communication of values and therapeutic change. *Archives of General Psychiatry,* 1960, *2,* 300–304.

Posthuma, A. B., & Carr, J. E. Differentiation matching in psychotherapy. *Canadian Psychological Review,* 1975, *16,* 35–43.

Rogers, C. R. The necessary and sufficient conditions of therapeutic personality change. *Journal of Consulting Psychology,* 1957, *21,* 95–103.

Rosenberg, M. J. The conditions and consequences of evaluation apprehension. In R. Rosenthal & R. L. Rosnow (Eds.), *Artifact in behavioral research.* New York: Academic Press, 1969.

Rosenthal, D. Changes in some moral values following psychotherapy. *Journal of Consulting Psychology,* 1955, *19,* 431–436.

Rosenzweig, S. Some implicit common factors in diverse methods of psychotherapy. *American Journal of Orthopsychiatry,* 1936, *6,* 412–415.

Rotter, J. B. Generalized expectancies for internal vs. external control of reinforcement. *Psychological Monographs,* 1966, *80,* (1, Whole No. 609).

Rush, A. J., Beck, A. T., Kovacs, M., & Hollon, S. Comparative effects of cognitive therapy and pharmacotherapy in the treatment of depressed outpatients. *Cognitive Therapy & Research,* 1977, *1,* 17–37.

Seeman, M., & Evans, J. W. Alienation and learning in a hospital setting. *American Sociological Review,* 1962, *27,* 772–782.

Seguin, C. A. *Love and psychotherapy.* New York: Libra Publishers, 1965.

Sloane, R. B., Cristol, A. H., Pepernick, M. C., & Staples, F. R. Role preparation and expectation of improvement in psychotherapy. *Journal of Nervous & Mental Disease,* 1970, *150,* 18–26.

Sloane, R. B., Staples, F. R., Cristol, A. H., Yorkston, N. J., & Whipple, K. *Psychotherapy versus behavior therapy.* Cambridge, Mass.: Harvard University Press, 1975.

Smith, H. *Forgotten truth: The primordial tradition.* New York: Harper Colophon, 1977.

Smith, N. L., Glass, G. V., & Miller, T. I. *Benefits of psychotherapy.* Baltimore: Johns Hopkins University Press, 1980.

Stampfl, T. G. Implosive therapy. In P. Olsen (Ed.), *Emotional flooding.* New York: Human Sciences Press, 1976.

Strupp, H. H. The nature of the therapeutic influence and its basic ingredients. In A. Burton (Ed.), *What makes behavior change possible?* New York: Brunner/Mazel, 1976.

Strupp, H. H., & Hadley, S. W. Specific vs. nonspecific factors in psychotherapy: A controlled study of outcome. *Archives of General Psychiatry,* 1979, *36,* 1125–1136.

Szasz, T. S. *The myth of psychotherapy: Mental healing as religion, rhetoric, and repression.* New York: Anchor, 1978.

Torrey, E. F. *The mind game.* New York: Emerson Hall, 1972.

Uhlenhuth, E. H., & Duncan, D. B. Subjective change with medical student therapists: II. Some determinants of change in psychoneurotic outpatients. *Archives of General Psychiatry,* 1968, *18,* 186–198.

Vaillant, G. E. Why men seek psychotherapy, I: Results of a survey of college students. *American Journal of Psychiatry,* 1972, *129,* 645–651.

Whitehorn, J. C., & Betz, B. *Effective psychotherapy with the schizophrenic patient.* New York: Jason Aronson, 1975.

Wilkins, W. Expectancies in therapy research: Discriminating among heterogeneous nonspecifics. *Journal of Consulting and Clinical Psychology,* 1979, *47,* 837–845.

Wolberg, L. R. *The technique of psychotherapy* (3rd ed.). New York: Grune & Stratton, 1977.

HANS H. STRUPP

THE OUTCOME PROBLEM IN PSYCHOTHERAPY: CONTEMPORARY PERSPECTIVES

Fabry Studios

Hans H. Strupp is Distinguished Professor of Psychology at Vanderbilt University. Previously he was on the faculties in the departments of psychiatry and psychology at the University of North Carolina, Chapel Hill. He obtained his doctorate in psychology at George Washington University in 1954 and his psychoanalytic training at the Washington School of Psychiatry. He is a diplomate in clinical psychology, American Board of Professional Psychologists.

Strupp has written over 175 articles and has written and edited a number of major books on psychotherapy, including *Explorations of the Therapist's Contribution to the Treatment Process* (1960), *Patients View Their Psychotherapy* (1969), *Changing Frontiers in the Science of Psychotherapy* (1972), *Psychotherapy: Clinical, Research, and Theoretical Issues* (1973), and *Psychotherapy for Better or Worse: An Analysis of the Problem of Negative Effects* (1977).

Strupp has received numerous awards, including the Helen Sargent Memorial Award from the Menninger Foundation, a Distinguished Professional Achievement Award from the American Board of Professional Psychology, a Distinguished Professional Psychologist Award from Division 29 (Psychotherapy) of the American Psychological Association (APA), and both a Distinguished Scientist Award and a Distinguished

Scientific Contribution Award from Division 12 (Clinical Psychology) of APA. Strupp is also on numerous editorial boards and is a fellow of the American Psychological Association, the Tennessee Psychological Association, and the American Association for the Advancement of Science. He has served as president of the Society for Psychotherapy Research and of APA's Division of Clinical Psychology.

HANS H. STRUPP

THE OUTCOME PROBLEM IN PSYCHOTHERAPY: CONTEMPORARY PERSPECTIVES

The birth of modern psychotherapy is commonly traced to Josef Breuer's famous patient Anna O. who, about a hundred years ago, gained relief from her hysterical difficulties by means of the "talking cure." Sigmund Freud, Breuer's young colleague, built on Breuer's early insights, and his subsequent discoveries of psychological dynamics ushered in a revolution which continues to have profound effects on contemporary clinical thinking and practice.

Nonetheless, despite enormous advances, modern psychotherapy is beleaguered today as never before. Avidly sought by thousands of troubled people who desire relief from an assortment of problems ranging from the classical neurotic conditions to personality disorders, alienation, loneliness, and existential despair, many diverse forms of psychotherapy are practiced by an expanding cadre of professionals, including psychiatrists, clinical psychologists, social workers, nurses, and pastoral counselors. Psychotherapy continues to be seen as a major weapon against personal and interpersonal difficulties besetting people's lives. On the one hand, it has become a billion-dollar industry, a set of treatments compensable by the government and private health-insurance companies. On the other hand, it is attacked by scores of critics who deny that there is such a thing as psychotherapy or who question its effectiveness (more recently, in comparison with psychotropic drugs) or advocate interventions claimed to be superior to traditional ones. Coupled with these doubts are the public's growing mistrust of science, medicine, and the professions, with their alleged preoccupation with economic and political power and their lack of concern for the consumer, and the accumulated frustration of a populace which desires simple and cost-effective solutions to the complex problems of our technological society.

Whatever psychotherapy purports to be or however it is defined, several things are clear today.

1. It is not a miracle drug or a panacea.

2. Although a substantial percentage of persons experiencing some form of psychotherapy report marked benefits, others in states of crisis overcome their difficulties through their own adaptive capacities or with the help of friends, clergymen, and others who may provide counsel.

3. Individuals who have made a better adaptation to adult living and who possess greater personality resources derive greater benefits from psychotherapy than persons who lack these strengths and who suffer from emotional disorders of long standing.

4. No single form of dynamic psychotherapy or behavior therapy is uniquely superior to others (except perhaps in a few narrowly circumscribed conditions).

5. A number of psychopathological conditions are not helped significantly by available forms of psychotherapy (or any other known treatment modality).

6. The extent to which intensive or prolonged psychotherapy produces radical reorganization of a patient's personality and, therefore, lasting change is questionable.

7. The quality of the interpersonal relationship established between a patient and a therapist plays an important part in determining the course and outcome of the therapy.

8. Once the patient has met certain criteria of suitability, the therapist's personal qualities appear to be more potent factors than any specific set of techniques he or she may use.

9. Finally, in the absence of the foregoing considerations, the quest for specific psychotherapeutic techniques for specific disorders (analogous to a drug) may turn out to be futile.

Why, in the light of this seemingly gloomy picture does the practice of psychotherapy continue to flourish? Why do therapists continue to be trained? Why do people continue to enlist the services of psychotherapists? The following discussion will address some of these thorny issues confronting society and the mental health professions. It should become apparent that one cannot speak of psychotherapy as a unitary treatment procedure apart from the person of the patient and the person of the therapist. Rather the personal qualities of the participants inevitably become intertwined in any therapeutic encounter. At the same time, it is possible for the therapist to employ his or her clinical acumen in understanding complex cognitive, symbolic, and emotional processes that lead to the formation of symptoms or other difficulties in living and to help the patient resolve or ameliorate some of these problems. Thus psychotherapy is both a personal and a technical enterprise, and many of the persistent misunderstandings derive from inadequate appreciation of these facts.

Definitions

In the broadest terms, psychotherapy is concerned with personality and behavior change. The patient who seeks help for a psychological problem desires change—he or she wants to feel or act differently—and the psychotherapist agrees to assist the patient in achieving this goal. The major issues in psychotherapy relate to what is to be changed and how change can be brought about. The first question entails definition of the problem for which the patient is seeking help (such as depression, marital difficulties, shyness, nail biting, sexual dysfunctions, or existential anxiety); the second question pertains to the process and techniques by means of which change is effected (such as support, ventilation of feelings, insight through interpretations, systematic desensitization, or assertiveness training). Ideally, one would like to be able to say that, given Problem X, the optimal approach is Technique Y. In practice, however, things are not so simple or straightforward; on the contrary, since many human problems are extraordinarily complex, so are the issues facing the therapist who attempts to deal with these difficulties in therapeutic ways. For the same reason, it is unlikely that there can be a single optimal approach to the solution of a psychological problem. Accordingly, the alleged distinctions between behavior therapy and the therapies based on psychodynamic principles pale in significance. To make this statement is not to deny that there may be fundamental distinctions between the philosophies and practices of behavior therapists and dynamically oriented therapists; but, in fact, no therapist practices a pure technique. Indeed, commonalities in all forms of therapy may turn out to be more crucial than the differences.

Part of the confusion besetting the field relates to the definition of psychotherapy as a treatment modality, analogous to medical treatment in which a physician ministers to a passive patient. This problem is complicated by the fact that modern psychotherapy has its roots in medicine. Thus, terms like patient, therapist, diagnosis, or etiology continue to be used. In truth, psychotherapy bears only a superficial resemblance to this model. Since it is undeniable that psychotherapy attempts to alleviate human suffering, however, the medical analogy persists. Furthermore, some conditions (e.g., depressions) appear to yield to psychotherapy as well as to pharmacological interventions, the latter being traditionally the province of physicians. Therefore, it may be asserted that psychotherapy appears to improve a person's mental health, a term that has always been fuzzy and the utility of which is increasingly being called into question. Nonetheless, for political as well as economic reasons, psychiatrists (as physicians) have found "remedicalizing" psychotherapy advantageous. As will be seen, this move runs counter to historical developments, turns back the clock, and jettisons hard-won advances.

It is important to remind ourselves that psychotherapy bears a much closer relationship to the teacher-student model. As early as 1905, Freud (p. 267) characterized psychoanalytic therapy as a form of "re-education" or "after-education," a position he never abandoned thereafter. He saw clearly, as most therapists have seen since, that psychotherapy, above all else, is a collaborative endeavor in which the patient, from the beginning, is expected to play an active part. By the same token, the vast majority of neurotic disorders—the prime conditions for which psychotherapy is used—are the product of maladaptive learning in early childhood, resulting in low self-esteem, dependency, and other forms of immaturity. To overcome these impediments, patients must be helped to mature and to become more autonomous, more self-directing, and more responsible. In order to feel better about themselves, their relationships with others, and their behavior in general, patients must learn to make changes within themselves and in their environment. The process of therapy is designed not to impose change on the patient but to create conditions that allow change to occur within the patient.

Therefore, psychotherapy is a learning process, and the role of the therapist is analogous to that of a teacher or mentor. Furthermore, if troublesome feelings, cognitions, attitudes, and patterns of behavior have been learned, the possibility exists, within limits, for unlearning or relearning. Conversely, where learning is impossible (for example, in conditions attributable to genetic or biochemical factors), psychotherapy has little to offer. Similarly, if the disturbance is due solely to factors in the person's social milieu (poverty, oppression, imprisonment) or if patients themselves do not desire change but change is mandated (for example, by a court of law or a school system), psychotherapists encounter great difficulties. Thus, psychotherapy works best if patients desire change of their own accord and are motivated to work toward it, if the environment in which they live tolerates the possibility of change, and if the inner obstacles to learning (defenses and rigidities of character) are not insurmountable. Since everyone, despite conscious assertions to the contrary, is deeply committed to maintaining the status quo, psychotherapeutic learning is rarely simple and straightforward.

No single definition of psychotherapy (or behavior therapy) has been given universal acceptance nor is it likely to be given such acceptance. Depending upon the therapist's theoretical orientation and other factors, psychotherapy is seen by some as a psychosocial treatment, by others as a special form of education, and by still others as a means of promoting personality growth and self-actualization—to cite but a few divergent views. Most therapists agree, however, that psychotherapy involves both a human relationship and techniques for bringing about personality and behavior change.

The Problem of Therapy Outcome

For the preceding reasons, the problem of treatment outcome is exceedingly complex and not conducive to simple answers. Nevertheless, the question of psychotherapy's effectiveness remains of central interest to many people. Still, unless the terms are properly defined, the question is even less meaningful than the comparable one, "Is surgery effective?" since interpersonal variables play a much lesser role in the latter.

The problem of psychotherapy outcome touches on many facets of human life, and conceptions of mental health and illness cannot be considered apart from problems of philosophy, ethics, religion, and public policy. Inescapably we deal with human existence, the person's place in the world, and ultimately we must confront questions of *value* (Strupp & Hadley, 1977). In the end, someone must make a judgment that a person's compliance with requests from others is a virtue or an indicator of pathological submissiveness; that a decrement of 10 points on the Depression Scale of the Minnesota Multiphasic Personality Inventory (MMPI) in the 90–100 range is a greater or a lesser improvement than a like change between 50 and 60; that in one case we accept a patient's judgment that he or she feels better whereas in another we set it aside, calling it "flight into health," "reaction formation," "denial," and so on. These decisions can be made only by reference to the values society assigns to feelings, attitudes, and actions. In turn, values are inherent in conceptions of mental health and illness as well as in clinical judgments based upon one of these models.

One of the great stumbling blocks in psychotherapy research and practice has been a failure to realize the importance of values. While researchers have rightfully dealt with technical and methodological issues and have made considerable gains in clarifying them, objective assessments and measurements have remained imperfect and imprecise. For example, it is a common finding (Garfield, Prager, & Bergin, 1971; Bergin & Lambert, 1978) that outcome assessments by patients, peers, independent clinicians, and therapists correlate only moderately. One may attribute this moderate correlation to the imperfection of the instruments and the fallibility of raters, but one should also be aware that raters bring different perspectives to bear and that the relative lack of correlation results partially from legitimate divergences in their vantage points.

As early as 1916, Freud saw the outcome issue as a practical one, and this may well be the best way to treat it. When all is said and done, there may be commonsense agreement on what constitutes a mentally healthy, nonneurotic person. Knight (1941) postulated three major rubrics for considering therapeutic change which still seem eminently reasonable: (1) disappearance of presenting symptoms, (2) real improvement in mental functioning, and (3) improved reality adjustment. Although most therapists and researchers may disagree on criteria and methods of assessing change, they would concur that therapeutic success should be demonstrable in the person's feeling state (well-being), social functioning (performance), and personality organization (structure). The first is clearly the individual's subjective perspective; the second is that of society, incorporating prevailing standards of conduct and normality; the third is the perspective of mental-health professionals whose technical concepts (e.g., ego strength or impulse control) partake of information and standards derived from the preceding sources but are ostensibly scientific, objective, and value free. As Strupp & Hadley (1977) have shown, few therapists or researchers have recognized these facts or taken their implications seriously. Therapists have continued to assess treatment outcomes on the basis of global clinical impressions whereas researchers have tended to assume that quantitative indices can be interpreted as if they were thermometer readings. Instead, values influence and suffuse all judgments of outcome.

There are other reasons for rejecting the traditional question "Is psychotherapy effective?" as neither appropriate nor potentially fruitful. It has become increasingly apparent that psychotherapy (or behavior therapy) as currently practiced is not a unitary process nor is it applied to a unitary problem (Kiesler, 1966). Furthermore, therapists cannot be regarded as interchangeable units that deliver a standard treatment in uniform quantity or quality (Parloff, Waskow, & Wolfe, 1978). Depending on differences in personality, education, intelligence, the nature of emotional difficulties, motivation, and other variables, patients are diversely receptive to different forms of therapeutic influence (Garfield, 1978). Finally, technique variables, since they are thoroughly intertwined with the person of the therapist, cannot be examined in isolation.

By now there are clear indications that these strictures are being taken more seriously by contemporary researchers (e.g., Sloane, Staples, Cristol, Yorkston, & Whipple, 1975), although as yet by few practicing therapists. A long-standing tradition among psychotherapists is to view their particular approach as the answer to every problem presented by patients, with scant recognition that another technique might be more appropriate in a given case. Freud's consistent refusal to view psychoanalysis as a panacea and his insistence upon carefully circumscribing its range of applicability stands as a notable exception. Neither therapists nor researchers can evade the necessity of working toward greater specificity in describing changes occurring in patients and evaluating the changes by reference to an explicit frame of values.

Research in Therapy Outcome

Research activity in the area of therapy outcomes has been voluminous and sustained (Bergin & Lambert, 1978). In the years since Eysenck (1952) charged that psychotherapy produces no greater changes in emotionally disturbed individuals than naturally occurring life experiences, researchers and clinicians alike have felt compelled to answer the challenge. Analyzing and synthesizing the data from 25 years of research on the efficacy of psychotherapy, Luborsky, Singer, & Luborsky (1975) have concluded that most forms of psychotherapy produce changes in a substantial proportion of patients—changes that are often, but not always, greater than those achieved by control patients who did not receive therapy. Other reviewers (e.g., Meltzoff & Kornreich, 1970) have reached similar conclusions. In an ingenious analysis, Smith & Glass (1977) have demonstrated that standardized measures across all types of therapy, patients, therapists, and outcome criteria show the average patient to have improved more than 75% of comparable control patients. In short, the preponderance of the evidence, interpreted in the most general terms, does not support Eysenck's pessimistic conclusion concerning psychotherapy, nor does it demonstrate behavior therapy as impressively superior to other forms.

The literature also reflects increments in the number of studies that are methodologically sound and clinically meaningful. Major investigations are exemplified by the studies at the University of Chicago Counseling Center (Rogers and Dymond, 1954), by the Menninger Foundation Project (Kernberg, Burnstein, Coyne, Appelbaum, Horowitz, and Voth, 1972), by the Temple study (Sloane et al., 1975), by the research of Paul (1966, 1967) and of DiLoreto (1971), and by the Vanderbilt Psychotherapy Project (Strupp & Hadley, 1979). Some of the primary aims of these studies were to contrast variations in treatment and to investigate the impact of patient and therapist variables in determining outcomes. Furthermore, in a host of investigations the impact of patient, therapist, and technique variables upon the process of psychotherapy has been explored (Orlinsky & Howard, 1978).

Patient Variables and the Problem of Diagnosis

Therapy outcomes obviously depend to a significant extent on patient characteristics. From the moment he or she meets a patient, the therapist seeks to define the nature of the problem in need of treatment or amelioration. The therapist becomes a diagnostician who attempts to identify a malfunction or a problem in order to take appropriate therapeutic steps. Diagnosing requires clinical understanding and an appreciation of the vast array of individual differences among patients. While seemingly simple, the problem is momentous in its implications for therapy and research.

As an illustration of the problem, therapists and researchers have come to realize that a phobia, a depression, or an anxiety state in one patient is not identical to a similar problem in another. Accordingly, it is hazardous for a variety of reasons to categorize or to type patients on the basis of the presenting difficulty or in terms of standard psychiatric diagnoses. Moreover, the utility of the classical diagnostic categories (hysteria, obsessive-compulsive neurosis, etc.) is limited for either therapeutic practice or research. Other systems of classification (in terms, for example, of defensive styles or of ego functions), while sometimes useful, have shortcomings of their own. The plain fact, long recognized by clinicians, is that patients differ on a host of dimensions—from intelligence, education, social class, and age to such variables as psychological-mindedness, motivation for psychotherapy, organization of defenses, and rigidity of character.

Human personality, furthermore, is organized, and personality organization often forms an integral part of the therapeutic problem. For example, phobic patients tend to be generally shy, dependent, and anxious in many other situations (Andrews, 1966). In addition, temperamental, genetic, social, and environmental factors of various kinds influence the patient's current disturbance. One must also recognize that the patient's life history, particularly interpersonal relationships in early childhood, may be crucially important for understanding and treating the current problem. The foregoing variables are typically intertwined in highly complex ways, resulting in a unique constellation.

Despite the uniqueness of individuals, there are commonalities in patients' problems. People react in diverse yet limited ways to stresses and crises (such as bereavement, disappointments, or rejection by important persons in their lives). So, while individual variations are real, all members of our culture have had somewhat comparable childhood experiences. For example, most of us have learned early in life that the expression of impulses must be curbed in the interest of social living; that is, we have learned discipline and acceptance of authority. To illustrate further, since Americans grow up in a relatively common culture, share the same language, and have common human desires, conflicts, and goals, others can understand our behavior and motives. For these reasons, as well as others, principles of personality functioning can be abstracted, and psychotherapy has the potential of becoming a scientific discipline. Sullivan's (1953) "one genus postulate" ("We are all much more simply human than otherwise") underscores the continuity of human experience regardless of ethnic differences or seemingly incomprehensible psychopathology.

In order to be maximally useful to a patient, therapists must sort and integrate the large mass of information that becomes available through clinical interaction and evaluation, formulate the therapeutic problem in terms that are meaningful both to participants as well as to society, and institute appropriate therapeutic procedures. In short, the psychotherapist and the therapy researcher must be sensitive diagnosticians, whose task is different from a one-time effort at pigeonholing individuals into diagnostic classes or categories.

The following implications should be noted:

1. Formulating the therapeutic problem and achieving consensus among interested parties, from the standpoint both of clinical practice and of research, is a task of the greatest importance. Thus, progress in studying therapy outcomes, both within and across therapeutic approaches, will remain seriously hampered unless dealing more effectively with this problem becomes possible.

2. Existing diagnostic schemes have a certain limited utility, as do theoretical formulations of patient problems stated in terms of presenting symptoms, difficulties, or targets. The latter are often troublesome because they are a statement of the patient's subjective feeling-state or problem which, as presented, may not lend itself to therapy. In one case,

patient and therapist may agree on the elimination of a phobia as the therapeutic goal. In another instance, however, the patient may state a vague or unrealistic target (like "becoming more popular" or "worrying less"). As therapy proceeds, the therapist often finds it necessary to reformulate the original target.

Moreover, in many instances focusing exclusively on one aspect of the patient's functioning (e.g., overt behavior) is insufficient. Rather, estimates of the totality of the patient's personality functioning and performance on a number of dimensions must be obtained even when a specific area is targeted for change. It is gradually being recognized that in all forms of psychotherapy patients will typically experience changes in their self-identity and self-acceptance; that is, regardless of behavioral change, successful psychotherapy produces changes in the patient's inner experience (Strupp, Fox, & Lessler, 1969), a realization previously rejected but now often accepted by some behavior therapists (Wachtel, 1977).

3. Diagnosis is a process which calls for the exercise of significant clinical skills. It must be systematic and lead to prognostic judgments that can be translated into therapeutic operations as well as outcome evaluations. In other words, the primary goal of psychodiagnosis should not be labeling but devising a realistic plan for therapeutic action.

4. The personality makeup and the behavioral patterns of the individual patient exert the single most important modulating effect on the therapist's total effort and, therefore, on the effort's usefulness. Disregarding or giving short shrift to this set of variables is tantamount to developing tools without considering the material with which one intends to work.

As society has begun to recognize the importance of making psychotherapeutic services available to a broad spectrum of the population, not merely to its affluent members, the problem of defining and identifying those individuals who can (or cannot) benefit from particular forms of therapy has become increasingly pressing. With this pressure has come the recognition that therapy must be tailored to the needs of individual patients and their problems, rather than the reverse (Goldstein & Stein, 1976). This aim is reflected in research efforts to socialize patients prior to psychotherapy (Orne & Wender, 1968; Hoehn-Saric, Frank, Imber, Nash, Stone, & Battle, 1964; Strupp & Bloxom, 1973), to increase their understanding of how therapy works, and to prepare them in other ways for therapy.

The study of patient characteristics in relation to therapeutic change, as Strupp & Bergin (1969) noted, for the most part has focused on one basic issue: How do patient variables influence and determine the immediate reaction to as well as the ultimate course of psychotherapy? The following question appears to be more significant: Which constellation of patient characteristics and problems are most amenable to which techniques conducted by which type of therapist in what type of setting? Thus, devising therapies that will benefit particular patients may be more important than the more common approach of trying to determine the kind of patient or the initial status which will respond best to fairly heterogenous types of therapy.

The Problem of Technique

Techniques are, of course, the core and raison d'être of modern psychotherapy, and they are anchored in theories of psychopathology or maladaptive learning. Psychoanalysis has stressed the interpretation of resistances and transference phenomena as the principal curative factor, contrasting these operations with the suggestions of earlier hypnotists. Behavior therapy, to cite another example, has developed its own armamentarium of techniques, such as systematic desensitization, modeling, aversive and operant conditioning, and training in self-regulation and self-control. In general, the proponents of all systems of psychotherapy credit their successes to more or less specific operations which are usually claimed to be uniquely effective. A corollary of this proposition is that a therapist is a professional who must receive systematic training in the application of the recommended techniques.

So far it has not been possible to show that one technique is clearly superior to another, even under reasonably controlled conditions (e.g., Luborsky et al., 1975; Sloane et al., 1975; Strupp & Hadley, 1979). The commonly accepted finding that approximately two thirds of neurotic patients who enter outpatient psychotherapy of whatever description show noticeable improvement (Garfield, 1978; Bergin & Lambert, 1978) likewise reinforces a skeptical attitude concerning the unique effectiveness of particular techniques. Finally, it often turns out that initial claims for a new technique cannot be sustained when the accumulating evidence is critically examined, as appears to be true, for example, of systematic desensitization in the treatment of phobias (Marks, 1978).

An alternative hypothesis has been advanced (e.g., Frank, 1973; Strupp, 1973) which asserts that psychotherapeutic change is predominantly a function of factors common to all therapeutic approaches. These factors are brought to bear in the human relationship between the patient and the healer. The proponents of this hypothesis hold that individuals defined by themselves or by others as patients, suffer from demoralization and a sense of hopelessness. Consequently, any benign human influence is likely to boost the patient's morale, which in turn is registered as improvement (Shapiro & Morris, 1978). Primary ingredients of these common nonspecific factors include understanding, respect, interest, encouragement, acceptance, forgiveness—in short, the kinds of human qualities that since time immemorial have been considered effective in buoying the human spirit.

Frank identifies another important common factor in all psychotherapies, that is, their tendency to operate in terms of a conceptual scheme and associated procedures which are thought to be beneficial. While the contents of the schemes and the procedures differ among therapies, they have common morale-building functions. Thus, they combat the patient's demoralization by providing an explanation, acceptable to both participants, for the patient's hitherto inexplicable feelings and behavior. This process serves to remove the mystery from the patient's suffering and eventually to supplant it with hope.

Frank's formulation implies that training in and enthusiasm for a special theory and method may increase the effectiveness of therapists, in contrast to nonprofessional helpers who may lack belief in a coherent system or rationale. This hypothesis also underscores the continuity between faith healers, shamans, and modern psychotherapists. While psychotherapists may operate on the basis of sophisticated scientific theories (by contemporary standards), the function of these theories may be intrinsically no different from the most primitive rationale undergirding a healer's efforts. In both instances, techniques of whatever description are inseparable from the therapist's belief system, which in successful therapy is accepted and integrated by the patient. Of course, some patients may be more receptive to, and thus more likely to benefit from, the therapist's manipulations than other patients.

From a different perspective, Rogers (1957) postulated a set of facilitative conditions (i.e., accurate empathy, genuineness, and unconditional positive regard) as necessary and sufficient conditions for beneficial therapeutic change. Thus, both Rogers and Frank deemphasize therapeutic techniques per se; instead, they elevate relationship factors to a position of preeminence.

While the hypothesis of nonspecific factors embodies a valuable idea, some technical operations may still be superior to others with particular patients, for particular problems, and under particular circumstances. For example, such claims are made by therapists who are interested in the treatment of sexual dysfunctions (Kaplan, 1974) and by behavior therapists who have tackled a wide range of behavior disorders (Marks, 1978). As yet, many of these claims are untested, and a great deal of research remains to be done to document that specific techniques are uniquely effective. Even so, there may be definite limits (largely those set by the patient's personality structure, as cited earlier) which no technique per se can transcend. To cite but one example: Sex researchers have come to realize that the success of treatment for sexual dysfunctions is often severely circumscribed by more or less deep-seated neurotic problems, of which the sexual difficulty is but one manifestation.

In any event, the problem clearly has important ramifications for research and practice. For example, if further evidence can be adduced that techniques per se contribute less to good therapy outcomes than has been claimed, greater effort may have to be expended in selecting and training therapists who are able to provide the nonspecific factors mentioned earlier.[1] We also need much better information concerning the kinds of therapeutic services that may be safely performed by individuals with relatively little formal training (paraprofessionals) as well as the limits set by their lack of comprehensive training. In any case, there may be definite limitations to what techniques per se can accomplish (Frank, 1974), limits that are set both by patient characteristics and by therapist qualities, including level of training.

The Person of the Therapist

As previously suggested, psychotherapy prominently involves the interaction of two or more persons, and the therapeutic influence is by no means restricted to the formal techniques a therapist may use. The patient, like the therapist, reacts to the other as a total person, hence both researchers and clinicians must become centrally concerned with the therapist as a human being. Of course, what has been said about enormous individual differences among patients applies with equal force to therapists. Indeed, it is difficult to fathom how in early psychoanalysis, as well as in many later research studies, therapists could have been treated as interchangeable units, presumably equal in skill and influence (Kiesler, 1966). Therapists, like patients, obviously differ in many dimensions (e.g., age, gender, cultural background, ethnic factors, level of professional experience, psychological sophistication, empathy, tact, and social values). Any or all of these may have a significant bearing upon a therapist's theoretical orientation, therapeutic techniques, and the man-

[1] This has been the thrust of a training program developed by Carkhuff and Truax (1965) and Carkhuff (1969) which relies heavily on developing the therapist's empathy and related interpersonal skills.

ner of interaction with and influence on a given patient. There can be little doubt that the therapist's personality is an important determinant of the therapeutic outcome.

The elusiveness of many therapist qualities has posed serious obstacles to research in this area. It is possible to specify human qualities a good therapist should possess (Holt & Luborsky, 1958) as well as those that may be harmful to patients (Hadley & Strupp, 1976). Because of the recent emphasis on the ancient medical principle "above all, do no harm," particular interest is currently being shown in those therapist qualities that may be detrimental to patients (Strupp, Hadley, & Gomes-Schwartz, 1977). Since therapists represent a combination of personality characteristics and qualities, dissecting strands in the therapist's total influence is difficult. Furthermore, patient personality characteristics demonstrably influence the therapist's effectiveness, a finding which supports the conclusion that patients must be selected more carefully to match the therapist's capabilities. Finally, therapists appear to be differentially effective with particular patients (Strupp, 1980a; 1980b; 1980c; 1980d).

It has frequently been mentioned that the effective therapist must be able to instill trust, confidence, and hope and to strengthen the patient's conviction in his or her own strength. Yet real as these variables undoubtedly are, they likewise have eluded quantification. It is becoming increasingly clear that single therapist variables, except perhaps glaring defects in the therapist's personality, are not likely to provide the answers sought by researchers and clinicians; instead, a combination of therapist attributes appears to form an integrated gestalt, to which the patient, other things being equal, responds positively, negatively, or neutrally. To have a therapeutic impact on the patient, the therapist's personality must have distinctive stimulus value or salience; therapists can never be impersonal technicians nor can they apply therapeutic techniques in a vacuum. At times, therapists must be capable of encouraging the patient to explore a particular feeling, belief, or attitude; at other times, they must wait patiently for the patient to arrive at his or her own solutions. They must be capable of distinguishing between the patient's neurotic and nonneurotic needs and resist entanglements in the patient's neurotic maneuvers. Above all, they must make a careful assessment of how much help is needed, what kind of help is needed, and what obstacles prevent the patient from reaching a constructive solution. In short, therapists must have a high level of personal maturity, clinical skill, and sensitivity. Concerted efforts to specify these qualities may yield important clues to the question of what is ultimately effective in psychotherapy.

The importance of the foregoing considerations has frequently been lost by the artificial distinction between therapists' personalities and techniques. For expository purposes, it is possible to describe techniques as if they existed apart from the person using them. In practice, however, they are never separate. If demonstrations are needed, all one has to do is to listen to the sound recording of any therapeutic interview. It becomes apparent that any therapist, regardless of his or her theoretical orientation, interacts with the patient as a total person. For example, all therapists will ask for clarifications, try to understand the patient's communications, and offer comments of various kinds. To be sure, one therapist may systematically attempt to identify and uproot a patient's neurotic beliefs; another may listen for a long time and sparingly offer interpretations of latent meanings in the patient's associations; a third may make homework assignments, and so forth. None of these techniques, however, are ever pure, and in all cases they are embedded in the human relationship between the participants. Furthermore, a trained therapist's interventions are guided by his or her understanding of the patient's problem at a particular time. This understanding is informed and guided by the therapist's clinical expertise or his or her knowledge of psychodynamics, of the nature of the patient's resistances, and of what, in terms of that understanding, might be helpful to say as well as how to say it. The therapist responds in terms of a cognitive map which gives direction and guidance. In the absence of such a map, which in essence is a refinement of commonsense understanding of another person's interpersonal difficulties, the therapist flounders. In sum, attempting a differentiation of technique and personality is basically meaningless. Instead, the two are inextricably intertwined, and they reflect the totality of the therapist's personality and professional experience.

The Therapeutic Alliance

In recent years, some psychoanalytic theorists (e.g., Greenson, 1967; Langs, 1973; Menninger & Holtzman, 1973) have identified the relationship between patient and therapist as a major therapeutic force. As Freud developed the technique of psychoanalytic therapy, he recognized that patients must become active partners who collaborate with the therapist in their cure. Freud distinguished between the patient's "observing ego" and "experiencing ego," postulating that the former represents the reasonable and rational part of the patient's personality which carries out the principal task of analytic therapy by forming an alliance and identifying with the therapist's efforts in analyzing the irrational (transferential) aspects of the patient's personality. Thus, the therapeutic relationship is composed of a real relationship (that is, the relationship between two adults, one of whom desires therapeutic change) and a transference relationship (represented by continual but unwitting tendencies on the patient's part to reenact neurotic conflicts with the therapist).

To the extent that factors within the patient or the therapist interfere with the establishment of a productive therapeutic alliance, therapeutic progress will be retarded or even vitiated. Premature termination or intractable dependency on the therapist are instances of such failure. Patients who have relatively intact and strong egos have a better chance of succeeding in analytic therapy (Horwitz, 1974; Kernberg, 1976) and perhaps in other forms of therapy as well. Although empirical studies of the therapeutic alliance are as yet scarce (Hartley, 1978), preliminary support for its importance comes from the Menninger project (Horwitz, 1974).

Superficially resembling any good human relationship, the therapeutic alliance provides a unique starting point for the patient's growing identification with the therapist, a point stressed by the proponents of the object relations theory (Fairbairn, 1952; Guntrip, 1971; Kernberg, 1976; Winnicott, 1965) who have spearheaded advances in psychoanalytic theory. According to these authors, the internalization of the therapist as a good object is crucial for significant psychotherapeutic change. The present writer (Strupp, 1969, 1973), among others, has likewise stressed the importance of the patient's identification with the therapist which occurs in all forms of psychotherapy. Since the internalization of bad objects has made the patient ill, therapy succeeds to the extent that the therapist can become a good object. Since the patient tends to remain loyal to the early objects of his childhood, defending their internalizations against modification, however, therapy inevitably becomes a struggle. Even from this cursory sketch it is apparent that patients' responsiveness to therapy, that is their ability to form a therapeutic alliance, is importantly determined by the quality of their early interpersonal relations with others.

Thus, the quality of the patient-therapist relationship, and of the alliance as it manifests itself throughout the interaction, appears to be a highly significant prognostic indicator of the forces working in favor of, or in opposition to, progress in therapy. Accordingly, it behooves clinicians and researchers to scrutinize the therapeutic alliance as well as its determinants.

Contemporary Issues

The foregoing overview warrants neither extravagant claims for nor total rejection of an enterprise which occupies an important role in contemporary society and has come to perform a useful function. Despite its diverse forms, psychotherapy offers a unique and humane approach to the vicissitudes of human adaptation, coping, and self-development. Clearly, there are many things psychotherapy cannot do, should not be expected to do, and should not claim to do. People in the field have barely begun to define the conditions under which particular interventions, hitherto lumped under the generic heading of psychotherapy, will succeed or will fail. Until this task is carried out by dispassionate and disciplined inquiry, sweeping conclusions about the effectiveness or ineffectiveness of psychotherapy are ill advised and decidedly premature. Nonetheless, it is possible today to be more certain about a number of issues and, in the light of accumulating clinical and research evidence, to formulate public policy. The field, however, is in serious danger of becoming swept up by political developments, at least some of which threaten to turn back the clock on hard-won scientific and professional progress. Foremost among these issues is the so-called remedicalization of psychotherapy. I shall set the stage for discussing this controversy by summarizing the previous exposition.

1. As we have seen, the essence of psychotherapy is a human relationship designed to produce personality or behavior change in a person traditionally called a patient or a client. In this professional relationship, therapists are enjoined to take responsibility for the safety and well-being of their patients. The nature of the relationship is further defined by ethical standards which are aimed at achieving optimal change while protecting the patient from exploitation and potential harm. To function adequately and responsibly in the therapeutic role, a therapist must have undergone appropriate training.

2. Psychotherapy (or any of its variants) is not a treatment modality or a set of technical procedures which can be precisely defined or administered in an impersonal manner. By contrast, all techniques function within the total context of a human relationship, and they can be no better than that relationship. Assuredly, technical operations may enhance changes achievable within a good therapeutic relationship. The preponderance of the available evidence, however, indicates that the human qualities of the patient and of the therapist and the nature of their relationship overshadow specific effects potentially attributable to technical maneuvers.

3. As a concomitant to the foregoing, the therapist does not treat a disease or a disorder but rather a human being who experiences more or less specific difficulties in his or her adjustment to life. It follows that there can be no impersonal treatment of a faceless patient by an anonymous therapist. Further, studying treatment outcomes based on such a model or assuming that a treatment can be developed which does not take full account of the personal qualities of the participants and the nature of their human interaction is futile.

4. Future research efforts must be aimed at matching a particular patient with a particular therapist for the purpose of achieving a human relationship in which the patient as a human being can feel respected, accepted, and understood. If this precondition is met, the success of psychotherapy is circumscribed by (a) the patient's ability to form a productive working relationship with the therapist, an ability that may be severely impeded by the damaging effects of earlier interpersonal experiences and the learning that has occurred within the context of these experiences; (b) the therapist's ability to understand the patient and to empathize with him or her; and (c) the therapist's technical skills in mediating learning experiences that the patient finds helpful. There may be many kinds of helpful experiences (for example, improved self-understanding, ventilation of affect, or assertiveness training), depending upon the patient's personality make-up, the nature of the problem, the changes desired by the patient, and the quality of the therapeutic relationship. It is highly questionable, however, whether any single technique is intrinsically superior to another, although there may be gradations of usefulness.

5. Finally, some patients appear to be good candidates for a psychotherapeutic relationship whereas others are not. By the same token, some therapists appear to have more appropriate personality characteristics and technical skills that may predispose them to be better therapists with particular patients. We cannot escape the conclusion that the value of what has been called psychotherapy depends heavily upon the encounter of two human beings and the extent to which such a relationship (in common parlance) clicks. This realization clearly raises difficulties because the pertinent variables are difficult to define; it also may imply that, depending upon appropriate patient and therapist variables, the applicability and the potential success of psychotherapy may be more circumscribed than has generally been believed. Thus, we may need better patients as well as better therapists. To recognize existing limitations, however, is no more than paying obeisance to reality which is often a hard taskmaster. No one faults medicine for its limited ability to correct nature's malformations or to reverse the damage created by

chronic conditions. One should expect no more from psychotherapy than to delineate realistically the conditions under which it flourishes or fails. Indeed, this delineation may be the process for evolving better alternatives.

The Remedicalization Debate

It is now becoming apparent that the future of psychotherapy, both as a form of clinical practice and as an area of scientific research, will be heavily influenced by political pressures. In part, these pressures have their roots in activities initiated by the federal government; to some extent, they also have fueled old struggles between the mental health professions. With regard to the latter, psychiatry is increasingly seeking an alliance with the powerful medical profession, opposing the sizable number of nonmedical mental health professions, among which clinical psychologists are the most numerous and influential. Thus, polarizations have occurred which may work to the detriment of patients, the mental health professions, and the future development of psychotherapy as a scientific and professional discipline.

The practice of psychotherapy in the United States has become an industry, and a growing number of claims for reimbursement of fees charged by mental health professionals are being presented to insurance carriers (third parties), both private and governmental. The questions therefore arise whether and to what extent such claims fall under the rubric of health care, which for insurance purposes is usually defined as medical treatment for a medical disorder. Directly related to the foregoing are the following issues: What is the nature of psychotherapeutic treatment? Is treatment safe and effective? For what conditions is it indicated? What tangible benefits does a unit of service yield? Who is competent to provide the service? How can criteria of professional competence be defined, measured, and enforced? What limitations should be placed on reimbursement? How can overuse and abuse be prevented? With some form of national health insurance looming on the horizon and the government's involvement in legislation for health insurance already a reality, the foregoing questions, among others, are being raised with increasing urgency. Responses are being sought from governmental agencies (e.g., the National Institute of Mental Health), the mental health professions, and experts within the mental health field.

Among the various issues, none is perhaps more salient than that relating to the safety and effectiveness of psychotherapy. The government's position that adequate scientific evidence on these points should be a precondition for reimbursement of services is understandable. But what constitutes acceptable evidence? Furthermore, by phrasing the question in this way, a number of implicit assumptions are being made whose reasonableness and validity are open to question. Among these assumptions, the following seem central:

1. If psychotherapy is to be reimbursed under health insurance, it must be defined as a form of medical treatment for a medical disorder. As a medical treatment, it must qualify as a health care technology whose risks and cost-effectiveness are to be assessed in accordance with procedures governing the testing of surgical interventions or drugs.

2. To assess the effectiveness and safety of a drug, clinical trials (i.e., experiments under controlled conditions) must be conducted. In clinical trials it is essential to provide stringent definitions of (a) the purity and dosage of the drug; (b) the nature of the disorder the drug is designed to ameliorate; (c) the character of the changes produced by the drug, including side effects and other adverse consequences; and (d) other pertinent variables which might influence the treatment.

3. Once clinical trials have been conducted, the procedures must be stringently followed in subsequent clinical applications. Monitoring the treatment to ascertain whether appropriate criteria are being met must also be possible. (This stipulation has given rise to the development of treatment manuals which seek to describe therapeutic procedures as explicitly as possible.)

As part of these requirements, the spotlight has been turned on the available research evidence to determine whether it might serve as an adequate basis for making the mandated determinations. In general, the conclusion is being reached that this evidence cannot. Major reasons appear to be the following:

1. While there now appears to be reasonable evidence that psychotherapy in general is moderately effective in the sense that the majority of patients tend to show measurable therapeutic gains, it is also possible to argue that these gains fall short of what is expected from fairly expensive and time-consuming treatments. At least in part, this problem is definitional and cannot be answered by scientific investigation.

2. It has not been possible to describe with sufficient stringency (a) the essential characteristics of the treatment; (b) the disorders psychotherapy has been designed to ameliorate; (c) the nature of the changes resulting from the interventions; (d) the durability of the changes achieved; (e) the relative merits of particular forms of psychotherapy with respect to a particular disorder; (f) the advantages of psychotherapy in comparison to other forms of intervention, such as drugs; (g) the training and qualifications of therapists necessary to administer a par-

ticular form of treatment; and (h) the circumstances under which a particular treatment is effective. Among the last group of factors one might include the patient's motivation to participate in the treatment, the availability of the treatment, the community resources, and a host of related variables.

3. Among clinicians and researchers, controversy persists on almost all of the foregoing issues. Furthermore, while considerable advances in research design, techniques, and methodology have been made over the past several decades and while the newer studies are more adequate than the older ones, research results do not readily translate into the kinds of precise decisions legislators and policymakers feel called upon to make.

Two kinds of solutions, neither of which is satisfactory, have suggested themselves: controlled research at an accelerated pace or legislative action based on available information. With respect to the former, Parloff (1979) has calculated that scores of investigations, at exorbitant expense, would have to be carried out to answer the questions posed by the government. Even under the most propitious circumstances, it would take many years before adequate evidence could be adduced. The second solution opens the door to decisions which would be heavily influenced by special interest groups rather than by scientific evidence. It might be argued that the scientific evidence in a field such as psychotherapy can never be sufficiently precise to undergird legislative efforts and that, in any event, political and economic considerations will take precedence. In short, compromise will always be necessary.

At present, the problem is being tackled by the government in efforts to step up targeted research (a major example is the collaborative study on depression, in which two forms of psychotherapy are being systematically compared with drugs) and by interpreters of the available evidence, incomplete as this evidence is. We witness the clash of various interest groups among the interpreters which seek to promote legislation favoring their particular aspirations. The battle will probably continue for years to come, and the results of scientific investigations may play only a limited role in the battle's outcome. Nonetheless, legislators and policymakers will predictably look to the scientific community for answers to the pressing questions mentioned above.

Obviously there is a serious paradigm clash between the exposition of psychotherapy presented in the body of this chapter and the clinical-trials approach currently being advocated by the government. It is also apparent that the latter approach is favored by those who are willing to accept a conception of psychotherapy as a form of health-care technology (with mandated reimbursement by insurance carriers) whereas the former is more congenial to those who have witnessed the evolution of modern psychotherapy as a psychological discipline. With respect to the latter, psychotherapy has gradually severed the ties with the disease model from which it took its start in Freud's day. In this view, if psychotherapy is not a health-care technology, it will logically not be reimbursable by health insurance. Thus, unless "health" is redefined to include both physical and mental health (in a rather broad sense), psychotherapy may not qualify under present or projected health insurance schemes.

A further argument is that psychotherapy is used disproportionately by members of the more affluent strata of society, from which is deduced that the public at large should not be expected to underwrite, either through tax dollars or voluntary contributions, benefits accruing predominantly to a relatively narrow segment of the population. Although, until recently, psychotherapy may have been relatively unavailable to a broader spectrum of the citizenry who might benefit from it, no one can deny that psychotherapy presupposes certain attitudes and motivations on the part of the consumer. Consequently, if these requirements are not met, the value of psychotherapy is correspondingly diminished. The charge that there is a necessary link between social class and ability to profit from psychotherapy, however, is not nearly so well documented as the critics allege. On the contrary, reasonable evidence shows that members of the lower economic classes, minorities, the elderly, and other groups can benefit from psychotherapy if the opportunities are provided and if therapists possess the requisite competence.

A Proposed Solution

It has become amply apparent that psychotherapy is in an embattled state. Much of the confusion is traceable to sharply divergent views of what psychotherapy is and what it is intended to do. This much is clear: If one disregards relatively minor problems of adjustment that are susceptible to instruction and training, psychotherapy deals essentially with problems in human living—man's view of himself and his place in the world—which importantly involve interpersonal relations. Anxiety, depression, alienation, and the host of symptoms psychotherapy is intended to ameliorate are manifestations of failures in human adaptation, including faulty assumptions about oneself, faulty ways of dealing with adult human reality, and faulty techniques of relating to one's contemporaries. As soon as one listens to a patient's story, one encounters unhappiness, frustration, and despair which find expression in diverse forms of psychopathology including psychosomatic symptoms, neurotic symptoms, and maladaptive character styles (characteristic ways of dealing with life's challenges). Basic to all of these difficulties are impairments in self-acceptance and self-esteem. These impairments, in turn, have their origins in a sense of weakness and helplessness—the basic condition of childhood. From this condition flows the wish for powerful, protective helpers on whose superior strength one hopes to rely. Therefore, the transference tendency is a fundamental and ubiquitous human trait that is set in motion as one encounters vicissitudes that factually or in fantasy exceed one's own strengths. Of course, this tendency is heavily compounded by traumas and adversities of childhood which have prevented the person from mastering the challenges and developmental crises faced by everyone in reaching adult maturity. In one form or another, every patient who enlists the services of a psychotherapist suffers from a realization of failure and defeat: His or her own personality resources are experienced as inadequate to cope with life.

Given this state of "demoralization" (Frank, 1974), there are numerous ways in which another person (therapist, friend, paraprofessional, clergyman, physician, etc.) can provide assistance and comfort. Respectful listening, reassurance, and advice are time-honored techniques that have been found useful by mankind since the dawn of history. These are the common or nonspecific factors to which much favorable change in all forms of psychotherapy can be attributed. Depending on the depth or pervasiveness of the patient's demoralization, these factors will exert a more or less lasting therapeutic effect. In general, their utility is commensurate with the extent to which the need of a powerful helper can be satisfied through a limited human relationship and whether one's own coping strengths can be shored up in this manner. In some cases, such help may be impressive; in many others, as we have come to realize, it is not. In order to provide help of this kind, a great deal of professional preparation is not needed, and many warm, understanding, and patient individuals can function in the role of a nonprofessional or quasi-professional helper.

But what can the professional psychotherapist offer? What fund of psychological knowledge allows him or her to transcend the baseline set by the foregoing? Such help can take one of two forms, the second of which impresses me as greatly more beneficial and desirable from a humane perspective.

The first approach takes full advantage of the therapist's position of power, largely established by the patient's transference tendency, that is, his desire for a powerful helper on whom he can rely and depend.

From this vantage point, it is possible for the therapist to indoctrinate, counsel, exhort, and guide the patient. This help may take the form of demonstrating to the patient the self-defeating quality of beliefs and assumptions about himself and others (such as "everyone must love me" or "by subordinating my desires to those of others I will gain their acceptance"); instructing a couple in more satisfying techniques of sexual enjoyment; and providing relaxation training to overcome anxiety generated in specific situations. Many so-called behavioral techniques capitalize on the powers conferred upon a professional helper by a patient seeking the assistance of an omnipotent transference figure. Crucial for the success of such endeavors is a patient who is relatively open to being influenced by such a helper, that is, one who while seeking help is not simultaneously opposing (resisting) the helper's assistance. Such patients may be described as well motivated and sufficiently independent and mature to follow, and thus take advantage of, the prescribed regimen. Many patients unfortunately do not meet these qualifications. In addition, all of these techniques partake of a certain directive, coercive quality which has often given rise to the charge of manipulation, behavior control, or brainwashing.

The second approach, which has its antecedents in Freud's discoveries, is based on the fundamental assumption that the most effective means of helping patients is to assist them in discovering for themselves the roots of their unhappiness and, in the process, to come to terms with these roots. These origins are regularly found in the child's existential dilemma of profound helplessness in a world that is experienced as hostile, rejecting, and misunderstanding. In these terms, the complex superstructure of neurotic symptoms, characterological distortions, and maladaptations is seen as an abortive attempt to solve problems which, given the child's biological and psychological dependence, could not be solved. The overvaluation of parental figures and the persistent wish for powerful protecting helpers is a necessary component of this constellation. For this reason, the analysis of the transference occupies an important role in psychotherapy based on psychoanalytic principles. Instead of allowing or encouraging the patient to perpetuate his dependency, the goal of therapy is to help the patient abandon his undue reliance on these fantasied images and to help him develop his own locus of control. In the process of working through, he discovers his own limitations (as well as those of others) and, in Freud's phrase, he learns to substitute ordinary human unhappiness for neurotic misery.

The process of discovering meanings and gaining insight into the mainsprings of one's motivations and behavior is necessarily time-consuming and costly. Moreover, it is not desired by a great many people who, in keeping with the transference paradigm, prefer magical solutions to rational ones. In furthering the objective of self-understanding or insight, however, the therapist must necessarily assume an expectant stance rather than a directive one. The therapist must allow the patient to proceed at his or her own pace, must follow rather than lead, and must limit activities to those which further the patient's self-understanding (such as summaries or interpretations). The therapist's goal is to help the patient understand and to promote change via such understanding rather than through directive or coercive means. The primary concern is that the patient's discoveries are to the greatest extent self-discoveries, that the changes occurring in the patient come largely from within rather than from without.

It follows that any activity on the therapist's part which is designed to promote change directly—through suggestion, indoctrination, or whatever directive means—uses rather than resolves the patient's transference tendency. Such capitalizing on transference is true of time-limited forms of dynamic psychotherapy in which the patient is pushed to accept interpretations designed to hasten change as well as all other forms that seek to impose change rather than foster it. From a pragmatic perspective emphasizing results rather than the process by which change is achieved, the difference may be inconsequential. In human terms, however, the difference is between subjugation (that is, the extension of control) and liberation. These are the fundamental choices open to any form of psychotherapy.

Does this preference mean that the best therapist is totally nondirective, committed to a therapeutic stance that opens the door to interminable treatment? Orthodox psychoanalysis has been faulted precisely on this point, and in many cases the criticism may have been justified. My answer is that, even within the model of self-discovery, it is possible—and, indeed, highly desirable—for the therapist to keep the dialogue focused, to avoid digressions, and to keep the patient on target. To be able to perform this therapeutic function, the therapist must have a thorough understanding of the major issues with which a patient is struggling. This understanding, in turn, permits the therapist to provide the necessary guidance and to keep the treatment from floundering. I further suggest that therapists of the future must receive much better training in carrying out these tasks, and research must seek to establish the extent to which these skills make a difference in process and outcome. At the same time, however, there is clearly a fine line between the latter kind of guidance, on the one hand, and directive control which imposes insights, solutions, and courses of action, on the other. To state the problem slightly differently: While personality and behavior change is clearly the goal of psychotherapy, how this change is achieved is not a matter of indifference. My own view is that a free society must be extremely sensitive to this issue and it must strenuously resist the imposition of change by coercive means, no matter how well intentioned the procedures may be. The price to pay may be a technology that is less potent, that takes a longer period of time, and that may be unsuitable for a sizable segment of the patient population.

Conclusion

The outcome of psychotherapy, like that of any complex educational process, is extraordinarily difficult to measure and evaluate. In this chapter I have attempted to document why this difficulty exists. Nonetheless, the task is not insuperable. Indeed, progress will be facilitated if psychotherapy is viewed in a broader interpersonal context and if analogies to a medical treatment are rejected. In my view, the true purpose of psychotherapy is to stimulate personality growth and to help the patient overcome obstacles impeding such growth. Patients need to learn how their developmental histories have interfered with their maturation, how patients stand in their own way, and how they might learn to lead more adaptive, satisfying, and fulfilling lives. Such learning is often very difficult and protracted because it is interfered with by longstanding, deeply engrained patterns of thinking, feeling, and acting. The basic question for the psychotherapist is how personality growth can be facilitated and hastened. Therapy without guidance results in chaos; forcible therapy has its own built-in defeats; the therapist's task is to find the optimum balance. The therapist, like the good parent, needs to know how to love without spoiling and to discipline without hurting, as Robert Waelder once defined the goal of education (1960).

References

Andrews, J. Psychotherapy of phobias. *Psychological Bulletin,* 1966, *66,* 455–480.

Bergin, A. E., & Lambert, M. J. The evaluation of therapeutic outcomes. In S. L. Garfield & A. E. Bergin (Eds.), *Handbook of psychotherapy and behavior change: An empirical analysis* (2nd ed.). New York: Wiley, 1978.

Carkhuff, R. R. *Helping and human relations: A primer for lay and professional helpers* (Vol. 1). New York: Holt, Rinehart and Winston, 1969.

Carkhuff, R. R., and Truax, C. B. Lay mental health counseling: The effects of lay group counseling. *Journal of Consulting Psychology,* 1965, *29,* 426–431.

DiLoreto, A. O. *Comparative psychotherapy: An experimental analysis.* Chicago: Aldine-Atherton, 1971.

Eysenck, H. J. The effects of psychotherapy: An evaluation. *Journal of Consulting Psychology,* 1952, *16,* 319–324.

Fairbairn, R. *Object relations theory of the personality.* New York: Basic Books, 1952.
Frank, J. D. *Persuasion and healing* (2nd ed.). Baltimore: Johns Hopkins University Press, 1973.
Frank, J. D. Psychotherapy: The restoration of morale. *American Journal of Psychiatry,* 1974, *131,* 271–274. (a)
Frank, J. D. Therapeutic components of psychotherapy. *Journal of Mental Disease,* 1974, *159,* 325–342. (b)
Freud, S. [On psychotherapy]. In J. Strachey (Ed. and trans.), *Standard Edition of the Complete Psychological Works of Sigmund Freud* (Vol. 7). London: Hogarth, 1953. (Originally published, 1905.)
Freud, S. [Analytic therapy]. In J. Strachey (Ed. and trans.), *Standard Edition of the Complete Psychological Works of Sigmund Freud* (Vol. 16). London: Hogarth, 1963. (Originally published, 1916.)
Garfield, S. L. Research on client variables in psychotherapy. In S. L. Garfield & A. E. Bergin (Eds.), *Handbook of psychotherapy and behavior change: An empirical analysis* (2nd ed.). New York: Wiley, 1978.
Garfield, S. L., Prager, R. A., & Bergin, A. E. Evaluating outcome in psychotherapy: A hardy perennial. *Journal of Consulting and Clinical Psychology,* 1971, *37,* 320–322.
Goldstein, A. P., & Stein, N. *Prescriptive psychotherapies.* New York: Pergamon Press, 1976.
Greenson, R. *The technique and practice of psychoanalysis.* New York: International University Press, 1967.
Guntrip, H. *Psychoanalytic theory, therapy, and the self.* New York: Basic Books, 1971.
Hadley, S. W., & Strupp, H. H. Contemporary views of negative effects in psychotherapy. *Archives of General Psychiatry,* 1976, *33,* 1291–1302.
Hartley, D. Therapeutic alliance and the success of brief individual psychotherapy. Unpublished doctoral dissertation, Vanderbilt University, 1978.
Hoehn-Saric, R., Frank, J. D., Imber, S. D., Nash, E. H., Stone, A. R., & Battle, C. C. Systematic preparation of patients for psychotherapy: I. Effects on therapy behavior and outcome. *Journal of Psychiatric Research,* 1964, *2,* 267–281.
Holt, R. R., & Luborsky, L. *Personality patterns of psychiatrists: A study in selection techniques* (Vol. 1). New York: Basic Books, 1958.
Horwitz, L. *Clinical prediction in psychotherapy.* New York: Jason Aronson, 1974.
Kaplan, H. S. *The new sex therapy: Active treatment of sexual dysfunctions.* New York: Brunner/Mazel, 1974.
Kernberg, O. F. *Object relations theory and clinical psychoanalysis.* New York: Jason Aronson, 1976.
Kernberg, O. F., Burnstein, E. D., Coyne, L., Appelbaum, A., Horowitz, L., & Voth, H. *Psychotherapy and psychoanalysis: Final report of the Menninger Foundation's psychotherapy research project.* Topeka: The Menninger Foundation, 1972.
Kiesler, D. J. Some myths of psychotherapy research and the search for a paradigm. *Psychological Bulletin,* 1966, *65,* 110–136.
Knight, R. P. Evaluation of the results of psychoanalytic therapy. *American Journal of Psychiatry,* 1941, *98,* 434–446.
Langs, R. *The technique of psychoanalytic psychotherapy.* New York: Jason Aronson, 1973.
Luborsky, L., Singer, B., and Luborsky, L. Comparative studies of psychotherapies: Is it true that "Everybody has won and all must have prizes?" *Archives of General Psychiatry,* 1975, *32,* 995–1008.
Marks, I. Behavioral psychotherapy of adult neurosis. In S. L. Garfield and A. E. Bergin (Eds.), *Handbook of psychotherapy and behavior change: An empirical analysis* (2nd ed.). New York: Wiley, 1978.
Meltzoff, J., & Kornreich, M. *Research in psychotherapy.* New York: Atherton Press, 1970.

Menninger, K. A., & Holtzman, P. S. *Theory of psychoanalytic techniques* (2nd ed.). New York: Basic Books, 1973.

Orlinsky, D. E., & Howard, K. I. The relation of process to outcome in psychotherapy. In S. L. Garfield & A. E. Bergin (Eds.), *Handbook of psychotherapy and behavior change: An empirical analysis* (2nd ed.). New York: Wiley, 1978.

Orne, M. T., & Wender, P. H. Anticipatory socialization for psychotherapy: Method and rationale. *American Journal of Psychiatry,* 1968, *124,* 1202–1212.

Parloff, M. B. Can psychotherapy research guide the policy maker? A little knowledge may be a dangerous thing. *American Psychologist,* 1979, *34,* 296–306.

Parloff, M. B., Waskow, I. E., & Wolfe, B. E. Research on therapist variables in relation to process and outcome. In S. L. Garfield & A. E. Bergin (Eds.), *Handbook of psychotherapy and behavior change: An empirical analysis* (2nd ed.). New York: John Wiley, 1978.

Paul, G. L. *Insight versus desensitization in psychotherapy: An experiment in anxiety reduction.* Stanford: Stanford University Press, 1966.

Paul, G. L. Insight versus desensitization in psychotherapy two years after termination. *Journal of Consulting Psychology,* 1967, *31,* 333–348.

Rogers, C. R. The necessary and sufficient conditions of therapeutic personality change. *Journal of Consulting Psychology,* 1957, *21,* 95–103.

Rogers, C. R., and Dymond, R. F. *Psychotherapy and personality change.* Chicago: University of Chicago Press, 1954.

Shapiro, A. K., & Morris, L. A. Placebo effects in medical and psychological therapies. In S. L. Garfield and A. E. Bergin (Eds.), *Handbook of psychotherapy and behavior change: An empirical analysis* (2nd ed). New York: Wiley, 1978.

Sloane, R. B., Staples, F. R., Cristol, A. H., Yorkston, N. J., & Whipple, K. *Psychotherapy versus behavior therapy.* Cambridge: Harvard University Press, 1975.

Smith, M. L., & Glass, G. V. Meta-analysis of psychotherapy outcome studies. *American Psychologist,* 1977, *132,* 752–760.

Strupp, H. H. Toward a specification of teaching and learning in psychotherapy. *Archives of General Psychiatry,* 1969, *21,* 203–212.

Strupp, H. H. Toward a reformulation of the psychotherapeutic influence. *International Journal of Psychiatry,* 1973, *11,* 263–327.

Strupp, H. H. Success and failure in time-limited psychotherapy: A systematic comparison of two cases (Comparison 1). *Archives of General Psychiatry,* 1980, *37,* 595–603. (a)

Strupp, H. H. Success and failure in time-limited psychotherapy: A systematic comparison of two cases (Comparison 2). *Archives of General Psychiatry,* 1980, *37,* 708–716. (b)

Strupp, H. H. Success and failure in time-limited psychotherapy: With special reference to the performance of a lay counselor. *Archives of General Psychiatry,* 1980, *37,* 831–841. (c)

Strupp, H. H. Success and failure in time-limited psychotherapy: Further evidence (Comparison 4). *Archives of General Psychiatry,* 1980, *37,* 947–954. (d)

Strupp, H. H., and Bergin, A. E. Some empirical and conceptual bases for coordinated research in psychotherapy. *International Journal of Psychiatry,* 1969, *7,* 18–90.

Strupp, H. H., & Bloxom, A. L. Preparing lower-class patients for group psychotherapy: Development and evaluation of a role-induction film. *Journal of Consulting and Clinical Psychology,* 1973, *41,* 373–384.

Strupp, H. H., Fox, R. E., & Lessler, K. *Patients view their psychotherapy.* Baltimore: Johns Hopkins Press, 1969.

Strupp, H. H., & Hadley, S. W. A tripartite model of mental health and therapeutic outcomes: With special reference to negative effects in psychotherapy. *American Psychologist,* 1977, *32,* 187–196.

Strupp, H. H., & Hadley, S. W. Specific versus nonspecific factors in psychotherapy: A controlled study of outcome. *Archives of General Psychiatry,* 1979, *36,* 1125–1136.

Strupp, H. H., Hadley, S. W., and Gomes-Schwartz, B. *Psychotherapy for better or worse: An analysis of the problem of negative effects.* New York: Jason Aronson, 1977.

Sullivan, H. S. *Conceptions of modern psychiatry.* New York: W. W. Norton, 1953.

Wachtel, P. L. *Psychoanalysis and behavior therapy.* New York: Basic Books, 1977.

Waelder, R. Basic theory of psychoanalysis. New York: International Universities Press, 1960.

Winnicott, D. W. *The family and individual development.* New York: Basic Books, 1965.

MICHAEL J. MAHONEY

PSYCHOTHERAPY AND HUMAN CHANGE PROCESSES

MICHAEL J. MAHONEY

Michael J. Mahoney is a professor of psychology at Pennsylvania State University, where he has been on the faculty since 1972 when he obtained his doctorate at Stanford in experimental psychopathology.

His interests in personal change processes, the interdependence of cognition, behavior, and affect, and the philosophic base of scientific inquiry are reflected in his published works. He is the author of numerous journal articles and book chapters and has been an author or editor of nine books, including *Cognition and Behavior Modification* (1974), *Behavioral Self-Control* (1974), *Scientist as Subject: The Psychological Imperative* (1976), *Permanent Weight Control* (1976), and *Psychotherapy Process: Current Issues and Future Directions* (1980). In addition to being on the editorial board of ten journals and book series, he was editor of *Cognitive Therapy and Research* from 1977 to 1981 and is currently editor of the *Clinical Psychology and Psychotherapy Series.* A member of numerous professional organizations, Mahoney is a fellow of the American Psychological Association.

MICHAEL J. MAHONEY

PSYCHOTHERAPY AND HUMAN CHANGE PROCESSES

The patterns and parameters of human change processes remain one of the oldest and most intriguing themes of thoughtful inquiry. Our libraries are filled with an inseparable mixture of fictional and nonfictional expressions and analyses of change and stability in human lives. And throughout these writings are pervasive assumptions about human nature, epistemology, and certain tacit universals of experience and existence (Durant & Durant, 1970; Foucault, 1970; Friedman, 1967, 1974; Polanyi, 1966; Russell, 1945). The persistence of our quest for knowledge—and especially knowledge about ourselves—is probably a reflection of formidable inclinations toward both meaning and power. Francis Bacon observed that "knowledge is power." The nature of that power was stated more explicitly in the ancient Chinese volume, the *I Ching or Book of Changes:*

> If we know the laws of change, we can precalculate in regard to it, and freedom of action thereupon becomes possible. (Wilhelm & Baynes, 1950, p. 283)

For their comments and suggestions I would like to thank Thomas D. Borkovec, Mark Burrell, Norman J. Lesswing, Keith E. Nelson, David S. Palermo, Jeri K. Sides, Debra Wallett, and Walter B. Weimer.

Our philosophic, scientific, and artistic literatures offer an expansive array of proposed laws or patterns of change, each with its prescriptions and proscriptions for living.

Only in the last century, however, have we come to appreciate more fully that the laws of change are interdependently reflected in the laws describing microscopic and macroscopic processes. The increasing recognition of this participatory system can be witnessed in areas as disparate as self-efficacy theory (Bandura, 1977), politics and economics (Hayek, 1967, 1978), biosocial evolution (Campbell, 1975; Wilson, 1975, 1978), and even the ordering processes of history and science themselves (Foucault, 1970; Weimer, 1979). It is therefore not surprising that many advocates of human potential and world peace are now turning their attention to the pivotal significance of personal change in cultural transformation (Ferguson, 1980; Land, 1973; Leonard, 1972).

But the average consumer of psychotherapy does not seek our services in altruistic hopes of facilitating cultural transformation. Although its meanings and measures seem to be shifting away from earlier connotations of pathology and personal inadequacy, psychotherapy continues to draw much of its energy from the covalent resources of human pain and human hope. Our socially sanctioned role as therapists is that of a guide and assistant—each of us using our individualized and ever-changing theoretical sextants to gauge movement and direction. And, from our privileged role as helpers, we must often witness the breadth and depth of human suffering, the awesome tenacity of human courage, and the humbling limitations of our own understanding. After sixteen years of studying, teaching, and practicing psychotherapy, I am increasingly impressed with both the capacity and the constrictiveness of human change processes.

Prefatory Remarks

This is perhaps a good point at which to insert some structural intentions for the observations that follow. To begin with, I am not writing as a representative of any particular school of thought, conventional or emergent. It has become increasingly clear in recent commentaries on eclecticism and convergence that the theoretical substrate of psychotherapy is undergoing widespread reappraisal (Garfield & Kurtz, 1976, 1977; Goldfried, 1980). Although I feel a deep sense of respect for the dialectics that are already underway between various schools of thought, I cannot honestly claim a comfortable niche in their contact. The point here is that I do not mean to present my remarks as emanating from an established theoretical corner. They are my impressions as a student and practitioner of psychotherapy.

A second prefatory remark has to do with the divergence between my present reflections on human change processes and what has been traditionally considered the literature and domain of psychotherapy process. Many models and instruments have been proposed as viable analyses and measures of therapeutic change (Burton, 1976; Howard & Orlinsky, 1972; Kiesler, 1973; Mahoney, 1980a; Orlinsky & Howard, 1978). I believe that these contributions have been most valuable in highlighting their individual limitations. Molecular analyses of communication patterns within sessions have yielded results that have been heuristically unsatisfying. Whether the reasons be instrument error, unwieldy magnification, or something else, the complexities of human change have not been adequately captured or conveyed by precise dissections of therapeutic transcripts. At the other extreme, the holistic complexity of personal development has been beautifully rendered by numerous "big picture" artists, but many of these megamodels seem to sacrifice disorderly particulars in the service of universal generalizations. I am not sure where to place my own contribution to all this—except perhaps by negation. I will not offer encyclopedic reviews of the molecular process research, nor will I pretend to offer a new megamodel of change. Instead, my remarks will be directed at five related themes that, in my opinion, are relevant to human change processes. Since I believe that psychotherapy process is an arbitrary subset of more fundamental processes of personal development and change, I will use the broader category as the admittedly spacious arena for my observations.

Finally, the comments that follow are an intentional hybrid of theoretical conjectures and clinical impressions. I have tried to communicate some of the assumptions and emerging hypotheses that guide my behavior as a therapist and stimulate my inquiries as a researcher. I have assumed that those who might find my work useful would be interested in both its practical and its theoretical dimensions. I have therefore attempted to illustrate some of my conjectures with clinical material. I am indebted to my clients not only for allowing me to share these experiences with you but also for helping me refine my theoretical impressions in the challenging reality of our exchanges. Although the library and laboratory have been valuable instructors in my life, the limitations of their lessons have been most clearly revealed to me in the context of my attempts to facilitate change in myself and others. Like many of my colleagues, I often despair at the size of the gap between our theoretical maps and the experiential territory they are supposed to represent. As I shall reiterate, there are strong arguments from the fields of epistemology and cognitive psychology to the effect that our ability to create adequate models of human experience may ultimately asymptote in a deeper appreciation of how limited our models must be and how instrumental our maps are in defining, distorting, and directing our endless explorations. All of this notwithstanding, I have become increasingly engaged by the challenge and responsibility of studying our patterns of stability and change. Although my clients have often disabused me of some treasured and entrenched illusions about process, the sting of their lessons has been amply compensated for by their intimate gifts of honesty, complexity, and courage.

Since I will be weaving through some wide-ranging areas of relevance, let me offer a crude sketch of the directions I will be taking. My remarks have been organized with the aid of five themes. I will begin by arguing that a fundamental challenge in our efforts to understand and direct our lives is the *problem of meaning.* Within that context I will discuss the significance of viewing the central nervous system as an organ of order and the implications of conceptualizing therapeutic change in terms of changes in personal meaning. My second focus will take us into the centuries-old debate about mechanistic determinism and personal causation. Under the rubric of *constructive ontology* I will share my impressions of this feud in an analysis of "the new look" in cognitive psychology and epistemology. The main assertion there will deal with our active role in co-creating the personal realities to which we react. To understand more adequately the nature of our contribution to individual meaning structures, I will then have to examine the processes of ordering and knowing. This realm is modestly understood, and my remarks there will be brief. In studying the evolution of complex phenomena and the organization of our nervous systems, I shall endorse the concept of *hierarchical structuralism*—the functional stratification of our experiential processes. I will briefly touch upon the convergent implications of several themes in neurobiology, psychoanalysis, cognitive psychology, and social evolution.

Up to this point the thrust of my remarks will have been (1) that personal experience is extensively embedded in an individual context of meaning, (2) that we are active participants in the creation and change of our meaningful contexts, and (3) that an adequate appreciation of this perspective requires an analysis of stratified ordering processes in the nervous system. Many of the themes developed in these first three areas will be reintegrated in the fourth and fifth. Under *oscillative processes in development* I will present some conjectures on the dynamics of change and on the essential tensions which define our experience of stability and mutation. Our myriad strategies for dealing with disequilibrium in ourselves and in our clients will afford me the opportunity to comment on such topics as the role of attention in change, the importance of resistance processes, and the tyranny of techniques in our attempts to help people change. I will conclude the main part of my paper with a section on *participatory vitalism* and the role of self-empowering hope in adaptation and change. My final remarks will translate all of this discussion into some questions and impressions about the practice of psychotherapy and the investigation of human change processes.

Phenomenology and the Primacy of Meaning

The first theme I shall emphasize is deceptive in its simplicity. It is the fundamental proposition that human experience is imbued with the pursuit, construction, and alteration of meaning. Bartlett (1932) proposed a similar notion in his documentation of the extent to which humans display an "effort after meaning." That we seek and create meaning, however, need not imply that our lives reflect a tropism toward some transcendant plane of ultimate ideals. By its very nature, meaning is a highly personal and idiosyncratic phenomenon. Except where our research instruments have sacrificed individual differences as trivial or troublesome, we seldom report identical perceptions of ostensibly identical events. This phenomenological variance may itself be a reflection of an embedded evolutionary wisdom at both the individual and collective levels.

At an individual level, the primacy of meaning does not necessarily lead to a retrenchment in phenomenalism or existential solipsism. Although we may each inhabit a private universe of personal meanings, we also share an extensive part of our world with other people. Indeed, much of our social intercourse is directed at defining discrepancies among received views of reality and dealing with them. Reality and meaningfulness have long been companion concepts, and their closeness is hardly coincidental. Threats to a meaning structure are often experienced as threats to reality by its adherents (Berger & Luckman, 1967). The primacy of meaning and this protection against its change are as much a reflection on our nervous systems as on the social systems in which they have developed.

Order and Contrast

Most contemporary observers of human behavior seem to concur in the notion that the brain and nervous system facilitate adaptation and growth via mechanisms that entail classification, contrast, and meaning.

Studies into the paleoneurology of our intelligence suggest that we bear the burden and blessing of a long and challenging biosocial evolution (Campbell, 1975; Jerison, 1973, 1976). Likewise, the literatures of cognitive psychology and psychobiology seem to be converging toward some intriguing implications that have relevance for our understanding and practice of psychotherapy (cf. Davidson & Davidson, 1980; Schwartz, 1978; Shaw & Bransford, 1977; Weimer & Palermo, 1974, 1981). The evolution of the nervous system was apparently influenced by its adaptive ability to order, organize, and translate experience into pragmatic action. The extant data on human perception and thought also suggest that much of our consciousness is dependent upon some form of contrast. As Foucault (1970) and others have noted, order may be constructed from a variety of patterns which share the critical feature of classificatory contrast. The content of knowing, if not its process, is tethered by such focalizing contrasts as agent and action, figure and ground, known and unknown. This dependency on contrast could be illustrated at many levels of information processing. For example, we could look at the meaning of the term "change" and discover that its definition is tied up with notions of stability, and vice versa. This type of definition is an illustration of conceptual contrast. A more primitive example might take the form of perceptual contrast patterns. Most of us look for a pattern in all visual arrays, only dimly aware that we actively evaluate a variety of potential tacit meanings. Our active role in perception will be a topic in the next section. For the moment, we need only note the search for order, the inclination to classify and assign meaning. This process is facilitated, of course, when different patterns of contrast are explored.

Contrast may also be illustrated in the less sensate realm of logic. The laws of identity and the excluded middle form the cornerstone of Aristotelian logic. The law of identity ($a = a$, $a \neq$ not - a) is an arbitrary vote for symbolic permanence. It protects the stability of a meaning within the boundaries of a given proposition. The law of the excluded middle states that a proposition must be either true or false; it cannot be both. It can, of course, be neither; but this conclusion usually renders the proposition literally meaning-less [sic]. Much of our moment-to-moment experience is imbued with this contrast-laden quest for meaning.[1] One irony here is that we seek order via contrast and, while we seem to gravitate toward consistency and invariance, we also

[1]There is at least one sense in which Eastern philosophies seem to invoke a more subtle form of contrast in their logic. Where Western notions of truth require the absence of self-contradictory assertions, some Eastern perspectives define truth as the harmonic assimilation of opposites. In these systems, the contrast between truth and untruth is more frequently expressed as a contrast between whole and part rather than consistency and contradiction.

learn most from the limits and contrasts of our experiential categories (Foucault, 1970; Hayek, 1952a, 1952b, 1978). In at least one sense, we represent open ordering systems which are "naturally" inclined to seek certain kinds of closure. Consistency and contrast seem to be our fundamental domains of exchange with the world.

Contextual Theories of Meaning

Translating this concept into the more familiar realm of our everyday contact with psychotherapy clients, we must first reiterate the importance of gauging the assumptive worlds which give meaning and significance to personal experience (Beck, 1976; Frank, 1973; Guidano & Liotti, in press; Raimy, 1975). Unless we appreciate the patterns by which individuals order their realities, we are unlikely to understand fully their requests for help. According to contextual theories of meaning (cf. Bransford & McCarrell, 1974; Jenkins, 1974; Macnamara, 1981; Pepper, 1942), the meaning of any given particular depends upon the context from which it is viewed. A vertical line may be read as a "one" or an "ell" depending on whether it is surrounded by letters or digits. Similarly, an experience may be granted different meanings from the vantage point of different contexts.

The everyday significance of this point was brought home to me several years ago in a family-style program for predelinquent children. I was working with a six-year-old black boy who was bright, sensitive, and abandoned. Over a period of years, he had come to reject his racial heritage and to torture himself with his blackness. A devout racist, he insisted that white people were inherently better than blacks. I was a live-in teaching parent and wanted to help this boy, Taylor, not only to accept but also to take pride in his ancestry. I had been encouraging him to acknowledge and express some of the resentment he felt for other blacks, but progress had been painfully slow. After a flash of inspiration I invited some friends to join us for dinner—a black businessman and his white wife. Taylor was politely distant throughout dinner and refused to talk with our guests. I was puzzled. That night when I went in to kiss him good-night, I found myself confronting two tear-filled eyes. It took me several minutes to recognize the naiveté of my plan. While I had been orchestrating an in vivo illustration of racial equality and raceless affection, Taylor had been watching a very different spectacle. Where I had seen two adults inpervious to the hues of their skin, my six-year-old friend had seen a successful black man who had rejected his own race in favor of a white wife. Our contexts were different, and with them the derivative meanings.

The contexts by which an individual orders experience may well be one of the most challenging and promising targets of effective psychotherapy. It is apparent that we are capable of shifting some of our frames of reference (Goffman, 1974) and that we are actively involved in the choice of some contexts. Thus, as Proffitt (1976) has illustrated, we seem to contract or buy into a particular framework from which to order experience. We purchase consistency and order by inventing or borrowing a context that captures and organizes our current experience patterns (Proffitt & Halwes, 1981). In this sense, meaning is accompanied by closure and by limiting reference points. In cases of chronic dysphoria these frameworks, I believe, are imbued with painful assumptions and self-fulfilling prophecies (Jones, 1977). Although there are wide individual variations, we should not overlook the possibility of common meaning structures within similar displays of self-preoccupation. For example, we should not be surprised to find that persons who seek therapy report danger and disappointment in their lives. While I am skeptical of attempts to map universal schemata corresponding to discrete nosological categories, my skepticism rests with our diagnostic categories as much as with our individual differences. The invariance within the variance is often fascinating, however, and it deserves our attention as researchers.

The practical relevance of the primacy of meaning has only recently begun to receive recognition in our experimental endeavors. While many workers have shifted their attention from the ostensive stimulus to the "stimulus as perceived" (Mahoney, 1974), the significance of that shift for our understanding of human change processes is still being evaluated. The data suggest that the significance may be quite impressive. In her review of the role of perceived control in subjective distress, for example, Thompson (1981) concludes that "reactions to potentially stressful events depend on their meaning for the individual" (p. 89). She goes on to note that our various strategies of cognitive and behavioral control may derive their power by changing the meaning of an event and its corresponding emotional and behavioral concomitants. Thompson's (1981) recommendations for future research are noteworthy:

> The challenge now is to discover the types of meanings that can be used and to explore how to help individuals develop the ability to assign meanings that will be the most beneficial to them. (p. 99)

The point is that most forms of personal distress and its treatment rely on the primacy of meaning and the centrality of meaning change in personal change. The implication is for researchers to seek into the contexts and contracts by which we assign and alter meaning.

I like to remind myself and my clients that our personal frameworks for meaning did not evolve in a function-free vacuum. No matter how painful and limiting our personal realities, they are the legacy of valuable developmental choices. We have adapted to idiosyncratic patterns of genetic potential and environmental possibilities. It is, of course, distressing to witness unnecessary suffering and avoidable constraints on personal freedom. But I believe we must also respect our fallible constructions of self and reality as having been functional allies in our attempts to cope with the vicissitudes of life. I shall return to this point in a later section when we take up the concept of healthy resistance.

Constructive Ontology

Thus far I have argued that the problem of meaning is fundamental to our understanding of human experience. I have not, however, offered a reference point from which to study the meaning of meaning. Cogent analyses of this concept have already been offered by a number of capable philosophers and scientists (Bransford & McCarrell, 1974; Frankl, 1978; Jenkins, 1974; Klemke, 1981; Pepper, 1942; Proffitt, 1976). There is one sense in which meaning—as the fiber of ordered value—can never be understood. Until we develop less dependency on contrast in our knowing processes, we are unlikely to appreciate the pervasiveness of meaning in our adaptation. We can, of course, divide experiences along categories of relative quantity of meaning—from most to least meaningful—but the dimension itself will still lack a figure-ground contrast.

The definitional difficulty is common to all branches of science and philosophy. One valuable lesson from our centuries of studying epistemology, cosmology, and the nature of explanation has been the ultimate retreat of our analyses into some form of commitment. This was the theme in Bartley's (1962) revolutionary volume on the nature of rationality and knowing processes. Our philosophical quests for uncaused causes, unexplained explainers, and undefined definers may well remind us of a saying sometimes attributed to Schopenhauer—namely, that "philosophy is the systematic misuse of a set of symbols specifically designed for that purpose." I find the meaning of meaning much less engaging than the processes operative in its development and change. A discussion of these processes brings us to yet another arena of interdisciplinary convergence.

Learning and Memory

As central as they are to the enterprise we call psychology, the concepts of learning and memory remain two of the most elusive fundamentals in our knowledge. We have made undeniable progress in these areas, but I do not know too many psychologists who feel comfortable with the adequacy of our understanding. Only in the last decade have we begun to move away from obtuse laboratory analogues and restrictive instruments of analysis. In my opinion, that move is long overdue. Clearly, the old experimental chambers of animal learning research and the early emphasis on associative learning in our memory laboratories have left us with a stockpile of potentially valuable details on microprocesses. But they have also diverted us from some very compelling and challenging questions about dynamic patterns of stability and change in a complex and open system.

It seems increasingly obvious that we are active participants in our environmental exchanges. Examples of this "reciprocal determinism" are abundant (Bandura, 1978; Jones, 1977; Mahoney, 1974). These complex patterns of attention, action, and reaction illustrate our participation in the ongoing exchange between person and environment. In my present argument for constructive ontology, I am concurring with some recent insights into our participation in the development and maintenance of functional ordering schemes—or schemata—that place limitations on the realm of assimilable experience.

If humans are, indeed, active participants in the reality constructions that shape their lives, we are well advised to study the processes involved in that participatory construction. Behavioristic and cybernetic models generally fall short in their analyses because of their metatheories of classical or strict determinism and, in the case of radical behaviorism, their anachronistic notions about the nature of scientific inquiry.[2] Whatever else it may require, an adequate analysis of human learning and memory processes must consider the complexities of an open system that acts upon the information encountered and alters it. And this statement brings us to the "new look" in human knowing processes.

[2]The difference between "determinate" and "deterministic" metatheories has been addressed by such writers as Hayek (1967, 1978) and Weimer (1981a, 1981b). Briefly, a determinate perspective recognizes the operation of rules and ordered relationships, but it does not claim the ability to forecast particular outcomes. Deterministic perspectives, however, often presume a linear sequence of discrete particulars (hence the label of "billiard ball determinism").

Cognitive Psychology

There have been many debates about what constitutes a bonafide revolution in science (Kuhn, 1962, 1970a, 1970b; Lakatos & Musgrave, 1970; Weimer, 1979). Without pursuing that tangent, let me suggest that we are witnesses of and participants in an exciting generation of change and development in our theories of human experience. This change is most apparent in the renewal of interest in cognition and in the role of psychological processes in our scientific constructions of reality. Since I have addressed the new look in epistemology in some of my previous work (Mahoney, 1976, 1979, in press), I shall confine my present remarks to cognitive psychology and the recent expansion of cognitivism in clinical psychology. Cognitive theories and therapies are increasingly in vogue and are being looked to for novel suggestions on stubborn issues in psychotherapy. Many of these therapies are reminiscent of the mind-cure movement which was noted with both alarm and fascination by William James (1901/1958) at the turn of the century, when writers such as Dubois (1906, 1908, 1911), Janet (1898), and Vaihinger (1911) were laying foundations for what would later become today's rational and cognitive therapies. These therapies are, to use his words, "deliberately optimistic" and "largely suggestive" and they display "an intuitive belief in the all-saving power of healthy-minded attitudes" (p. 88).

Much of my own writing and research has been in rational and cognitive therapies, and it is therefore not surprising that I would call attention to their promise. But much of what is being popularized in today's wave of cognitivism seems superficially mediational and unnecessarily restrictive in its notions of contemporary cognitive psychology. The "cognitive revolution" (Dember, 1974) has not been confined to expansions of cognitive notions in our various specializations. While the rest of psychology has been becoming energetically more cognitive, cognitive psychology has taken a dramatic step toward becoming more "motoric." The step has hardly been unanimous, but those who have suggested it are beginning to offer some fascinating reappraisals of our notions of attention, perception, memory, and action. Conventional models of cognition have portrayed the human brain as an active but subservient witness to experience—a logical collector of pieces to a large puzzle. This model is reflected in an emphasis on sensory input and a preoccupation with stimulus-response analyses. In commenting on these sensory metatheories of cognition, Weimer (1977) wrote the following:

> Common to these positions is an implicit motion that cognition is to be understood "from the outside inward," that it is a matter of the

> structuring of sensory information by intrinsically sensory systems, and that the products of cognition must somehow subsequently be married (in a peculiar sort of shotgun wedding) to action. (p. 270)

It is this leap from input to output that has stymied associationism ever since its inception. How does the human brain manage to translate sensation to perception, let alone action? This puzzle was posed by Höffding in his critique of associationism in 1891 and is thus called "the Höffding step." How does sensory input become meaningful? And what are the transformational processes that turn the lead of perception into the gold of behavioral adaptation?

Sensory metatheories of cognition would have us follow the stimulus from sensory receptors through perceptual filters, iconic stores, the crowded streets of short- and long-term memory, and finally into some cybernetic mechanism or executive routine that decides upon and initiates a reaction. With all due respects, this mysterious transition from input to output reminds me of a cartoon by Sidney Harris (Figure 1). The new models of human cognition are called "motor theories" because they emphasize the active and instrumental role of the person in all cognitive processes. Where sensory theories emphasize the role of feedback in learning, motor theories combine feedback mechanisms with feedforward mechanisms. The latter might be likened to variably flexible "intentions" for experience which serve to protect and expand its current structure. Feedforward mechanisms are actually preontological in the sense that they place limits on the nature and range of assimilable experience. Their hypothesized operation is consistent with a sizable literature in cognitive psychology as well as with some recent neurological findings that the cortex transmits information "downstream to subcortical structures for preprocessing" (Weimer, 1977, p. 275). Contemporary representatives of these motor theories include Hayek (1952b), Shaw and Bransford (1977), Turvey (1974), and Weimer (1977). Although they could be illustrated in a number of ways, feedforward mechanisms are most familiar to the clinician when they are compared with projection processes. When one examines Figure 2, for example, one is tempted to view it as yet another rendition of Rorschach. One of the more enjoyable interpretations of this figure suggested that it depicts Popeye kissing Olive Oyl. An experienced psychometrician may be inclined to edit and censor meanings fed forward, especially if projection is viewed as an externalization of rejected parts of the personality. The stimuli used for conventional projective testing have no "real" meaning—hence, the presumed warrant for assigning responsibility to the respondent. In the present illustration, however, my ambiguous stimulus does have some real-world contact in that I know how it was created.

Figure 1. The leap from input to output in associationism. (© 1977 by Sidney Harris, *American Scientist Magazine.* Printed by permission.)

Where other persons may construct various perceptions of the figure, I am at least partially tethered by memories of a full moon over Nantucket and this crude first attempt at a hand-held time exposure photograph.

Mechanism, Mysticism, and Motor Theories

The significance of motor theories and feedforward mechanisms goes far beyond that conjectured by Kant and Freud in their respective conjectures on synthetic *a priori* knowledge and the projection of personal

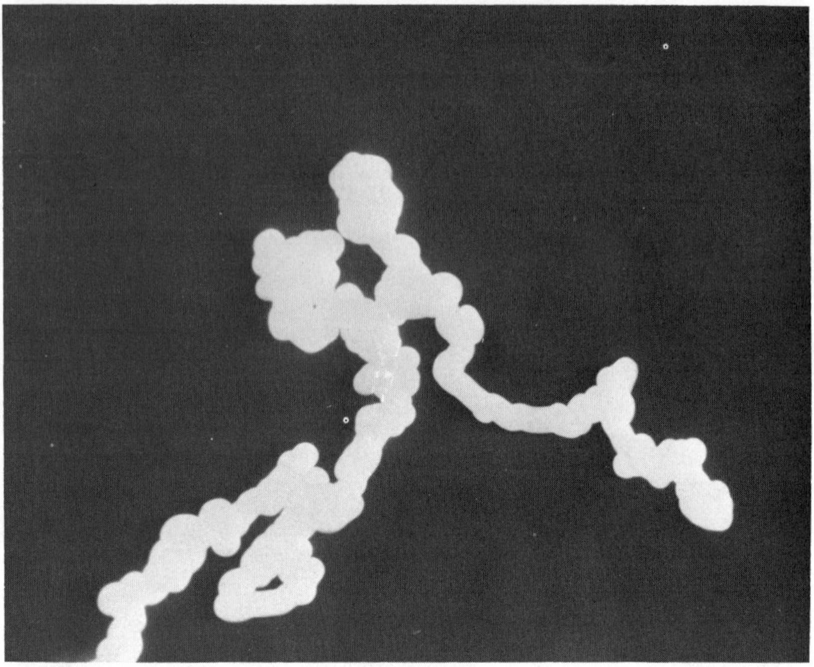

Figure 2. An illustration of feedforward mechanisms.

realities onto external configurations. We co-author the scripts of our lives, so to speak, within the confines of our senses and our idiosyncratic ordering processes. When we confront the extent of our participation in the meaning of our experience patterns, the relevance of constructive ontology for adjustment becomes more obvious. Do we do to ourselves what we fear our environment may do? Do we self-spectate, self-judge, and self-doubt *because* we fear public inspection, evaluation, and mistrust? I doubt that the cause and effect process is that simple. Yet there is a clear implication that we co-create our personal fates and our reactions to their vicissitudes.

Epictetus may have been wise in invoking us to examine our attitudes toward an experience more closely than the experience itself. That invitation—made some 20 centuries ago in Western culture—was a startling call to process as contrasted to content. *Content* and *process* are terms that serve here to illustrate what I believe could be one of the most progressive paradigm shifts in contemporary psychology—namely, the transcendence of a lively theoretical dialectic between the mechanists and the mystics.

On one hand, the mechanists are typified by behaviorists, cyberneticians, and other specialists in closed systems. Their contributions on the molecular determinants of predictable behavior are a potentially valuable asset in our self-understanding. Their focus, however, is on the role of the person as a transducer of energy. Their flow diagrams are essentially linear and anchored at both ends in the public domain of observable stimuli and observable responses.

On the other hand, the mystics are illustrated in their extremes by cosmotropic theories in which the person is a channel or a generator of energy or both. Some of these models reframe personal responsibility as a Karmic assignment, and many grant the individual generous capacities for intelligence and well-being. Reality as seen by the conscious "outer mind" is often protrayed by these writers as a patently crude and confining illusion that recedes only for those who seek and attain enlightenment. In some forms, mystical ontology asserts that we are active agents in the material existence of objects.[3]

The essence of the contrast here may ultimately rest on tacit assumptions of an epistemological sort. The mechanists seem to view reality as a matrix of discrete causal events, while the mystics seem to like fluid, probabilistic, and holistic metaphors. One group likes to view the world from without, the other from within. I do not pretend to have an unequivocal resolution to this debate, but I do have some opinions on the warrant for their assumptions and claims. Without belaboring the specific contentions of the mechanists, mystics, and motor theorists, I would argue that, at the present time, the motor theorists appear to offer a "progressive problem shift" (Lakatos, 1970) without violating too much of the embedded wisdom of the two extremes. It might be more accurate to bring motor theories into this dialogue not as a contender so much as a commentator on the contrast. Indeed, we are the sculptors of our experience, but we must work within tangible boundaries of power. There is a remarkable consistency between motor theories of cognition and some of the more modest renditions of transpersonal psychology (cf. Walsh & Vaughan, 1980). In one sense, they are strange companions, but their paths of inquiry seem to have brought them into parallel directions. I personally find the extreme mechanists least credi-

[3]There is some irony in the fact that John Wheeler—the astrophysicist who coined the term "black hole"—has given unintentional ammunition to proponents of holographic and mystical models of the universe (Brush, 1980). Wheeler's interpretation of recent developments in quantum mechanics suggests that "our consciousness affects that which we are conscious of" (Brush, p. 432)—a statement that understandably invites the interest of parapsychologists. According to Wheeler, we are contributors to a "participatory universe." For a discussion of some of the confusions and complexities in this argument, see Weimer (1981a).

ble, followed closely by the mystics. I sleep with the motor theorists, but I keep an eye open.

The point of the foregoing discussion is that constructive ontology—the phenomen of active participation in our reality constructions—appears to be a viable and working hypothesis. As Cris Williamson notes in one of her songs, we are both "the changer and the changed." How often have we observed or suspected that our clients are unwitting culprits in their own life crises? How often do we witness repetitive patterns of dysfunction and distress that are fueled and directed by idiosyncratic patterns of contracted meaning?

In this sense, one of our major tasks as therapists and theorists lies in the realm of identifying the structures and processes through which our clients construct and construe their everyday existence. Motor theories do not provide a miraculous solution to the problem of translating awareness into action. They do, however, highlight the extent to which our experience is tacitly prepared for us by our central nervous system. Motor theories also suggest that a promising direction for research on intervention strategies may involve a shift away from what the therapist does to the client and toward what the client does to himself or herself.

Hierarchical Structuralism

My third major theme deals with the nature and form of relationships within and among our central nervous system (CNS) ordering processes. This theme is one which bears important implications for our models of relatively stable patterns of individuality and unconscious processes and for the omnipresent issues of motivation and resistance in psychotherapy.

The nervous system can be viewed as a survival-enhancing structure whose primary functions include the maintenance of basic life-support systems. The senses provide the brain with much of its information about internal and external realities, but we must appreciate the variable influence of feedforward mechanisms in focusing and assimilating that information. As Hayek (1952b) and others have noted, we seem to be neurologically "wired" to classify our experiences and to transform the "buzzing booming confusion" of sensation into some codified and dynamic representation of the world. Research on memory and forgetting is basically directed at investigating our intriguing abilities to transcend spatiotemporal boundaries via these hypothesized internal representations. Not surprisingly, we find that our learning and memory abilities are themselves related to certain skills of categorization and condensation. Performances with "meaningful" material are almost always superior to those obtained when the test materials cannot be assimilated into prior ordering systems.

The point I am moving toward here might be paraphrased by saying that our CNS ordering processes are themselves ordered. They are not only organized and holistically integrated, but they also appear to be functionally stratified. Of course, this stratification is one of the central features of the myriad perspectives subsumed under the rubric of structuralism. For present purposes, I am using the term *hierarchical structuralism* to refer to the contention that our knowing processes are functionally stratified. Put another way, there appear to be patterns of nonreciprocal interaction within the human nervous system. Our theories of language, of personality, and even of the physical universe are imbued with reflections of presumed stratification. We talk about cardinal and surface traits, primary and secondary reinforcement, primary and secondary thinking processes, and deep and surface structures. Here the validity of our models may be less relevant than the frequency with which our brains seem to impose stratification and structure on experience.

Structuralism and Cognitivism

The theme of structuralism is one that invites both contention and confusion in that it often invokes mixed metaphors and semantic ambiguities. Since many of us rely on our visual system to instantiate the concept of structure, we may find ourselves limited and misled by some of the nuances of that system. Some of these problems seem to be receding, however, in recent analyses of the development and dynamics of complex systems. The growing acknowledgement of an interdependence between structure and function is evident in literatures that span several disciplines. Most pertinent here are the structural analyses that have become increasingly popular in personal and socialized belief systems and in analyses of hierarchical structure in biological evolution (e.g., Ayala & Dobzhansky, 1974; Campbell, 1974, 1975; Goldstein & Blackman, 1978; Kuhn, 1970a; Lakatos, 1970; Pattee, 1973; Zeleny, 1980). For the sake of brevity, let me move past the interdisciplinary convergences here and focus on the potential significance of this notion for our work as therapists.

To begin with, the idea of ordination within CNS ordering processes suggests that some of these processes may be more basic or fundamental than others. This notion is hardly new or alien to theorists who are comfortable with stratified or layered models of human consciousness (Valle & vonEckartsberg, 1981). It is more likely to present problems for those writers who question the value of inferred mediational processes in our analyses of behavior. For them, stratified mediational processes are simply a deeper and more costly excursion into an infinite abyss. They seem to view structuralism with less disdain than "cognitivism." Thus, in *About Behaviorism* Skinner (1974) argues that

> A small part of [one's] inner world can be felt or introspectively observed, but it is not an essential part, . . . and the role assigned to it has been vastly overrated. . . . It is impossible to estimate the havoc [that theories about internal states and processes] have wreaked . . . [upon] effort[s] to describe or explain human behavior. (pp. xii–xiii)

The increasing skirmishes between behaviorists and cognitivists are a reflection of issues that run much deeper than the epistemological wisdom of operationism, the logical warrant for parsimony, and the essence of scientific method. Beneath the surface arguments are recurrent hints of tacit assumptions about determinism, personal causation, teleonomy, and the complexity of CNS processes that comprise and potentiate human experience.

I digress on this point partly to separate structuralism from cognitivism and partly to preview a forthcoming assertion. In 1974, I attempted a comparison of nonmediational and mediational models of human behavior (Mahoney, 1974). My conclusion at that time was a cautiously optimistic endorsement of the value of cognitive psychology for clinical work. As previously noted, we have recently witnessed a remarkable growth of interest in clinically relevant cognitive processes and cognitive-behavioral therapies. Several aspects of this "cognitive revolution" have concerned me (Mahoney, 1980b), but my fascination with CNS ordering processes remains undaunted. Far from being "vastly overrated" (Skinner, 1974), the "inner world" is probably the least understood and potentially most revealing frontier in contemporary science. Although I sometimes worry that the extreme cognitivists may try to seal themselves within the organism in an inverted reflection of their behavioral colleagues, I generally trust that we are moving toward a less dichotomous set of vantage points from which to examine ourselves.

Although the cognitive-behavioral therapies have gone in the direction of integrating intrapersonal and external influence processes, I believe that our models still have a long way to go. Private speech, self-statements, and communicable fantasies are apparently important elements in personal adaptation and growth (Beck, 1976; Mahoney, 1974; Mahoney & Arnkoff, 1978; Meichenbaum, 1977; Pope & Singer, 1978; Singer, 1974; Singer & Pope, 1978). Our analyses of CNS ordering processes cannot hope to be adequate, however, so long as we treat the most easily measured surface structures as if they were the whole of human consciousness. Words and other public expressions of inner experience are generally crude and distorting representations of our phenomenology. In a quest for public consensus, such as that of science, we are fortunate to have these expressions, however crude they may be. But we are committing a costly error of translation if we equate what our clients say with what they think and how they feel. Likewise, our preoccupations with cognitive contents may be diverting attention from the critical patterns in cognitive processes. The valuable data base of surface structures—or observable particulars—need not be abandoned in order to expand our analyses into the more elusive and yet more basic deep structures and dynamics of human experience.

Unconscious Processes

With this assertion we have entered the territories of depth psychology, linguistics, transformational theories, and unconscious processes—a tropical jungle of which the diversity and the fertility present ample opportunities for entanglement, confusion, and obfuscation. I have argued elsewhere that unconscious processes—or tacit ordering processes in the CNS—seem to be increasingly difficult to ignore given the extant arguments and data (e.g., Bowlby, 1979b; Hayek, 1952b, 1978; Mahoney, 1980a, 1980b; Nisbett & Wilson, 1977; Polanyi, 1966; Shaw & Bransford, 1977; Shevrin & Dickman, 1980; Weimer, 1977). In his stimulating analysis of the structure and functions of the nervous system, Hayek (1952b, 1978) leaves little doubt as to the centrality of unconscious processes in everyday experience. For example, in his discussion of "the primacy of the abstract" (1978), his propositions are spelled out quite clearly:

> The contention which I want to expound and defend here is that . . . all the conscious experience that we regard as relatively concrete and primary, in particular all sensations, perceptions and images, are the product of a super-imposition of many "classifications" of the events perceived. . . . What I contend, in short, is that the mind must be capable of performing abstract operations in order to be able to perceive particulars, and that this capacity appears long before we can speak of a conscious awareness of particulars. . . . When we want to explain what makes us tick, we must start with the abstract relations governing the order which, as a whole, gives particulars their distinct place. (pp. 36–37)

The most obvious implication of this kind of analysis is one that has been defended and attacked since the turn of the century—namely, that the scope of our inquiry must be broad enough to accommodate experiences that are not consciously experienced. On a more personal and pragmatic level, there is also the invitation to reappraise our assumptions and proscriptions in this domain. Elsewhere I have outlined in more detail my own earlier resistance to the notion of unconscious processes (Mahoney, 1980b). It has taken several years for me to recognize these prejudices and achieve some measure of emancipation from them, and I suspect that there are still others that will present themselves from time to time. Many social scientists are understandably reluctant to shift their focus from public observables to the seemingly less secure realm of private processes. There are arguments for parsimony, arguments against explanatory fictions, and threatening implications that these cognitivist excursions into mentation are a dangerous step away from science.

I believe that these arguments are well-intentioned and that one can, indeed, point to historical instances where the invocation of tacit mediational processes have apparently encouraged more obfuscation than progress. At the same time, I think we would be naive and reckless in our theory construction either to deny their potential significance or to allow our theories to be confined by Freud's (or anyone else's) notions of unconscious processes. While there may not be an adequate contemporary theory of deep structures, I believe that there is some valuable wisdom in the extant speculations on foundational processes in experience (Ellenberger, 1970).

By way of illustration I shall share a few experiences that contributed to my own increased respect for unconscious processes in personal adjustment and development. Several years ago, when I began to explore some more open-ended assessment techniques with my clients, I was impressed with the richness of their self-reports. They offered some hints of ordering patterns that had not been apparent in their earlier records of private speech patterns. Until then my clients' self-monitoring assignments had been structured in accordance with my own theoretical assumptions about their belief systems. The emphasis in my clinical assessment had been clearly rationalistic, and much of my attention in therapy was directed at the identification and change of maladaptive beliefs. The novelty and the potential relevance of their responses to my newer techniques were sufficient, however, to pique my clinical and scientific interests, and I was soon encouraging clients to share segments of their "stream of consciousness" during our sessions. The essence of my technique was not unlike that of free association except that I used a gentle induction of trusting relaxation and would occasionally interrupt a client's report to illustrate significant themes.[4] Because of the utility of this procedure in offering in vivo instantiations of tacit world views, I now explore the benefits of "streaming" with many of my clients. An extensive literature on some dimensions of this process already exists (Klinger, 1971; Pope & Singer, 1978; Singer & Pope, 1978). In an effort to increase the clinical utility of these streams, several colleagues and I are developing a system of classifying their contents and patterns.

Another contribution to my increased respect for unconscious processes has come from explorations of my own feedforward mechanisms. I do not claim to be intimately familiar with and accepting of those processes, but I have become increasingly respectful of their influence in my personal and professional life. Over the years, I have tried to expose myself to a wide range of theoretical models. My research on psychological processes in science reflects this interest in personal and social processes in knowing. I have tried to remain open to the value of heterogeneity and tacit features of invariance. Besides having some genuine personal motives, I have been interested in gleaning the embedded bits of wisdom in our attempts to help each other. My experiences in psychotherapy workshops, retreats, and individual therapies have deepened my appreciation for my own tacit scaffoldings. A hopeful skeptic, I have had the privilege of exploring both the experiential and the theoretical dimensions of these different approaches. In the process of learning about them, of course, I also have learned a lot about myself. For example, I have come to recognize the intensity of my resistance to "non-talking cures"—the evocative therapies and other interventions that deviated from my comfortable role as a spectating therapist. I also have become aware of my continual testing of a therapy in ways that subtly reduced its chances of infiltrating my core assumptions about change. And I have come to appreciate the persistence and pervasiveness of some chronic patterns of uncomfortable self-consciousness.

These are hardly earthshaking insights, and they may not have the rhetorical force of a few dramatized case histories. My remarks serve only to expand a point that has already fueled our dialectics for quite some time—namely, that our "normal waking consciousness" may, in the words of William James (1901/1958) be "but one special type of consciousness" (p. 298). The nature, functions, and patterns of other types of experience present a formidable problem for depth psychologies. Hierarchical structuralism suggests that our understanding of human experience might be enriched by a more balanced appreciation of core ordering processes and their associated expressions. Needless

[4]This technique may be similar to some of the experimental procedures used by Kulpe and Buhler in their early investigations of imageless thought.

to say, the challenge is a formidable one, and it is all the more complicated by its immersion in paradigm politics and by the myopia that always makes forecasting a progressive problem shift difficult (Lakatos, 1970). The declining popularity of orthodox psychoanalysis (Garfield & Kurtz, 1976) could reflect a rejection of unconscious determinants in our causal analyses. Such a rejection might be both premature and excessive if we place any stock whatsoever in the cutting edge of contemporary psychobiology, epistemology, and cognitive psychology. And the most central question is not one of salvage: that is, what should we retain of Freud's hypotheses? In some ways, the new look offered by today's structuralists may require some sweeping shifts in old notions of determinism and causation. As a brief illustration, one of Hayek's (1978) passing comments on the "sub-conscious" will suffice:

> It is generally taken for granted that in some sense conscious experience constitutes the "highest" level in the hierarchy of mental events, and that what is not conscious has remained "sub-conscious" because it has not yet risen to that level. . . . If my conception is correct . . . [we are not aware of much that happens in our mind] not because it proceeds at too low a level but because it proceeds at too high a level. It would seem more appropriate to call such processes not "sub-conscious" but "super-conscious," because they govern the conscious processes without appearing in them. (p. 45)

This perspective challenges the basic strategy of moving unconscious material "upward" into awareness. Indeed, it highlights the naiveté of two-dimensional structuralism as well as some of our tacit arrogance about the role of awareness in experience. A message that seems to be frequently repeated by modern structuralists has already been noted here in reference to meaning change and psychotherapy—namely, that an adequate analysis must address process as well as content.

Related to the theme of hierarchical structuralism is the emergent hypothesis that there may be a correlation between stratification and mutability. The most basic schemata for experience—those that bear on such issues as causation, the trustworthiness of sense data, identity, and self-world relationships—these core schemata are probably more difficult to change than the more peripheral ordering processes (Mahoney, 1980b). This greater resistance to change may be due to their chronological primacy in the developing organism. Experiences that occur early in the lifespan—especially if they are autonomically intense and repeated—seem to leave a noticeable mark on the developing person (Ainsworth, 1979; Bowlby, 1973, 1979a; Sroufe, 1979). Such experiences need not be critical or insurmountable to constitute formative influences in the development of personal meaning structures. (For the vying opinions on this issue, see Kagan, 1976; Kagan, Kearsley, & Zelazo, 1978; Lipsitt, 1979; and Rutter, 1972.) That such early experiences are formative is all too apparent in psychotherapy clients. It is also apparent that change, when it is effected, seems to consolidate rather than eliminate prior patterns of adaptation. As reflected in our literatures on extinction, relapse, and recidivism, earlier patterns of thought, feeling, and action are seldom eradicated. More often they appear to be competing candidates for experience, and they often seem to win the competition during a client's struggle toward personal change. In a manner that may reflect the wisdom of individuality within evolution, new scaffoldings for experience may offer an option to override previous schematic patterns. When the override is experienced as a failure, the organism wisely falls back on the old and familiar schemata for its directives.

Oscillative Processes in Change

Retracing my remarks thus far, I have talked about the primacy of meaning, personal responsibility in the construction of meaning, and the stratification of our CNS ordering processes. In this section, I would like to pull these themes together. Our earlier discussion of meaning noted that human consciousness appears to be permeated with contrasts and polarities. The main conjecture in this section is that these contrasts may be related to the experience of disequilibrium and the energization of human change processes. Although binary cybernetic metaphors seem less than adequate in describing our internal processes, in another sense the concept of contrast may offer some helpful directions for our theorizing.

Let us return for a moment to the assertion that the nervous system is an organ of classification and order. This assertion presumes an ability to differentiate and relate—to identify perceptual invariants (Gibson, 1966) and to create functional, pragmatic, or "meaningful" webs of relationship among our representations of reality. Polanyi (1966), Hayek (1952b, 1978), and others have cogently argued that our awareness of the tacit or abstract rules employed by the nervous system may be inherently limited by our abilities to classify, correlate, and—in a sense—"perceive" our own ordering patterns. Also, our most respected models of our universe invoke sharp contrasts between such categories as matter and energy, part and whole, good and evil, reality and unreality. This is not to say that there are no gray areas between a set of polarities but only to note the frequency with which we rely on contrasting reference points to stabilize and define a dimension.

This same reliance on certain kinds of contrast may well be operative in our personal constructions of reality and in our capacities for change. Just as Thomas Kuhn (1977) has come to defend the role of an "essential tension" in the dynamic progression of scientific thought, we may find ourselves confronting a similar concept in the realm of personal thought. If so, this concept could have implications for the processes of change in and outside psychotherapy. If meaning change lies at the core of personal change—and if meaning is itself a fedforward relationship between our CNS scaffolding and the furniture of experience—then personal change may involve some tacit and explicit restructurings of our assimilating processes. In ways reminiscent of Piaget's concepts of assimilation and accommodation, our exchanges with the world around us may involve hierarchical expansions in our conceptual scaffoldings.

Equilibrium and Emotional Processes

The concepts of equilibrium and disequilibrium permeate our psychological theories and our therapeutic interventions. We acknowledge that the human nervous system appears to have incorporated a "negative feedback logic" in its structure and functions. The lower- and mid-brain structures seem to be teleonomically wired to protect homeostasis. When we are within the limits of acceptable deviation from our "set points," we are more likely to be experiencing the equanimity of equilibrium. When we violate the boundaries of that contrast, however, we enter the domain of disequilibrium and usually initiate actions to restore balance to our *milieu interieur* (Bernard, 1865/1957). This same metaphor permeates our theories of personality and psychotherapy in that our clients' most common request—and a therapist's most comfortable goal—is usually equilibration. In psychotherapy, the elusive balance that is sought is most often located in the domain of emotive processes. I would like to take a few moments here to comment on some of the ramifications of that emphasis.

I share the concern expressed by several existential and humanistic therapists about the extent to which contemporary psychotherapies have assented to an equilibration model of personal well-being (e.g., Bugental, 1965, 1978; Maslow, 1971). When clients request our assistance in reducing and controlling the pain and debilitation of their personal struggles, I believe our most humane intentions lie in the direction of that assistance. What seems less certain is whether our attention should remain unilaterally focused at the level of emotional control.

With the possible exception of some transpersonal and existential-humanistic therapies, virtually all of our intervention attempts stem from a metatheory that uses harmony, balance, or equanimity as its tacit direction. I have recently begun to wonder whether that direction—as precious as I believe it may be to our well-being—fully captures the dynamics of our human predicament. In our attempts to rapidly reduce emotional turbulence, I sometimes wonder if we are not rushing to quiet the messenger long before we have comprehended the message. The bulk of our specifiable techniques for helping seems to be aimed at achieving emotional satisfaction, directly or indirectly, without our more fully examining the role of contrasts and feelings in our personal experience.

Few psychologists would question the importance of studying the nature and functions of emotionality in human development (cf. Lewis & Rosenbaum, 1978; Plutchik & Kellerman, 1980; Yarrow, 1979; Zajonc, 1980). It seems clear that emotional changes are bound up with significant personal changes. It is also clear that we manifest a long-standing tradition of conceptualizing emotions as both expressions and driving forces in those changes. What I find most intriguing at the moment are the hypothesized oscillative processes that superordinate the emotive ones. By "oscillative" I do not necessarily mean temporal shifts in valence or configuration—although I believe that gross oscillative patterns are readily apparent in our adaptation (Aschoff, 1981; Ferguson, 1980; Land, 1973). In its present use, "oscillative" refers to the dynamic tension between contrasts in our ordering processes. Parallel notions can be found in Kuhn's (1977) essential tension, metatheories of dialectics, opponent-process theories of motivation (e.g., Solomon, 1980), two-factor learning theory (Mowrer, 1960a, 1960b), axiology (theories of value), and a wide range of metatheories that echo the yin and yang of a holistic approach.

The extant strategies for dealing with emotional contrasts seem to fall into one or more of the following categories:

1. *discharge,* which is evidenced in evocative and cathartic therapies (Nichols & Zax, 1977);
2. *control,* which is really a superordinate concept for those therapies that pit the person "against" his or her emotive processes;
3. *denial,* which is usually accomplished via a diversion of the experienced energy;
4. *confrontation,* which overlaps with the first two in its acknowledgement and engagement with emotive processes (cf. Rachman, 1980);
5. *reframing,* which attempts to redefine the contrast; and
6. *transcendence,* in which the contrast is not only redefined, but also used.

My remarks here are not intended to endorse a particular strategy so much as to reflect upon all of them. I do, however, want to comment on what appear to be converging paths in our secular wanderings. For example, consider the following commentary on the processes of change:

> General kinds of "cognitive pendulums" or systematic shifts with development apply. . . . Among these are: (1) shifts from rapid acquisition of new skills and rules to limited growth while old skills and rules are repeatedly applied, and (2) shifts from one quality to its opposite, as from broad to narrow, from stable to unstable, and from loosely-related components to a highly integrated and complex level.

Out of context, these could be the words of a cognitive theorist or a transcendentalist. In reality, they are a description of developmental linguistics (Nelson & Nelson, 1978, p. 226).

Another gem of apparent convergence comes from the worlds of physics and chemistry. For his revolutionary theory of "dissipative structures," Ilya Prigogine (1980) was recently awarded a Nobel prize. Aside from challenging the second law of thermodynamics and our revered concept of entropy, Prigogine's theory comments on the role of oscillative contrasts in the development of any open system. His theory and data suggest that disequilibrium—when it reaches a critical criterion—helps to drive an open system in the direction of restructuring its ordering processes. The initial structures for assimilating and balancing energy contrasts must transform in order to accommodate the disequilibrium. The principle underlying dissipative self-organization, called "order through fluctuations," has already stimulated some intriguing hypotheses about personal and social development (cf. Ferguson, 1980; Jantsch, 1980; Zeleny, 1980). As shown in Figure 3, the process of dissipative self-organization is one that clearly reflects the spontaneous development of a higher level of order within the system.

When I first learned of Prigogine's work, I was struck by its parallels in psychotherapy. I was particularly interested in the processes of transformation, hoping that the fields of chemistry and physics might offer some useful metaphors for my work in helping clients to restructure—or, perhaps more accurately, metastructure—such notions as identity, role, adequacy, and acceptable meaning. Of particular heuristic and practical interest has been the idea that episodes of psychological disequilibrium may reflect and/or stimulate fundamental restructuring processes in the central nervous system. If this is the case, our analyses must withdraw to a more molar vantage point, and our efforts to achieve rapid emotional equilibration must be reappraised. This line of thinking

Figure 3. The Belousov-Zhabotinskii Reaction: Chemical scroll waves illustrate the development of spontaneous "order through fluctuations." Photograph by Fritz Goro. From *From being to becoming: Time and complexity in the physical sciences* by I. Prigogine. Reprinted by courtesy of W. H. Freeman and Company.

is buttressed by a growing number of oscillative theories in personal and systems development (cf. Ayala & Dobzhansky, 1974; Campbell, 1975; Capra, 1975; Davidson & Davidson, 1980; Ferguson, 1980; Hayek, 1952b, 1978; Kuhn, 1977; Lakatos & Musgrave, 1970; Land, 1973; Leonard, 1972; Pribram, 1980; Progoff, 1975; Russell, 1945; Weimer, 1977, 1979, 1980; Zukav, 1979). Therapists who have focused on transformational processes in change have suggested that our therapeutic interventions may be more helpful when they direct the energy of crisis toward basic reconstructions of personal meaning. Brugh Joy (1978), for example, comments as follows:

> Realizing that the specific problem of the client is only the shadow of a much deeper pattern dynamic, the Transformational therapist does not start at the problem level, the level at which the client perceives

> the difficulty. Instead, the Transformational therapist tries to comprehend the pattern level of consciousness, which is manifesting the "problem," and to focus the transmutational energy there. Nothing of much value . . . will happen if the client's awareness is allowed to remain in the perspective of the problem. (p. 216)

Joy describes the three major paths to problem resolution outlined by the Tibetan Buddhist approach: (1) *transmutation,* which is roughly equivalent to a restructuring of cognitive-experiential processes via the development of higher-order scaffolding; (2) *ennoblement,* which consists in reframing the problem as an important life task; and (3) *distanced manifestation,* which entails a joint effort to allow the problem to manifest itself fully while one simultaneously disidentifies from it. A fourth strategy, evidently not endorsed by the Tibetan Buddhists, is simply to wear the problem out. This strategy seems to be the unfortunate predicament of all too many psychotherapy clients.

An intriguing question for researchers interested in oscillative processes and personal change has to do with the parameters and patterns involved in the transformation of meaning. Emotional arousal has long been recognized as a facilitator of belief change (Frank, 1973; Nichols & Zax, 1977; Sargant, 1957). The necessity and functions of affective disequilibrium remain only modestly understood, however. Should the psychotherapy client be encouraged to develop skills for coping with such dysphoria or for controlling it? Should the disequilibrium be "ennobled" and the problem reframed? What are the effects of symptom prescription on the meaning assigned to personal distress? The developing literatures on autopoiesis and dissipative structures suggest that spontaneously ordering open systems may get locked into unprogressive cycles of instability or stagnation when their self-organizing processes are thwarted (cf. Jantsch, 1980; Prigogine, 1980; Zeleny, 1980). Is there a warrant to draw a parallel here to the client who is stuck in a chronic pattern of self-defeating efforts which seem to transform the solution into a problem? These are issues that warrant our thoughtful attention.

Attention and Effort

To illustrate further the potential relevance of oscillative processes for our theoretical investments, I shall conclude this section with some emergent hunches about the interrelationships among our arbitrary dimensions of contrast, value, meaning, and emotionality. First, it would not be surprising to find that attentional processes lie at the heart of therapeutic change. With their apparent connection to our concepts of vigilance, meaning, and the direction of experience, these processes seem to premonitor and construct the focal areas of our moment-to-moment engagements in life. Despite the probable centrality of attentional processes in meaning change, however, I doubt whether significant personal change can be effected via superficial strategies of stimulus control and focalized meditation. Since attentional processes are likely to be a reflection of more fundamental ordering processes, there may be more practical yield in those approaches that attempt to sketch the metastructures to which attention is subservient. The literatures of paradoxical intention, symptom prescription, and psychological reversals, for example, point to the limited mutability of both the contents and processes of attention (Apter, in press; Bandler & Grinder, 1975, 1979; Frankl, 1978; Haley, 1973; Raskin & Klein, 1976; Svebak & Stoyva, 1980; Watzlawick, 1978). My hunch is that therapies that look beneath attentional processes may yield more promise than those that restrict their focus to that dimension. This is not, however, an invitation to narcissistic depth. I agree with Kopp (1978) that although unexamined life may not be worth living, "the unlived life is not worth examining" (p. 72). A balanced appreciation of the dynamic interplay between feedforward and feedback mechanisms may be our most reasonable hope at this time.

A second theme that is placed in focus by oscillative processes is the role of effort and surrender in personal well-being. Contemporary western ideologies continue to reflect an impatient preoccupation with increasing the boundaries of personal causation (Fogle, 1978). We long to control our feelings, our actions, and our lives (cf. Perlmuter & Monty, 1979), and our attempts to do so often involve attentive effort (cf. Pribram & McGuinness, 1975). Embedded in our desperate quest for control is a metatheory of personal and public freedom. And much of that freedom is libertarian in flavor: it seeks freedom from its contexts rather than freedom within them (Hayek, 1978; Weimer, Note 1). The net message to our cultural participants is to try harder. Little wonder, then, that we appear to lead the world in dysphoria and stress-related diseases. The Eastern alternative to effort is surrender, a kind of passive intentionality that attempts to integrate and utilize the contrasting powers of internal and external influence. By many Western readers, surrender is read as defeat and equated with a submissive deference to fatalistic processes. The accuracy of this translation is questionable, however, inasmuch as the meaning of transparadigmatic concepts can never be accurately grasped from the context of a foreign perspective (cf. Radnitzky, 1981; Walsh, 1980).

The practical implications of the effort/surrender issue merit our close attention. To me, the relevance of this issue seems most apparent in disorders that involve sympathetic/parasympathetic conflicts—anxiety, insomnia, and several sexual dysfunctions. Here there are clearly times when effort seems to get in the way of progress, and I am comfortable encouraging patience, gentleness, and some kind of self-trust. But does this pattern extend beyond the abovementioned instances of autonomic coordination? At this point, I must say "I do not know." In all honesty, however, I would add that I am actively exploring this possibility in my work as a therapist and that I am encouraged by the results to date. My most credible successes have thus far come in areas where a client has been struggling with apparent resistance processes. I shall therefore close this section with a few comments on the significance of these processes for meaningful change.

Resistance

I begin by respectfully separating this concept from its Freudian legacy. Although there are clear parallels, my use of the term "resistance" derives more from cognitive psychology, psychobiology, and clinical practice than from classical psychoanalytic theory. The reality of resistance also seems to be less controversial than its meaning. Our literature on stress reduction, lifestyle change, and psychotherapy seems to echo the vastness of our resistance to change. Relatively little clinical experience is needed to confront the ambivalence behind many therapeutic undertakings. This conflict about change can be experienced and expressed in many different ways. In my experience as a therapist, I have found that resistance processes are most apparent when significant meaning structures are being challenged. This resistance may occur early in therapy, but it is more common when disequilibrium is intense and demanding. The parallel to dissipative structures and to critical instability thresholds is a tempting one to draw in that resistance to change seems to intensify with the demands for that change. My first point here is to comment on the wisdom of such resistance in a hierarchically structured complex system. There is a sensed survival value in protecting and perpetuating old reality constructions—especially those which are most central to our experience. Probably these constructions feed-forward an active reluctance to be examined or changed.

In his insightful analysis of what a scientist may experience during the revolution and evolution of paradigms, Imre Lakatos (1970) has offered an intriguing interdisciplinary comment on intrapersonal resistance processes. Lakatos argues that the "hard core" of a belief system is functionally surrounded by a "protective belt" whose function is to divert reality tests away from the hard core. This diversion is accomplished by the contrasting subprocesses of the protective belt—a "negative heuristic" that directs one away from certain paths of engagement and a "positive heuristic" that encourages patterns that do not threaten the hard core of a paradigm. How many of us have seen comparable processes in ourselves and our clients? How often do we foreclose on credibility before experiencing the returns of an excursion beyond familiar ordering patterns? And how often are our clients locked into "neurotic" patterns of insecurity by rejecting old scaffoldings almost as vigorously as they avoid alternative ones?[5]

Freud is said to have abandoned hypnosis because it sidestepped the processes of resistance. My own experiences as a therapist have led me cautiously to agree that a vast amount of personal energy seems to be channeled into the avoidance of certain changes. For example, several of my clients seemed to have identified with their problems to the point that symptomatic improvements were frightening assaults on identity. When I asked one chronically depressed man what he thought it would take for him to change, he answered, "I guess I would have to be someone else." After several months of therapy, another woman reported experiencing unprecedented periods of well-being but lamented that they could not be authentic if *she* were experiencing them.[6] The same woman offered a vivid illustration of the protective role of resistance to the examination or change of core ordering processes. When we first began to work intensively on the process as well as on the content of her depression, I used stream of consciousness as both an assessment and a reactive examination of her attentional patterns. During her second experience with streaming, she experienced intense terror and bolted upright from the exercise. My inquiries revealed that she was experiencing what she called "tunnels." She described these tunnels.

[5]It is interesting to speculate that the "protective belt" postulated by Lakatos may involve many of the ego functions hypothesized by personality theorists. Western metatheories encourage a strengthening of the ego, while many Eastern ideologies contend that the ego must be weakened and stripped away in healthy development. A structuralist compromise might take the form of redirecting the protective focus of such processes so that a higher order structure can emerge.

[6]In cases where symptomatology has merged with personal identity, techniques of distancing or disidentification may be valuable. These techniques, which are espoused by a wide range of therapies, encourage the individual to develop a boundary between identity and the particulars of experience. They may also aid in extricating a person from a meaning structure to the point that the structure can be recognized as a formerly tacit operational scheme. The problem with distancing techniques may not be unlike that noted in our discussion of effort and surrender—viz., their appropriateness may vary with time, the nature of the problem, and personality components. They may also accentuate and amplify issues of identity and control.

Figure 4. A depressed client's rendition of a self-protective "tunnel."

> They come in when I'm in trouble. They keep me away from things and they won't let anything in . . . just enough to function.

When I asked her if she could draw one, she said that they were not really visual. Part of the time she felt the presence of a tunnel, but only occasionally did she "see" something resembling one. As depicted by her drawing in Figure 4, it was—in her own words—"more like seeing *through* them." Our later work in therapy has led both my client and me to conclude that the experience of her tunnels varied with her being asked to examine some of her most basic assumptions. In later months, she experienced the tunnel phenomenon many times as she moved through our therapy sessions and her own change processes. These experiences became less frequent and less isolative, but they remained a frequent reminder of the protection given to our fundamental ordering processes.

My strategy for dealing with cognitive entrenchment processes is not unlike that espoused by others who have voiced a respect for the role of resistance in therapy (e.g., Bugental, 1978; Haley, 1973). I try to deal with it in a manner that reduces the need for entrenchment and yet uses that same protective energy in the service of a progressive shift in personal paradigms. Several years ago I believed that these shifts might be accomplished via precipitous "cognitive clicks" similar to those experienced in such figure-ground transformations as the Necker cube (see Figure 5; Mahoney, 1974). More recently I have come to appreciate that those clicks are seldom climactic. They seem to be important reflections of a shift in personal meaning, and they may occasionally suggest a transformation of formidable personal significance. This finding was illustrated for me in the case of a woman who had been severely incapacitated by agoraphobia for almost six years. Two years of psychoanalysis had apparently exacerbated the problem. Although she had reached terminal behavior on a cognitive-behavioral program of therapy, her subjective distress and incapacitation remained extreme. During almost two years of work with me, she reported intense "waves" of autonomic arousal and cognitive disequilibrium. These culminated in a brief period of diffuse affect and courageous personal struggle, after which the agoraphobia suddenly dissipated. When I asked her to describe her experience, I was struck by the magnitude of the shift:

> You know, [parts of my past] seem like a dream . . . in the sense of its being hard to remember *that* life as anything but so far away in both time and mind—it's hard even to feel it anymore—I *remem-*

ber, but it's like . . . the whole thing . . . was just this 5- or 6-year interruption in my life.

Precipitous shifts like this one are relatively rare both in and outside psychotherapy, perhaps because of the self-protective aspects of core CNS ordering processes. From my own limited experience with significant personal transformations, such shifts appear to be correlated with long and intense engagement with formerly tacit features of one's hard core (cf. Bugental, 1978; Guidano & Liotti, in press). If we hope to ex-

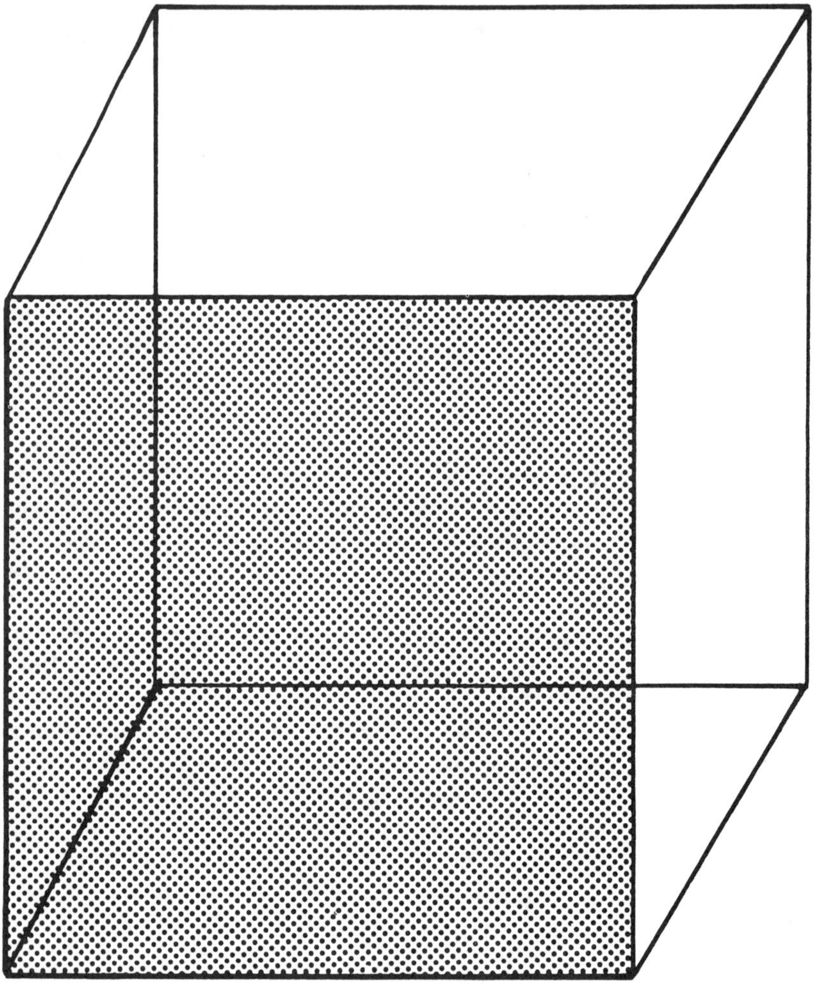

Figure 5. The Necker cube.

pand our understanding of human change processes, we must respect the inherent self-protective mechanisms within complex open systems. With that understanding, we can hope to learn to recognize our clients' multifaceted "escapes from freedom" (Fromm, 1941) and to facilitate their attempts to overcome the limitations of prior meaning structures.

Participatory Vitalism

The fifth and final theme for my remarks has to do with the concept of hope and its role in personal change and well-being. Although its absence is often acknowledged as a factor in affective disorders, hope remains one of those ethereal topics that has escaped serious scientific attention.[7] In recent years it has begun to make so ubiquitous an appearance in our theories that one wonders how long we can continue to overlook it. In Burton's (1976) collection of contemporary theories of psychotherapy process, we find the theme of hope permeating the thinking of some of our most respected authorities. Judd Marmor speaks of the role of "faith, hope, and expectancy" in a client, and Leon Salzman titles his contribution "The Will to Change." Albert Bandura's comments reflect his growing respect for "self-efficacy" and the parameters determining self-perceptions of adequacy. Jerome Frank offers the thesis that "a major function of all schools of psychotherapy is to restore morale" (p. 73). Viewing demoralization as a frequent characteristic of persons who seek therapy, he argues that a successful therapy must be able to combat "feelings of helplessness, hopelessness, impotence, and isolation" (p. 79). A parallel endorsement of autonomy, self-direction, and personal adequacy is offered by Hans Strupp and by theorists representing a number of other approaches.

The apparent consensus on the role of hope in psychotherapy may not be surprising given the frequency with which we encounter this concept in our literatures of philosophy, religion, biography, and fiction (Barrett, 1967; Durant & Durant, 1970; Friedman, 1967, 1974; Hendin, 1978; Russell, 1945). Whatever it is, hope appears to be a perennial theme in our analyses of the human condition. I bring it into the present discussion because I believe that its importance merits reiteration. I would also like to believe that contemporary psychology can make a valuable contribution to our understanding of its role in personal well-being.

Let me begin by offering a tentative definition of hope as an expectation of or trust in the satisfactory value of future experience. Rather

[7]It is noteworthy that Mowrer's (1960a, 1960b) two-factor learning theory incorporated hope and fear as central and related elements in motivation and learning.

than dwell on the semantics of the concept, I shall plunge more directly toward some pragmatics. My main contention here can be outlined as follows. Since we appear to be active participants in constructing and influencing the realities which, in turn, shape us, we bear some responsibility for the nature of our exchanges with the world. Our control is, of course, often limited, so that the boundaries of causal responsibility—as contrasted with physical and social accountability—may fluctuate across exchanges. Hope appears to be an influential factor in our multifaceted involvements with life processes at individual and social levels. To the extent that we value such involvements, we are well advised to respect the power of hope and our own role in its generative processes.

Teleonomy and Growth

The concept of hope cannot be adequately addressed without touching upon its connections with such themes as love, faith, humanism, and vitalism. As Maurice Friedman (1967, 1974) has so aptly noted in his analyses of the "hidden human image," our everyday exchanges with each other, ourselves, and the world around us are richly imbued with a web of assumptions about human nature, cosmology, determinism, existential absurdities, pragmatics, and so forth. One of the themes that seems to recur quite frequently in our widely varying ideologies is that of *vitalism* or, in the language of evolutionary biologists, *teleonomy* (Ayala & Dobzhansky, 1974). As I understand the term, teleonomy refers to inherent ordering processes which serve to direct the maintenance and growth of open systems. Where teleology implies a tacit or explicit destination, teleonomy connotes more of a flexible direction. I say "flexible" because clearly inherent ordering processes must contend with unpredictable constraints in their expression. Thus, in his attempt to integrate the wisdom of biological reductionism and evolutionary vitalism, Donald Campbell (1974) notes that our development—as persons and systems—is influenced by our encounters with selective "natural laws" which often stimulate and preserve novel patterns of adaptation.

Of course, notions of growth, energy, and dynamic processes in development have been recorded for centuries. Henri Bergson developed the first clear philosophy of vitalism and linked reality, life, and values to an *élan vital,* or vital force, which might be described in the lyric words of Gibran (1923) as "life longing after itself." Although vitalism was soon overshadowed by the movements toward existentialism, positivism, and pragmatism, its continued presence is not difficult to discern in our poetry, fiction, and reflections on human directions (e.g., Barrett, 1967; Ferguson, 1980; Hendin, 1978). As Friedman (1967) and others have noted, Bergson's idealistic rendition of vitalism committed "the fatal error of assuming that any movement onward is also upward" (p. 72). While we may be wise to respect and value the teleonomic dimensions in our lives, we must also contend with the existential responsibilities inherent in the processes of living. Hence, the heading of "participatory vitalism." We are participants in the dynamic exchange that constitutes a human life. We are simultaneously cause and effect, choice and chance, figure and ground. Our understanding is incomplete, and our power is often limited; and yet the demands of life remain frequently unsympathetic.

This is where hope may be recognized as an elusive ether that permeates all perseverance. Our studies into human suffering leave little doubt about the preciousness of hope, while our records of war and destruction tell us that excessive hope—inspiration—can also be directed in the service of inhumane goals. Out of all the life forms on our planet, we appear to be most capable of transcending time and space. We remember, consciously and otherwise, the constructed lessons of past experience, and we lean toward our future with a preparatory mixture of hope and fear. I concur with Jerome Frank (1974, 1976) that the people who most often seek our assistance in psychotherapy suffer from an imbalance in these inclinations. That imbalance is often understandable in light of their life history and personal sensitivities. I also believe that their dysphoria is often a valuable element in energizing and directing their life. But without hope there is little engagement in either life or change, and without engagement there is little left that we recognize as human.

Responsible Hope

Significant personal change is seldom achieved without sacrifice, suffering, and a kind of loneliness that eludes description. In reflecting on his own energetic life as a philosopher, family man, and humanitarian, Bertrand Russell (1967) noted the preciousness of human love in relieving "that terrible loneliness in which one shivering consciousness looks over the rim of the world into the cold unfathomable lifeless abyss." The loneliness and suffering experienced by psychotherapy clients sometimes harks from a kindred dimension. And, in those periods of their utmost vulnerability and need, we may recognize both the value and the importance of our crude assistance as therapists.

The processes of psychotherapy are indistinguishable from more generic processes of change, and they are therefore operative before and after our privileged exchanges with a client. In this sense, it is difficult to imagine those processes being completed or finished within any given period of personal development. Within the time-limited relationship that constitutes intensive psychotherapy, however, there is often a need to deal with attributions of power and the wellsprings of hope. As tempting as being set on a pedestal by a client may seem, I do not feel comfortable with attributions that credit the power of my person, theory, or techniques at the expense of a client's appreciations of his or her own role in both the development and transformation of a change crisis. This is not to deny my assistance nor to overrate the boundaries of their personal causation. I also believe that there may be a healthy function to some forms of heroism. My point here is that the "retreat to authorities" (Bartley, 1962) must eventually find itself in the personal arena of commitment and trust. A client who trusts in my competency must first trust in his or her skill in the selection of a trustee. The analysis, when pursued far enough, always returns us to "home"—to personal meaning structures and their pragmatic obligations. And psychotherapy, when it begins to asymptote in its yield, usually finds the client acknowledging his or her readiness to move forward in life without professional assistance and with a deeper appreciation of personal resources.

Reflections and Concluding Remarks

I have reflected along five interrelated themes—the primacy of meaning, the role of feedforward mechanisms in our constructions of meaning, the stratification of our ordering systems, the oscillative processes in stability and change, and the value of responsible hope. Although my remarks have sometimes approached the arrogance of a formal hypothesis, they have usually remained tentative and discursive. Those familiar with my work will not be surprised by that tentativeness. I am a "cautious optimist," and my remarks probably emanate from some tacit structures well removed from my awareness. I do have the opportunity to copy edit my remarks, of course, so I accept responsibility for what I have said. All in all, I think I have given a fairly honest accounting of my present thoughts and intuitions about therapy.

One of the primary goals of this paper has been to raise questions about the fundamental processes of human change. Progressive inquiry always leads to more questions than answers, more opening than closure. Rather than summarize or review my remarks, let me therefore conclude with a few emergent questions and a brief commentary on the conduct of psychotherapy. My questions begin with some fundamentals and move toward particulars:

1. How might we improve our understanding of change processes? Is our current scientific knowledge being avoidably constrained by theoretical filters, inappropriate assessments, and technical tyranny?

2. To what extent are we aware of tacit feedforward processes in our conceptions and enactments of therapy? How would the quality of our therapy be influenced by our becoming more or less parochial in our ideological boundaries?

3. To what extent do our graduate training programs offer students the most meaningful and relevant experiences for their careers as helping professionals?

4. What would be the effects of widening our conceptions of science to accommodate qualitative as well as quantitative research?

5. What would be the effects of moving away from molecular techniques and toward the study of therapy in its broader context as a personal and cultural exchange?

6. What are the most important questions for directing our research programs?

I think that these questions could be helpful in refining our understanding of human change processes. I would also hope that no one person would be expected to have confident answers to these queries.

My own responses would necessarily reflect a deepening appreciation for the complexity and potential of human growth processes. In my privileged role as a socially sanctioned adviser, I have sensed the formidable depth and breadth of a person's capacities for adaptation and development. I have tried, often unsuccessfully, to help people free themselves from stubborn patterns of suffering and self-limitation. But I have also had the honor of witnessing moderate and occasionally dramatic changes in my clients—changes in self-concept, reality constructions, and the fluctuating interface of these crude constructs. I have never "cured" a client of a mental disease; I do not know what that would be like. But I have seen people transcend and transform painful constraints on their personal freedom, and the experience has felt like something I would like to facilitate better. That clients' progress has seldom been painless or rapid makes me worry about the implications of the recent trend toward prescriptive brevity in psychotherapy. With the growing emphasis on accountability by government and health care agencies comes a temptation to dilute our therapies and to define success in terms of what we know we can achieve in less than 20 sessions. Sometimes that time is plenty. Sometimes it is just what the client needed. But what do we do about persons who are struggling with tenured core schemata that constrict or complicate their lives? What do we do about the clients who need more time? I believe we are in trouble when the length of therapy—whether short or long—is equated with its quality. Some clients—and admittedly some of us therapists—need more time than others. That is reality. We are naive if we believe we can force human change processes into certain statutes of limitation.

I believe that psychotherapy can offer helpful assistance in human adaptation and development; that it can be a catalyst for the kinds of transformations, sharp and subtle, that nurture a life toward a fuller expression of its identity in the dynamic contexts of an open system. The kind of psychotherapy I am talking about remains an elusive ideal for today's practitioners. It has not been captured by any of the competing ideologies. Nor does it lie hidden behind our annual progression of new techniques. Techniques are valuable but crude expressions; they are ritualized communications about *our* constructions of reality and *our* intentions for our clients (Mahoney, in press). It is *beneath* our techniques—in the murky realm of those constructions and intentions—that we may sense our grasp of human change processes. And it is beneath the familiarity of our role as therapists that we may come to sense and appreciate our privileged roles as guides, advisers, and observers of the human pilgrimage.

Therefore I would like to close with an acknowledgement of the unity of our intent, if not of our methods. In the next few decades, psychotherapy may well face one of its most formative challenges. In my opinion, that challenge is not in the demand for demonstrated impact. Instead, it is in our reaction to those demands. Unless we are prepared to meet those demands with a courage born of conviction, we may risk compromising our humanitarian foundations. Relevance, effectiveness, and cost-efficiency are legitimate requests, but let us not lose sight of the more basic issues of value on which they are based. However it may be conceptualized or enacted, psychotherapy reflects both an intention and a commitment to help people. Let us not overlook either of these in the debates on our status as a science, art, or service. I believe that we already have much to offer and that the responsibilities of having a "window on the human soul" (Bugental, 1978, p. 150) have never been so apparent. Let us therefore agree to share our experiences in ways that respect and foster the life processes to which our profession is committed. We will best serve our profession and our clients when we act with integrity on our best intentions.

References

Ainsworth, A. D. S. Infant-mother attachment. *American Psychologist,* 1979, *34,* 932–937.

Apter, M. J. *The experience of motivation: A theory of psychological reversals.* New York: Academic Press, in press.

Ayala, F. J., & Dobzhansky, T. (Eds.). *Studies in the philosophy of biology: Reduction and related problems.* Berkeley: University of California Press, 1974.
Aschoff, J. (Ed.). *Handbook of behavioral neurobiology: Vol. 4. Biological rhythms.* New York: Plenum, 1981.
Bandler, R., & Grinder, J. *The structure of magic: A book about language and therapy* (2 vols.). Palo Alto, Calif.: Science and Behavior Books, 1975.
Bandler, R., & Grinder, J. *Frogs into princes: Neuro linguistic programming.* Moab, Vt.: Real People Press, 1979.
Bandura, A. Social learning perspective on behavior change. In A. Burton (Ed.), *What makes behavior change possible?* New York: Brunner/Mazel, 1976.
Bandura, A. Self-efficacy: Toward a unifying theory of behavioral change. *Psychological Review,* 1977, *84,* 191–215.
Bandura, A. The self system in reciprocal determinism. *American Psychologist,* 1978, *33,* 344–358.
Barrett, W. *The illusion of technique.* New York: Doubleday, 1967.
Bartlett, F. C. *Remembering.* Cambridge: Cambridge University Press, 1932.
Bartley, W. W. *The retreat to commitment.* New York: Alfred A. Knopf, 1962.
Beck, A. T. *Cognitive therapy and the emotional disorders.* New York: International Universities Press, 1976.
Berger, P. L., & Luckman, T. *The social construction of reality: A treatise in the sociology of knowledge.* Garden City, N.Y.: Anchor, 1967.
Bernard, C. *An introduction to the study of experimental medicine.* New York: Dover, 1957. (Originally published, 1865.)
Bowlby, J. *Separation: Anxiety and anger.* New York: Basic Books, 1973.
Bowlby, J. *The making and breaking of affectional bonds.* London: Tavistock, 1979. (a)
Bowlby, J. Knowing what you are not supposed to know and feeling what you are not supposed to feel. *Canadian Journal of Psychiatry,* 1979, *24,* 403–408. (b)
Bransford, J. D., & McCarrell, N. S. A sketch of a cognitive approach to comprehension: Some thoughts about understanding what it means to comprehend. In W. B. Weimer and D. S. Palermo (Eds.), *Cognition and the symbolic processes* (Vol. 1). Hillsdale, N.J.: Erlbaum, 1974.
Brush, S. G. The chimerical cat: Philosophy of quantum mechanics in historical perspective. *Social Studies of Science,* 1980, *10,* 393–447.
Bugental, J. F. T. *The search for authenticity: An existential-analytic approach to psychotherapy.* New York: Holt, Rinehart, & Winston, 1965.
Bugental, J. F. T. *Psychotherapy and process: The fundamentals of an existential-humanistic approach.* Reading, Mass.: Addison-Wesley, 1978.
Burton, A. (Ed.), *What makes behavior change possible?* New York: Brunner/Mazel, 1976.
Campbell, D. T. Evolutionary epistemology. In P. A. Schlipp (Ed.), *The philosophy of Karl Popper* (Vol. 14, Books I and II). *The library of living philosophers.* LaSalle, Ill.: Open Court Publishing, 1974.
Campbell, D. T. On the conflicts between biological and social evolution and between psychology and moral tradition. *American Psychologist,* 1975, *30,* 1103–1126.
Capra, F. *The tao of physics.* New York: Bantam, 1975.
Davidson, J. M., & Davidson, R. J. (Eds.). *The psychobiology of consciousness.* New York: Plenum, 1980.
Dember, W. N. Motivation and cognitive revolution. *American Psychologist,* 1974, *29,* 161–168.
Dubois, P. *The influence of the mind on the body.* New York: Funk & Wagnalls, 1906.
Dubois, P. *The psychic treatment of nervous disorders.* New York: Funk & Wagnalls, 1908.
Dubois, P. *The education of self.* New York: Funk & Wagnalls, 1911.

Durant, W., & Durant, A. *Interpretations of life: A survey of contemporary literature.* New York: Simon & Schuster, 1970.

Ellenberger, H. F. *The discovery of the unconscious.* New York: Basic Books, 1970.

Ferguson, M. *The Aquarian Conspiracy: Personal and social transformation in the 1980s.* Los Angeles: J. P. Tarcher, 1980.

Fogle, D. O. Learned helplessness and learned restlessness. *Psychotherapy: Theory, Research and Practice,* 1978, *15,* 39–47.

Foucault, M. *The order of things: An archeology of the human sciences.* New York: Random House, 1970.

Frank, J. D. *Persuasion and healing* (2nd ed). Baltimore: Johns Hopkins Press, 1973.

Frank, J. D. Psychotherapy: The restoration of morale. *American Journal of Psychiatry,* 1974, *131,* 271–274.

Frank, J. D. Restoration of morale and behavior change. In A. Burton (Ed.), *What makes behavior change possible?* New York: Brunner/Mazel, 1976.

Frankl, V. E. *The unheard cry for meaning: Psychotherapy and humanism.* New York: Simon & Schuster, 1978.

Friedman, M. *To deny our nothingness: Contemporary images of man.* Chicago: University of Chicago Press, 1967.

Friedman, M. *The hidden human image.* New York: Dell, 1974.

Fromm, E. *Escape from freedom.* New York: Holt, Rinehart, & Winston, 1941.

Garfield, S. L., & Kurtz, R. Clinical psychologists in the 1970s. *American Psychologist,* 1976, *31,* 1–9.

Garfield, S. L., & Kurtz, R. A study of eclectic views. *Journal of Consulting and Clinical Psychology,* 1977, *45,* 78–83.

Gibran, K. *The prophet.* New York: Knopf, 1923.

Gibson, J. J. *The senses considered as perceptual systems.* Boston: Houghton Mifflin, 1966.

Goffman, E. *Frame analysis: An essay on the organization of experience.* New York: Harper, 1974.

Goldfried, M. R. Toward the delineation of therapeutic change principles. *American Psychologist,* 1980, *35,* 991–999.

Goldstein, K. M., & Blackman, S. *Cognitive style: Five approaches and relevant research.* New York: Wiley, 1978.

Guidano, V. V., & Liotti, G. *Knowledge organization and emotional disorders: A structural approach to psychotherapy.* New York: Guilford, in press.

Haley, J. *Uncommon therapy.* New York: W. W. Norton, 1973.

Hayek, F. A. *The counter-revolution of science: Studies on the abuse of reason.* New York: Free Press, 1952. (a)

Hayek, F. A. *The sensory order.* Chicago: University of Chicago Press, 1952. (b)

Hayek, F. A. *Studies in philosophy, politics, economics.* Chicago: University of Chicago Press, 1967.

Hayek, F. A. *New studies in philosophy, politics, economics, and the history of ideas.* Chicago: University of Chicago Press, 1978.

Hendin, J. *Vulnerable people: A view of American fiction since 1945.* Oxford: Oxford University Press, 1978.

Howard, K. L., & Orlinsky, D. E. Psychotherapeutic process. *Annual Review of Psychology,* 1972, *23,* 615–668.

James, W. *The varieties of religious experience.* New York: New American Library, 1958. (Originally published, 1901.)

Janet, P. *Neurosis and fixed ideas.* Paris: Alcan, 1898.

Jantsch, E. The unifying paradigm behind autopoiesis, dissipative structures, hyper- and ultracycles. In M. Zeleny (Ed.), *Autopoiesis, dissipative structures, and spontaneous social orders.* Washington, D.C.: American Association for the Advancement of Science, 1980.

Jenkins, J. J. Remember that old theory of memory? Well, forget it! *American Psychologist,* 1974, *29,* 785–795.

Jerison, H. J. *Evolution of the brain and intelligence.* New York: Wiley, 1973.

Jerison, H. J. Paleoneurology and the evolution of mind. *Scientific American,* 1976, *234,* 90–101.

Jones, R. A. *Self-fulfilling prophecies: Social, psychological, and physiological effects of expectancies.* Hillsdale, N.J.: Erlbaum, 1977.

Joy, W. B. *Joy's way: A map for the transformational journey.* Los Angeles: J. P. Tarcher, 1978.

Kagan, J. Resiliency and continuity in psychological development. In A. M. Clarke and A. D. B. Clarke (Eds.), *Early experience: Myth and evidence.* New York: Free Press, 1976.

Kagan, J., Kearsley, R. B., & Zelazo, P. R. *Infancy: Its place in human development.* Cambridge, Mass.: Harvard University Press, 1978.

Kiesler, D. J. *The process of psychotherapy: Empirical foundations and systems of analysis.* Chicago: Aldine, 1973.

Klemke, E. D. (Ed.). *The meaning of life.* Oxford: Oxford University Press, 1981.

Klinger, E. *Structure and functions of fantasy.* New York: Wiley, 1971.

Kopp, S. *An end to innocence: Facing life without illusions.* New York: Bantam, 1978.

Kuhn, T. S. *The structure of scientific revolutions.* Chicago: University of Chicago Press, 1962.

Kuhn, T. S. Logic of discovery or psychology of research? In I. Lakatos and A. Musgrave (Eds.), *Criticism and the growth of knowledge.* Cambridge: Cambridge University Press, 1970. (a)

Kuhn, T. S. Reflections on my critics. In I. Lakatos and A. Musgrave (Eds.), *Criticism and the growth of knowledge.* Cambridge: Cambridge University Press, 1970. (b)

Kuhn, T. S. *The essential tension: Selected studies in scientific tradition and change.* Chicago: University of Chicago Press, 1977.

Lakatos, I. Falsification and the methodology of scientific research programmes. In I. Lakatos and A. Musgrave (Eds.), *Criticism and the growth of knowledge.* Cambridge: Cambridge University Press, 1970.

Lakatos, I., & Musgrave, A. (Eds.). *Criticism and the growth of knowledge.* Cambridge: Cambridge University Press, 1970.

Land, G. T. L. *Grow or die: The unifying principle of transformation.* New York: Dell, 1973.

Leonard, G. B. *The transformation: A guide to the inevitable changes in humankind.* Los Angeles: J. P. Tarcher, 1972.

Lewis, M., & Rosenbaum, L. A. (Eds.). *The development of affect.* New York: Plenum, 1978.

Lipsitt, L. P. Critical conditions in infancy: A psychological perspective. *American Psychologist,* 1979, *34,* 973–980.

Macnamara, J. Meaning. In W. B. Weimer and D. S. Palermo (Eds.), *Cognition and the symbolic processes* (Vol. 2). Hillsdale, N.J.: Erlbaum, 1981.

Mahoney, M. J. *Cognition and behavior modification.* Cambridge, Mass.: Ballinger, 1974.

Mahoney, M. J. *Scientist as subject: The psychological imperative.* Cambridge, Mass.: Ballinger, 1976.

Mahoney, M. J. Psychology of the scientist: An evaluative review. *Social Studies of Science,* 1979, *9,* 349–375.

Mahoney, M. J. (Ed.). *Psychotherapy process: Current issues and future directions.* New York: Plenum, 1980. (a)

Mahoney, M. J. Psychotherapy and the structure of personal revolutions. In M. J. Mahoney

(Ed.), *Psychotherapy process: Current issues and future directions.* New York: Plenum, 1980. (b)

Mahoney, M. J. Clinical psychology and scientific inquiry. *International Journal of Psychology,* in press.

Mahoney, M. J., & Arnkoff, D. B. Cognitive and self-control therapies. In S. L. Garfield and A. E. Bergin (Eds.), *Handbook of psychotherapy and behavior change* (2nd ed). New York: Wiley, 1978.

Marmor, J. Common operational factors in diverse approaches to behavior change. In A. Burton (Ed.), *What makes behavior change possible?* New York: Brunner/Mazel, 1976.

Maslow, A. H. *The farther reaches of human nature.* New York: Viking, 1971.

Meichenbaum, D. *Cognitive behavior modification.* New York: Plenum, 1977.

Mowrer, O. H. *Learning theory and behavior.* New York: Wiley, 1960. (a)

Mowrer, O. H. Learning theory and the symbolic processes. New York: Wiley, 1960. (b)

Nelson, K. E., & Nelson, K. Cognitive pendulums and their linguistic realization. In K. E. Nelson (Ed.), *Children's language* (Vol. 1). New York: Gardner Press, 1978.

Nichols, M. P., & Zax, M. *Catharsis in psychotherapy.* New York: Gardner Press, 1977.

Nisbett, R. E., & Wilson, T. D. Telling more than we can know: Verbal reports on mental processes. *Psychological Review,* 1977, *84,* 231–259.

Orlinsky, D. E., & Howard, K. I. The relationship of process to outcome in psychotherapy. In S. L. Garfield & A. E. Bergin (Eds.), *Handbook of psychotherapy and behavior change* (2nd ed). New York: Wiley, 1978.

Pattee, H. H. (Ed.). *Hierarchy theory: The challenge of complex systems.* New York: George Braziller, 1973.

Pepper, S. C. *World hypotheses: A study in evidence.* Berkeley, Calif.: University of California Press, 1942.

Perlmuter, L. C., & Monty, R. A. (Eds.). *Choice and perceived control.* Hillsdale, N.J.: Erlbaum, 1979.

Plutchik, R., & Kellerman, H. *Emotion: Theory, research, and experience* (Vol. 1). New York: Academic Press, 1980.

Polanyi, M. *The tacit dimension.* New York: Doubleday, 1966.

Pope, K. S., & Singer, J. L. *The stream of consciousness: Scientific investigations into the flow of human experience.* New York: Plenum, 1978.

Pribram, K. H. Mind, brain, and consciousness: The organization of competence and conduct. In J. M. Davidson & R. J. Davidson (Eds.), *The psychobiology of consciousness.* New York: Plenum, 1980.

Pribram, K. H., & McGuinness, D. Arousal, activation and effort in the control of attention. *Psychological Review,* 1975, *82,* 116–149.

Prigogine, I. *From being to becoming: Time and complexity in the physical sciences.* San Francisco: W. H. Freeman, 1980.

Proffitt, D. R. *Demonstrations to investigate the meaning of everyday experience.* Unpublished doctoral dissertation, Pennsylvania State University, 1976.

Proffitt, D. R., & Halwes, T. Categorical perception: A contractual approach. In W. B. Weimer and D. S. Palermo (Eds.), *Cognition and the symbolic processes* (Vol. 2). Hillsdale, N.J.: Erlbaum, 1981.

Progoff, I. *At a journal workshop.* New York: Dialogue House Library, 1975.

Rachman, S. Emotional processing. *Behaviour Research and Therapy,* 1980, *18,* 51–60.

Radnitzky, G. The complementarity of western and oriental philosophy. *Social Science,* 1981, *56,* 82–87.

Raimy, V. *Misunderstandings of the self.* San Francisco: Jossey-Bass, 1975.

Raskin, D. E., & Klein, Z. E. Losing a symptom through keeping it: A review of paradoxical treatment techniques and rationale. *Archives of General Psychiatry,* 1976, *33,* 548–555.

Russell, B. *A history of western philosophy.* New York: Simon & Schuster, 1945.

Russell, B. *The autobiography of Bertrand Russell.* London: George Allen and Unwin, 1967.

Rutter, M. *Maternal deprivation reassessed.* Baltimore: Penguin, 1972.

Salzman, L. The will to change. In A. Burton (Ed.), *What makes behavior change possible?* New York: Brunner/Mazel, 1976.

Sargant, W. *Battle for the mind.* New York: Harper & Row, 1957.

Schwartz, G. E. Psychobiological foundations of psychotherapy and behavior change. In S. L. Garfield & A. E. Bergin (Eds.), *Handbook of psychotherapy and behavior change* (2nd ed). New York: Wiley, 1978.

Shaw, R., & Bransford, J. (Eds.). *Perceiving, acting, and knowing: Toward an ecological psychology.* Hillsdale, N.J.; Erlbaum, 1977.

Shevrin, H., & Dickman, S. The psychological unconscious: A necessary assumption for all psychological theory? *American Psychologist,* 1980, *35,* 421–434.

Singer, J. L. *Imagery and daydream techniques in psychotherapy and behavior modification.* New York: Academic Press, 1974.

Singer, J. L., & Pope, K. S. (Eds.). *The power of human imagination: New methods in psychotherapy.* New York: Plenum, 1978.

Skinner, B. F. *About behaviorism.* New York: Knopf, 1974.

Solomon, R. L. The opponent-process theory of acquired motivation: The costs of pleasure and the benefits of pain. *American Psychologist,* 1980, *35,* 691–712.

Sroufe, L. A. The coherence of individual development: Early care, attachment, and subsequent developmental issues. *American Psychologist,* 1979, *34,* 834–841.

Strupp, H. H. The nature of the therapeutic influence and its basic ingredients. In A. Burton (Ed.), *What makes behavior change possible?* New York: Brunner/Mazel, 1976.

Svebak, S., & Stoyva, J. High arousal can be pleasant and exciting: The theory of psychological reversals. *Biofeedback and Self-Regulation,* 1980, *5,* 439–444.

Thompson, S. C. Will it hurt less if I can control it? A complex answer to a simple question. *Psychological Bulletin,* 1981, *90,* 89–101.

Turvey, M. T. Constructive theory, perceptual systems, and tacit knowledge. In W. B. Weimer and D. S. Palermo (Eds.), *Cognition and the symbolic processes* (Vol. 1). Hillsdale, N.J.: Erlbaum, 1974.

Vaihinger, H. *The philosophy of as if.* Berlin: Reuther & Reichard, 1911.

Valle, R. S., & vonEckartsberg, R. (Eds.). *The metaphors of consciousness.* New York: Plenum, 1981.

Walsh, R. N. The consciousness disciplines and the behavioral sciences: Questions of comparison and assessment. *American Journal of Psychiatry,* 1980, *137,* 663—673.

Walsh, R. N., & Vaughan, F. (Eds.). *Beyond ego: Transpersonal dimensions in psychology.* Los Angeles: J. P. Tarcher, 1980.

Watzlawick, P. *Change: The language of therapeutic communication.* New York: Basic Books, 1978.

Weimer, W. B. A conceptual framework for cognitive psychology: Motor theories of the mind. In R. Shaw & J. Bransford (Eds.), *Perceiving, acting, and knowing.* Hillsdale, N.J.: Erlbaum, 1977.

Weimer, W. B. *Notes on the methodology of scientific research.* Hillsdale, N.J.: Erlbaum, 1979.

Weimer, W. B. Ambiguity and the future of psychology: *Meditations Leibniziennes.* In W. B. Weimer and D. S. Palermo (Eds.), *Cognition and the symbolic processes* (Vol. 2). Hillsdale, N.J.: Erlbaum, 1981. (a)

Weimer, W. B. Hayek's approach to the problems of complex phenomena: An introduction to the theoretical psychology of *The Sensory Order.* In W. B. Weimer and D. S. Palermo (Eds.), *Cognition and the symbolic processes* (Vol. 2). Hillsdale, N.J.: Erlbaum, 1981. (b)

Weimer, W. B., & Palermo, D. S. (Eds.). *Cognition and the symbolic processes* (Vol. 1). Hillsdale, N.J.: Erlbaum, 1974.

Weimer, W. B., & Palermo, D. S. (Eds.). *Cognition and the symbolic processes* (Vol. 2). Hillsdale, N.J.: Erlbaum, 1981.

Wilhelm, R., & Baynes, C. F. (trans.). *The I Ching or book of changes.* Princeton: Princeton University Press, 1950.

Wilson, E. O. *Sociobiology: The new synthesis.* Cambridge, Mass.: Harvard University Press, 1975.

Wilson, E. O. *On human nature.* New York: Bantam, 1978.

Yarrow, L. J. Emotional development. *American Psychologist,* 1979, *34,* 973–980.

Zajonc, R. B. Feeling and thinking: Preferences need no inferences. *American Psychologist,* 1980, *35,* 151–175.

Zeleny, M. (Ed.). *Autopoiesis, dissipative structures, and spontaneous social orders.* Washington, D.C.: American Association for the Advancement of Science, 1980.

Zukav, G. *The dancing Wu Li masters: An overview of the new physics.* New York: William Morrow, 1979.

Reference Note

1. Weimer, W. B. *Rationalist constructivism, scientism, and the study of man and society.* Manuscript in preparation.

ANNETTE M. BRODSKY

SEX, RACE, AND CLASS ISSUES IN PSYCHOTHERAPY RESEARCH

Annette M. Brodsky is chief psychologist/director of training and associate professor in the department of psychiatry at the Harbor-UCLA Medical Center. Previously she was on the faculties of the University of Alabama at Tuscaloosa and Southern Illinois University at Carbondale, and she was staff psychologist at the United States Disciplinary Barracks, Fort Leavenworth. Brodsky obtained her doctorate in clinical psychology at the University of Florida in 1970.

Brodsky's research has focused on the areas of women's issues and psychotherapy. She has contributed more than 40 journal articles, book chapters, and monographs relevant to sex role issues. She edited *The Female Offender* (1975), co-edited (with Rachel Hare-Mustin) *Women and Psychotherapy: An Assessment of Research and Practice,* and produced *Sex-fair pyschotherapy stimulus films* (1979). Brodsky is a fellow of the American Psychological Association (APA) and is past president of Division 35. In addition to serving on a number of APA committees, she has been an active member of the Association for Women in Psychology, the Alabama Psychological Association, and the Southeastern Psychological Association. In 1981 she was awarded the Krasner Memorial Award by Division 29 (Psychotherapy) of the American Psychological Association.

ANNETTE M. BRODSKY

SEX, RACE, AND CLASS ISSUES IN PSYCHOTHERAPY RESEARCH

The variables selected for this paper might have included other demographic characteristics of patients or therapists as well as sex, race, and class. Sexual orientation, age, size, physical handicaps, or physical attractiveness are other characteristics that make individuals vulnerable to stereotyping, discrimination, and thus differential treatment. Rabkin (1977) gives her description of the patients who are welcomed as good therapeutic candidates as "young, physically attractive, well-educated, members of the upper middle class, intelligent, verbal, willing to talk about and take responsibility for their problems, possessing considerable ego strength, and showing no signs of gross pathology" (p. 173). I would add: white, female, native-born Americans, natively English speaking, and heterosexual.

Some of the issues for the populations discussed in this paper are familiar to all minority groups, while some are unique to one or a few. Those characteristics that appear favorable to one segment may well be the bane of another. Thus, depression may be a problem for women of most cultures and for both sexes of the lower classes in this country, but some of the most impoverished, restricted women in the world show low rates of clinical depression (Ananth, 1978). Some types of women (a single parent or an older family woman) might find a relationship with a male therapist more rewarding than other types (a single woman, a young family woman) who would probably prefer a female therapist (Orlinsky & Howard, 1980). A woman might be expected to have a better therapy outcome with a woman therapist if she is diagnosed as schizophrenic (Stein, Green, & Stone, 1972) and if the therapist is of the same race (Fry, Kropf, & Coe, 1980). But if she were a first generation Asian-American, she probably would not have made use of mental health services and, if she did seek therapy and did not speak English, she probably would not have received a bilingual therapist. If a translator were used, there is a good possibility that the affective messages she tried to communicate might not be read correctly from her nonverbal cues (Sabin, 1975).

These statements indicate that the available research literature says much about the impact of social class, race, and gender as characteristics of both therapist and patient. Also, many problems, mostly methodological, complicate the state of our knowledge. At the least, there appears to be a healthy change toward recognition of the importance of person attributes in psychotherapeutic outcome (Orlinsky & Howard, 1980; Hynan, 1981). That this series of lectures includes a major paper on these topics indicates both an awareness that they are important and, perhaps, a commitment to them that is token because it attempts to cover the diverse issues in a single presentation.

I accepted the task of trying to integrate these issues for two reasons: first, I did not believe that holding out for a Master Lecture on each would be productive, and, second, for all the work that has been done in each area, almost nothing has been attempted in comparing groups or in applying the techniques and designs useful in one area to another. Later I will address effective incidents of this cross-fertilization.

I also feel the need to clarify my representativeness as the author of a Master Lecture on all three variables. My own expertise is primarily in sex role issues in psychotherapy. Since the various racial (cultural) groups have developed enormous literatures specific to their own cultures, I have consulted personally with several individuals who are experts steeped in the psychotherapy literature and clinical issues of either Afro-American, Asian-American or Hispanic groups.[1] I chose these particular minority groups as a focus because they constitute a relatively large percentage of the population in the United States and because relevant research literature on pyschotherapy issues is available. Spanish-speaking groups now have a mental health journal (*Hispanic Journal of Behavioral Sciences*), a journal that abstracts Spanish publications (*Spanish Language Psychology*), and a Spanish Speaking Mental Health Research Center at UCLA which provides an annotated computer

[1]I would like to acknowledge the guidance to the literature on minorities offered by Stephen Lopez, Steve Morin, Dan Romero, Gail Wyatt, and Joe Yamamoto.

printout of 195 publications on treatment. The National Institute of Mental Health (NIMH) has released Volume I of the *Handbook of Asian-American/Pacific Islander Mental Health* (Morishima, Sue, Teng, Zane, & Cram, 1979), which includes an annotated bibliography of published materials. I am aware of no special publication on mental health of Afro-Americans that guides one to the available literature. Medline searches on ethnic issues in psychotherapy are unimpressive. The sex role literature on mental health is voluminous, particularly for the last decade, and there are bibliographies by NIMH (Zukerman, 1979) and JSAS (Midlarsky, 1977) and two specialized journals, *Psychology of Women Quarterly* and *Sex Roles.*

In order to make sense out of the three variables and the three cultures represented under race, I have also chosen to focus primarily on traditional one-on-one psychotherapy of adults rather than on specific treatment programs or special subgroups. Thus, I am eliminating specific issues regarding children, group therapies, alternative therapies, and special programs for drug abuse, battering, criminal populations, and so forth, although these factors may be included in global reviews.

Commonalities of All Minority Groups

All minorities have characteristics as a group that set them apart from the majority. While these characteristics may differ from group to group, the sense of not falling into the mainstream of the majority population is a shared isolating experience. Thus, Morin and Charles (in press) talk about the "pain" of gay men and lesbians hearing therapists talk of "normal" sexual or intimate relationships as goals of therapy. These pronouncements may not be addressed to the homosexual individual per se, but they may readily be read into general professional presentations by leading therapists or from the media or even in the professional literature on psychotherapy. The association of "different" as pathological is a stigma whether it refers to color, social class, sexual orientation, national origin, or gender.

Underutilization of mental health agencies is commonly discussed as an issue for Asians, Hispanics, and blacks, and, particularly, for lower social classes. The issue here is twofold. One, why is the particular group not appearing in numbers commensurate with its percentage of the community's population? Two, why is the retention of the minority group in treatment programs less than that of the majority culture? It is noteworthy that overutilization has been the issue for women (Chesler, 1972).

Stereotyping is a difficult situation that is shared by diverse minority groups. While the stereotypes may differ, often the effect is similar. Individuals lose their identity to the therapist's perception of their group membership characteristics, and treatment may be based on the stereotype rather than on the patient's specific problems. Finally, differential treatment may result because of actual discriminatory practices. Therapists, being products of their own backgrounds, operate with prejudices and values of varying degrees of awareness. Objectivity may be a goal not always achieved because one's biases are difficult to discover, even when they are pointed out (Brodsky, 1980). In addition, being sensitive to bias toward one group may not ensure equal sensitivity to another.

The Bems (1970) in a classic demonstration of sex bias in "liberal thinking" college students used the following example:

> Suppose that a white male college student decided to room or set up a bachelor apartment with a black male friend. Surely the typical white student would not blithely assume that his black roommate was to handle all the domestic chores. Nor would his conscience allow him to do so even in the unlikely event that his roommate would say: "No, that's okay, I like doing housework. I'd be happy to do it." We suspect that the typical white student would still not be comfortable if he took advantage of this offer, if he took advantage of the fact that his roommate had been socialized to be "happy" with such an arrangement. But change this hypothetical black roommate to a female marriage partner, and somehow the student's conscience goes to sleep. At most it is quickly tranquilized by the thought that "she is happiest when she is ironing for her loved one." (p. 90)

In a review on therapist-client racial similarity, Sattler (1977) states about the countertransference dynamics of the white female therapist with the black male client: "This combination intensifies all of the threats to masculine pride involved in the subordinate position of client and may evoke, for the white female therapist, all of the menacing mythology of interracial sex" (p. 254). Perhaps it is my white femaleness that takes offense at this statement. There are probably instances in this paper which will offend blacks, Hispanics, Asians, American Indians (because I did not include their specific issues), and others. Such is the nature of the subtlety of biases and the necessarily limited perspective a single individual can bring to cross-cultural issues.

Research on Bias Toward Minorities

The literature is rife with charges of bias in psychotherapy against almost all minorities. Reviews of bias against blacks, Hispanics, Asians, and women are only representative of the voluminous space occupied in professional journals in the last two decades documenting cases, citing surveys, and offering analogues demonstrating incidents of bias. These reports may exhibit varying levels of sophistication, anger, empirical purity, and tact; but the evidence has not gone unnoticed. Critics abound to challenge studies of therapist bias, and methodology has been the major battleground.

The literature on psychotherapy with women offers a good example. Bias was charged in the design of experiments where men were subjects and the conclusions were generalized to both sexes. When women were subjects, such generalization was less likely. As early as 1948, Herschberger (1970) parodied interpretations about women's motivations by insensitive male investigators. Thus, Josie the female chimp at the Yerkes Primate lab related her story:

> When Jack takes over the food chute, the report calls it his "natural dominance." When I do, it's "privilege"—conferred by him. . . . While I'm up there lording it over the food chute, the investigator writes down "the male temporarily defers to her and allows her to act as if dominant over him." Can't I get any satisfaction out of life that isn't *allowed* me by some male chimp? Damn it! (p. 10)

It was not until the 1970s that serious investigations of bias against women in therapy emerged. By 1973, the Task Force on Sex Bias and Sex Role Stereotyping in Psychotherapeutic Practice (APA, 1975) was formed to address the issues raised by psychologists about the treatment of women. Within a few years, guidelines for therapy with women (APA, 1978), minority women (Olmedo & Parron, 1981), the culturally different (Sue, in press), and homosexuals (Livingood, 1976) made their appearances in the literature. The empirical research, however, did not always support the bias charges. In general, there is only weak support for the theory that therapist sex or sex role has a bearing on patient outcome (Garfield & Bergin, 1978; Parloff, Waskow, & Wolfe, 1978). The classic psychotherapy research studies of the 1960s and early 1970s rarely analyzed by sex of subject and almost never by sex of therapist. Reanalysis of old data had been considered but, because of the rapid changes in sex role attitudes in the last decade, was rejected as useful only for historical purposes (Brodsky & Hare-Mustin, 1980).

Different questions arose concerning research bias against blacks. Eliminating blacks from data collection has been easier than analyzing their responses as a separate group. In fact, some evidence shows that systematic elimination of black subjects occurs because of institutional racism. In a study by Weiss and Kupfer (1974), the virtual absence of blacks on a psychiatric research ward was investigated. The authors concluded that certain factors appeared salient as staff attitudes: Blacks were a research risk because they might leave the ward before the study was over; blacks were a possible physical danger to female staff; blacks would create extra work by resisting procedures; and black subjects would consider the research to be like Nazi medical experiments because they would feel like guinea pigs at the mercy of researchers. Perhaps in the light of publicity about the Tuskegee syphilis experiment, the staff and the subjects had reason to be alerted to the anxiety that blacks might have about participation in research.

Stereotypes of Minority Groups

That stereotyping exists in treatment of minorities and women is not a new issue. Empirical documentation to delineate the stereotypes is more recent. Broverman, Broverman, Clarkson, Rosenkrantz, and Vogel (1970) stirred quite a fuss with their results from an adjective-checklist rating by clinicians of the healthy adult male, female, and sex-unspecified adult. Clinicians were found to have described similar characteristics for men and sex-unspecified healthy adults but different characteristics for women. In a rare instance of adaptation of design from a sex bias study to one for minorities, Lopez (1977) applied the technique to the description of Mexican-Americans, finding that Mexican-Americans were described as healthier than Anglo-Saxon Americans.

Even ethnic groups, themselves the objects of stereotypes, have distinct stereotypes of other ethnic groups. Thus Finney (1968) had 72 male and 85 female students rate 11 ethnic groups and themselves on a semantic differential measuring compliance, activity, desirability, strength, hostility, and conscientiousness. Chinese, Japanese, and Koreans were rated compulsive; Portuguese, Filipinos, and Puerto Ricans were rated hysterical; Hawaiians were rated hysterical and compulsive; and whites were rated neutral. The hysteria and compulsiveness ratings were attributed to these groups by both persons from outside groups and persons in whom the characteristics were stereotypically labeled. Similarly, in Lopez's study on Mexican-American stereotyping by therapists, all therapist groups, including bicultural and bilingual therapists, often stereotyped Mexican-Americans equally (Lopez, 1977).

What is known about each group that may be descriptive of its uniqueness as a cultural group is difficult to separate from stereotypes that serve only as Barnum statements (red flags that one is talking about a certain group member, but diagnostically serving no purpose in providing individual descriptive information). Thus, Haller (Note 1) found that diagnostic reports of adolescent girls often used descriptions such as "attractive" or "passive" that did not differentiate the individual other than to clue the reader to the fact that she was female. With this problem rarely addressed in the literature, one can document only what describes a group and hope that researchers will attend more to separating stereotypes from diagnostic descriptors that predominate in a specific group.

Inconsistencies in the findings of stereotyping and bias can be found even where the evidence would seem from the discursive literature to be fairly clear. Most of the studies are characterized by the investigation of one or a few minority groups on few dependent measures. Designation of the characteristics of the therapist population is rare. Bloombaum, Yamamoto, and James (1968) found that Mexican-Americans were most stereotyped on such characteristics as superstitiousness and impulsiveness. Blacks and then Jews, Chinese-Americans, and Japanese-Americans followed. The nationality of the therapists, however, was not indicated.

Cultural Issues in Therapy with Blacks

Blacks have been stereotyped as failing to meet the therapeutic criteria of verbal fluency, motivation, and "psychological mindedness" (Mayo, 1974). Mayo attributes the persistence of these stereotypes to "certain culture-specific variables that serve effectively as barriers to traditional outpatient treatment" (p. 472).

Like Yamamoto's data on lower social classes and minorities (Yamamoto, James, & Palley, 1968), Mayo's finding was that black females were more acceptable in therapy than black males. The females were diagnosed as less severely disturbed although they had more suicide thoughts and attempts than males.

The barriers Mayo identifies include high visibility of color, the use of black English, which is often seen as a deficiency rather than as a language in its own right. Cultural (or ghetto) behaviors, including ideosyncratic cognitive styles such as "volunteering nothing," along with the use of monosyllables, the occasional stuttering, and the repetition of certain phrases, are often interpreted as "pan-stupidity." Nonverbal behaviors of avoiding eye contact and frequent glancing around a room may represent orienting oneself to place rather than suspiciousness or "sizing up what can be ripped off" as interpreted by interviewers.

Adebimpe (1981) reviewed psychiatric diagnoses of black patients and found some evidence that hallucinations and delusions occurred more frequently among blacks but noted that, while delusions and hallucinations were associated with a definitive diagnosis of schizophrenia in whites, they were not so associated in black patients, an indication that these symptoms do not have the same diagnostic import across race. Affect may appear different as well. Carter & Haizlip (1972) attributed the frequent description of flat or inappropriate affect in blacks to a mask that white therapists and diagnosticians cannot readily decipher. Suspicious-looking behavior in blacks may well be highly adaptive rather than pathological.

Blacks attain higher Minnesota Multiphasic Personality Inventory (MMPI) baselines on a number of scales, particularly schizophrenia. Also, different baselines are found on other inventories including the Eysenck Personality Inventory. Thus some question exists as to the appropriateness of applying general norms to blacks and to other minority cultures.

For example, undergraduate college students in Hawaii of Chinese, Japanese, and Anglo-Saxon–American descent were tested on six self-report depression scales including the Beck Depression Inventory (BDI), the KAS-Hogarty Depression Scale (KAS), the Minnesota Multiphasic Personality Inventory (MMPI), the Multiple Affect Adjective Checklist (MAAC), and the Zung Depression Scale (ZDS). While all groups were within normal limits of depression, group differences showed Chinese females significantly higher on MAAC, MMPI, and ZDS and Japanese females higher on BDI and KAS. The relationship between measures differed for separate groups. The authors concluded that the measures of depression cannot be considered equivalent when used across ethnic groups (Marcella, Sanborn, Kameoka, Shizuru, & Brennan, 1975).

Blackness and lower social-class status have been confounded frequently by researchers. As Yamamoto (1978) has pointed out, researchers investigating lower social classes rarely differentiate among minorities. Institutional racism against blacks has been obvious throughout the professional literature for decades. That blacks are discriminated against because of the visibility of their minority status is as well documented as any other factor about the treatment of blacks. In comparative studies across cultural groups, blacks typically hold down the extreme end of the continuum indicating discriminatory attitudes by therapists (Bloombaum, Yamamoto, & James, 1968). Unfortunately, such data are continually represented as new discoveries (Jones &

Seagull, 1977). I think we can conclude that, in the United States, racism against blacks still exists and is more prevalent than for any other group. Now it is time to move on and provide the direction for positive treatment of blacks by the majority culture therapist.

Language Issues in Non-English-Speaking Minorities

Common to most cultural groups that have immigrated to the United States, particularly within recent generations, are language problems. The assessment and treatment of patients whose primary language is other than English presents more than the obvious need for translations. Because bilingual therapists do not exist in sufficient number to accommodate patients for whom such a therapist would be desirable, the use of translators has been frequent.

With regard to assessment, a few findings bear on the language issue. Del Castillo (1970) noted that psychotic symptoms were more prevalent when foreign-born patients were interviewed in their native language rather than in English. If the patients learned both languages together and were equally facile in either, however, the symptoms were equally prevalent in interviews in both languages. Del Castillo posited an unconscious vigilance when one tries to express oneself in a nondominant language, such that the effort to translate may control symptom expression, particularly that of the contact with reality. Marcos and Alpert (1976) discussed the implications of bilingualism in patients with proficiency in both languages. They noted that if one language has dominance over the other, that language will be used to interpret the other. This translation process may be even more complex if a third language is involved. As an example, a recently arrived Portuguese psychologist at my hospital can speak English only with some difficulty, but she needs to use English in order to understand Spanish-speaking patients who do not speak Portuguese. Eventually all languages for her must be translated first to Portuguese. Marcos and Alpert (1976) suggested that in therapy patients may complicate affective processes through the use of language unavailability, language splitting, or language switching. Thus they cited cases in which certain experiences were emotionally available only in the language the patient was using when they occurred. The need to avoid emotional material may lead to what Marcos and Alpert referred to as "splitting," refusing to own negative affects by understanding them only in a second language where the affective association is blunted. Thus the psychotic patient may hear threatening voices in the second language but friendly voices in the dominant (first-learned) language. On the one hand, switching languages permits the patient to be resistant. It provides a vulnerability to repression, compartmentalization, and denial. On the other hand, some positive aspects of using more than one language in therapy include the potential for the obsessive patient to return to childhood in the earlier emotional language or for an hysteric to use a more abstract, less emotionally charged, secondary language for communicating highly stressful situations (Marcos & Alpert, 1976).

The issue of needing to speak in a subordinate language in order to communicate with a monolingual therapist may add an additional stressor to the patient. Tonaka, Oyama, and Osgood (1963) found that speaking in the nondominant language produces a linguistic stress for individuals. Grand, Marcos, Greedman, and Barroso (1977) studied movements of Spanish-speaking schizophrenics who were fluent in English as a second language. The 10 subjects were presented recorded Spanish and English interview questions by videotape. These interviews were judged by two Spanish-speaking judges and two English-speaking judges. The English interview produced the higher pathology ratings. The patients were also noted to use more body touching movements under stress during the English interviews. One implication is that nonverbal cues may be used to aid the therapist working with a patient whose dominant language is other than that used in treatment.

Although there is not yet enough evidence to make more firm generalizations about the therapeutic effect of different languages in therapist and patient, the need for sensitivity to the potential restrictions is already documented. Sabin (1975) reported on two case studies in which psychiatrists were able to pick up the severity of mental thought disorder of the patient through translators, but both therapists missed the affective communication that the patient's depressed mood was the primary issue. Both patients committed suicide the day of the initial interview. The psychiatrists had noted the discussion of suicide but dismissed suicide as an imminent possibility. In one case, a woman stated, "I will die if my son is lost"; but this statement was interpreted as bizarre thinking rather than as the message that "I will take my own life if my son is taken away from me due to my not being well enough to retain custody." Sabin suggested that the difficulty may be a matter of distancing from those with whom we do not share common cultural backgounds. For example, data indicate that we ignore depression in lower-class patients because the middle-class medical staff have less ability to empathize when the patient is of another race or class.

Other Issues for Foreign-Born Minorities

Therapy issues for non-English-speaking minorities extend beyond the language barrier. Adopting a language may be an indicator of speed of acculturation of immigrants or refugees, but relinquishing ethnicity may be a stronger indicator of acculturation. Observations concerning Mexican women and the process of acculturation (Melville, 1980) revealed the drive for upward mobility often resulted in ambitious Mexican women's learning English and adopting American customs faster, while their less acculturated, lower-income counterparts tended to cling to the ethnic customs and depend on the group for economic and moral support. Melville suspected that a return to ethnicity might ensue later for the upwardly mobile woman when racial discrimination became more evident, but no data on this trend were available.

Stereotypes of minorities may be fed by lack of distinguishing information from individuals who have either language or cultural barriers that inhibit communication. Morales (1971) referred to the Mexican virtue of enduring stress passively and wondered if an aggressive Mexican would be seen differently from an aggressive American because aggression is not anticipated. Overinterpreting cultural factors may be as much a fault as emphasizing dynamic interpretations without considering cultural origins of behavior. The description of Asians or blacks as paranoid may be confounded with cultural behavior that is appropriate for coping in an alien environment. But a thought disorder may also exist (Yamamoto, 1978). Overgeneralizing among groups may contribute to misdiagnosis as well.

Where the families of foreign-born patients interact with treatment, sensitive issues arise. The dependence on and control of family members varies from culture to culture, and family traditions in most non-American cultures are considerably stronger than they are in the American culture. Conflict because of receiving therapy for family-related problems may override any benefit that may ensue. Asian women from traditional families who have experienced rape or spouse abuse may be unable to leave the situation or to avail themselves of help from an agency without the threat of disgrace to family honor if such behavior is revealed to an outsider. Encouraging the victim to seek help within the extended family in dealing with the situation may be the only reasonable measure available if the cultural mores of the woman are sufficiently traditional. Therapeutic technique such as assertive training may be another conflictual issue in the context of male-female roles in traditional Asian marriages. Yamamoto (1978) raised these and other comparative cultural issues that have received no research attention, particularly with regard to their potential for "culturally dissonant treatment" by unaware therapists.

Very little research has compared data across cultures. Tsung, Tardiff, Donetz, and Goresky (1978) examined ethnicity and patterns of help-seeking behavior. They discovered that among the severely disabled mental patients in a community the Chinese were kept in families longer, the Anglo-Saxon and Middle Europeans were referred by families or selves to multiple community agencies, and native Indians were referred by themselves or by others (usually nonfamily persons) to legal and social agencies. For all groups, a lack of agency coordination was common, although most of the patients eventually received inpatient intervention.

Women as a Minority

Women outnumber men in the population of all cultures and classes. They have been considered a minority, however, because of stereotyping and discrimination based on their sex that has designated them to inferior status. In relation to men of their own race and class, women tend to receive less income and less social status at all levels of education. White women receive less income than black men, but black women receive less income than white women (Hyde & Rosenberg, 1980).

Issues specific to women as a group go beyond discrimination and stereotyping. The development of higher rates of phobias (Chambless & Goldstein, 1980), hysterical traits (Walowitz, 1972) and depression (Weissman, 1980) in women as opposed to men has been attributed at least in part to sex role training. Research on women's issues has made enormous strides in the last decade, and program evaluation of new and alternative therapies are emerging in the psychotherapy literature (Brodsky & Hare-Mustin, 1980).

Women of minority groups do not necessarily suffer "double jeopardy," although some issues are indeed additive when minority status is a factor as well as sex. Thus, on the one hand, uneducated minority women have the lowest income of all sex/race combinations. On the other hand, the black woman has been described as professionally more serious than her white counterpart (Epstein, 1973), and counselors have been advised to help black women at professional levels take advantage of the negative stereotype of their aggressiveness in a work situation (Jeffries, 1976).

Minorities and Mental Health Utilization

Most minorities (with the notable exception of women) have been cited for underuse of mental health facilities and, particularly, for low representation in psychotherapy. Asian researchers report Asian Americans to be greatly underserved (Nguyen & Kim, Note 2) suggesting that this is often erroneously concluded to be due to their discomfort revealing family problems, the better adjustment of Asians regarding mental health, the closer-to-average income of Asians as opposed to other minorities, or other stereotypic myths that they are a particularly successful minority.

Lopez (Note 3) reviewed the literature on Chicanos and the use of mental health facilities and questioned the uncritical acceptance of the low utilization rates based on frequently flawed studies. Explanations for underuse by Mexicans included their supportive family structure, their use of *curanderos* and other alternative mental health resources, the inaccessibility of facilities, and stereotyping and discrimination by the therapist. Lopez critically examined these studies (Lopez, in press) and concluded that Chicanos were using a significant number of facilities "in parity with their representation in the community." He found that over the last two decades increasing percentages of Mexican Americans were accommodated by mental health services. The grievances about underutilization in the 1960s and early 1970s found in the literature may well have been accurate at the time, and they may have achieved what was sought: the funding of services to Mexican Americans and the alerting of the professions to a potential, unmet need.

The utilization issue may have seemed more salient when the particular minority studied represented a small segment of the population. With the exception of women and members of the lower social class, all minorities are indeed minorities in number. This situation may change shortly, however. Currently, Los Angeles is no longer a Caucasian majority, the Caucasians having less than 50% of the census. Latinos currently represent 46% of the population, and this figure is rising.

Lower Social Class Issues

Utilization remains an issue for the lower social classes, however, as do assorted variables on the quantity and type of treatment offered. Reviews of empirical studies examining acceptance into psychotherapy, retention in treatment, status of therapist, attitudes of therapist, expectation of client, and outcome of treatment have periodically appeared over the last decade (Meltzoff & Kornreich, 1970; Jones, 1974; Rabkin, 1977; Schubert & Miller, 1980; Garfield & Bergin, 1978). The bulk of these studies summarized according to selection and acceptance for therapy, acceptance of therapy by the patient, therapist assignment, type of therapy received, duration and amount of therapy, and outcome of therapy. The studies showed that the lower-class patient is more likely than the middle-class patient to be referred through hospital clinics, legal agencies, and other non-self-referrals. Therapists see lower-class individuals as rigid, inarticulate, suspicious, apathetic, passive, wanting symptomatic relief, or unable to profit from treatment. The patients, who expect pills and shots, are not "psychologically minded" and want action and direction from the therapist. Lower-class patients are less likely to be accepted and selected for therapy, particularly if the therapy is insight oriented and analytic. Lower-class patients are more likely not to return after the first session, not to follow through if they do return, not to profit from treatment, and not to wait for therapist concurrence to terminate. They are more likely to get organic treatment, no treatment, or group therapy. They can expect inexperienced therapists, shorter treatment, and physical therapies. They more likely will be less satisfied or less improved, although they show *better* outcome results in brief therapy or emergency treatment than do middle-class patients.

The individual studies show more complex relationships. Perhaps the more interesting evidence is that many of these results are not subject to generalization when one examines the conditions and the raters. In one study (Sloane, Staples, Cristol, Yorkston, & Whipple 1976), the therapist's impression of the patient's suitability for therapy was found unrelated to outcome. Lower-class patients have sought and appreciated insight-oriented psychoanalysis when the option was understood and available. Long-term psychotherapy was shown to be more effective for lower-class patients than for others (Goldensohn, 1981).

For whatever reasons that active, short-term therapies were offered to lower-class patients, these therapies have not proven to be necessarily inferior to analytic, long-term treatment. The active, direct, problem-solving approaches that lower-class patients report they want may actually have better outcome for many patients regardless of social or economic class. Active and positive participation has been linked to success in psychotherapy (Orlinsky & Howard, 1978).

Modifications of Treatment for Minorities

Preparing and modifying traditional treatment approaches for lower-class patients has been reported with some success. Schlesinger and

James (1969) suggested using symptom directed measures first and insight later, while using a more active role throughout. Yamamoto and Goin (1965) added that treatment be more flexible, brief, supportive, and reality oriented. The development of specific films, role plays, and pretherapy information sessions has been seen in the last decade. Heitler (1973) described an "anticipatory socialization interview" in which lower-class patients, who tend to be grossly misinformed about therapy, learned to address the values and expectations they brought which differed from those of their therapists. As a result, more accelerated, more adequate working alliances and longer retention were noted, as were ratings by the therapists that the patients were more comfortable and likable in group therapy.

Acosta, Evans, Yamamoto, and Wilcox (1980) developed a unique videotape to prepare Asian patients for psychotherapy. The videotape used cartoons picturing appropriate responsiveness to key issues that Asians have been shown to have difficulty relating to therapists, such as trusting the therapist with confidences, asserting oneself about a question for or a disagreement with the therapist, and telling the therapist if an appointment will not be kept.

Strupp and Bloxom (1973) described a role-induction film, which they claimed was evaluated better than an interview induction, which in turn was evaluated better than a control population in terms of favorable therapy experience of lower-class patients entering group therapy. Goldensohn (1981) found that lower-class patients responded less well to short-term than to extended treatment, but that Medicaid patients' rates of utilization were higher than those of employed groups when irregular attendance and early dropouts were ignored. Goldensohn's approach included the use of simple language in nonprofessional terminology, role playing, family therapy as a treatment of choice, emphasis on functional competence rather than self-actualization, intervention in real life settings, and use of natural helpers such as spouses, parents, and friends. An interesting facet of his approach is that these modifications were developed in a private practice of psychoanalysis through the Health Insurance Plan of New York. As Medicaid fees rise, the certainty of allocation of lower-class patients to community clinics has lessened, and treating the poor has had broader appeal to the private sector.

Kulka, Veroff, and Douvan (1979) noted that the income differences in self-referral that existed in 1957 did not exist in 1977. When lower classes did seek help in 1977, however, they were still less likely to go to a psychiatrist or to a psychologist than to other mental health personnel.

Patient-Therapist Matching

A common issue among minorities is the relationship between therapist and patient where the therapist is of the dominant culture and the patient of the minority. Much has been written to show that such pairing is fraught with potential difficulties in understanding, empathy, communication, and stereotyping (Chesler, 1972; Berzins, 1977; Sattler, 1977). Although therapist-patient matching for race and sex may be desirable (Fry, Kropf, & Coe, 1980), an obvious problem exists in finding enough currently practicing therapists of the cultural backgrounds and languages of the growing minority populations. Such requirements as being bilingual, gay, lesbian, black, or female may be difficult to accommodate. Demands for matching on these variables may serve a political purpose of drawing the deficiencies of the dominant culture to the profession's attention, but remediation will not be accomplished by sex changes, learning new languages, serving time in other parts of the world, or going into the ghettos to experience the life styles of the patients. While some of these adaptations are being done voluntarily by enthusiastic therapists and by innovative programs in multiethnic cities, the majority of therapists will no doubt continue to restrict practice to patients who meet their criteria of "good" candidates. Very little energy has been expended to examine the effectiveness of models for training in cross-cultural therapy. Lerner (1972) provided an exceptional study in a long-term project with ghetto blacks; and Yamamoto, Dixon, and Bloombaum (1972) described a positive result, based on 10 hours of lectures, to raise awareness of psychiatric residents to issues of black patients. Currently training in cross-cultural competencies is underway for Asians, Hispanics, and American Indians (Sue, in press), but guidance from these projects for majority therapists not in specific training programs is not yet readily available.

Matching on race, sex, or sexual orientation may increase compatibility; but there is evidence that even clients are aware that such matching may not be as important as the competence of the therapist. Thus Seigel (1974) found that blacks chose competence over ethnic similarity when given the preference. Now if only we could assess competence to everyone's satisfaction. The Task Force on Sex Bias and Sex Role Stereotyping in Psychotherapeutic Practice (APA, 1975) attempted to clarify that sexist or racist therapy is necessarily incompetent but that sexism and racism are not the only incompetencies a therapist may exhibit. Also, being of the same sex or race does not insure against the therapist's being racist or sexist. In fact, clients may be aware that therapists of their own race and sex may be biased. Thus Chesler (1972) found that women actually preferred male therapists to female therapists in the late 1960s; such data, however, do not hold constant through the 1970s (Sherman, 1980). Black patients may show a preference for middle-class white therapists over middle-class black therapists with the explanation that they may be afraid that the black middle-class therapists no longer identify with black issues (Wyatt, Powell, & Bass, 1981). The issue of matching may not concern some therapists. Being told that one is unsuitable to conduct therapy with a lower-class patient, a patient who speaks another language, or a patient from a minority at great social distance from one's own culture is not often disturbing unless one financially needs such patients. Thus the burden for the meeting of diverse cultures in therapeutic relationships has been more an issue of social consciousness than one of great interest to majority practitioners or researchers.

Methodology Issues

If one accepted only the evidence from well-controlled, double-blind, large-N, statistically significant, empirical studies in referred journals, there would be no paper on any of the variables discussed in this presentation. The nature of demonstrating bias, indeed of demonstrating outcome in psychotherapy, is fraught with restrictions in research design, controls, availability of subjects, objectivity of researchers, funding, and so forth. The history of psychotherapy research continues as the pendulum of research swings from the need for getting good experimental data to the need for keeping the data close to the real situation. The history of research on women's treatment issues offers a pristine example.

Naomi Weisstein (1969) protested that psychology knew nothing about women because psychology had never studied women. The knowledge of women in treatment was based almost exclusively on clinical intuition and individual reports. Thus she made the plea for inclusion of women's issues in the empirical research on clinical psychology. At that time, the protest was quite appropriate. Psychotherapy researchers had been analyzing the verbal content of therapy sessions, or the process variables that could be isolated from the therapy session, and a variety of other concrete aspects of the pyschotherapeutic endeavor (APA, 1975). Psychotherapy research was coming of age as an empirical field of study. Sex, either by itself or as a control in selecting subjects or analyzing results, was not one of the popular variables. Over the decade that followed, feminists blitzed the APA conventions with papers on sex discrimination in therapy and on the statistics of female authorship of journal articles. They also presented critiques of articles and of areas of programmatic research that ignored women's reactions when these reactions did not coincide with those of men (Horner, 1972). New ways of looking at masculinity and femininity were offered (Bem, 1974), and new measures to assess sex role attitudes and women's issues were developed (Beere, 1979).

Research on women was being included in the ranks of the established methods of psychology. Dissertations were examining sex roles; APA journals were publishing reviews (Worell, 1978; Smith, 1980); psychiatry journal articles on women's issues were becoming more data based (Seiden, 1976). But an unfortunate phenomenon occurred. When bias and discrimination were discovered, later replications tended to moderate the effect (Alper, 1973; Bem, 1974); or the studies which most effectively produced a main bias effect were discounted for their methodology (Stricker, 1977; Smith, 1980; Stearns, Penner, & Kimmel, 1980). Explanations of this phenomenon were forthcoming: Abramowitz (1978), one of the leading researchers of analogue studies on bias toward minorities and women, admitted that analogues were vulnerable to politics. The selectivity of the protocols chosen could easily favor a particular result. In addition, therapist subjects had become quite aware of sex role studies and probably were on guard as to their responses in such a behaviorally restricted sample of attitudes toward patients (Davidson & Abramowitz, 1980). Finally, when addressed directly about the purpose of the analogue study, many therapist subjects by the 1980s were aware of the nature of the studies in regard to sex discrimination, and those who were unaware answered the questions differently, usually in the direction of more bias (Livingston, Note 4).

So attempts to make bias studies more scientific via analogues may have backfired. Prescriptions to return to single case studies and clinical field studies are now in vogue (Brodsky & Hare-Mustin, 1980). An integration of paradigm I (experimental control groups, direct manipulation of experimental variables) with paradigm II (clinical case studies, in-depth inspection of the total situation in the field) is perhaps the direction of choice if one wishes to avoid the pitfalls of either single approach (DeHardt & Lerman, Note 5).

Although the literature on lower social classes and minorities may not be directly parallel to that of women's issues, the problems of methodology are quite similar. Analogue studies have not shown bias against blacks (Blake, 1973; Schwartz, Note 6), but reviews of the clinical literature indicate that strong impressions of such bias are apparent to clinicians and reviewers (Jones, 1974; Sattler, 1977).

Another caution regarding methodology may be indicated. We have known for years that researchers typically have an investment in results in a particular direction and that this investment often results in ideosyncratic positive findings (Rosenthal, 1966). One needs to bear in mind that all researchers working on issues of race and sex bias are vulnerable to their own perspectives. Studies and reviews which conclude negative results for bias are not themselves bias free in design. Stricker's critique of the research on psychotherapy and women (Stricker, 1977) has been criticized for expecting tougher criteria for studies showing bias toward women than for studies that did not confirm bias. DeHardt and Lerman (Note 5) have taken to task the reviews like Smith's (1980) which use meta-analyses across studies as an attempt to conclude that average bias is low or nonexistent. Thus they ask, "If in one sample of 40 females, 28 have been raped; and in 12 samples of 40 females each, none has been raped; and in one sample of 40 males, 28 were raped; is it fair to conclude that on the average rape does not occur?" (p. 14)

The methodology battle is larger than sex roles or minority issues in pyschotherapy. Psychotherapy research has been plagued by the complexities of the situation being studied. In all fairness, however, the developing, fledgling research areas in psychotherapy need to be treated with more openness, more forgiveness, and more attention to the kernels of possible truths uncovered. Certainly, one need not act as if bias is rampant in the therapist population at large. But complacency as a result of one or two failures to replicate a finding of bias is not warranted either. The best of our knowledge would point to an interaction effect in most of the minority, sex role discrimination issues (Orlinsky & Howard, 1980). The discrimination effect may not be the dominant feature in ratings of outcome, but its contribution may well be important in answering the question posed so often by so many: "Who is most effective with whom using what techniques in which settings?"

Conclusion

Three major points can be concluded from this presentation. First, many studies and much anecdotal evidence exist to demonstrate that person attributes of race, sex, and social class have an impact on who gets therapy, from which practitioners, for how long, and of which type. Second, the differential impact of these variables mcst likely appears in interaction with other variables of importance to psychotherapy rather than in isolation as a main effect. Third, the nature of the impact of these variables is not stable but is prone to change with the shift in sensitivity and awareness of the population of therapists and the acculturation of the population of patients.

I personally conclude from the literature of both empirical and intuitive accounts that there is sufficient racism, sexism, and classism among therapists to warrant the continued exploration of positive approaches to train therapists to deal with their biases. We do not need more documentation of therapist shortcomings; we need more evaluation of specific approaches with specific patients by specifically trained therapists to improve therapeutic outcome for minorities and women.

Reference Notes

1. Haller, D. L. *Attribution of sex-stereotypic descriptors to adolescent females in psychotherapy.* Unpublished Master's thesis, University of Alabama, 1975.
2. Nguyen, T. D., & Kim, S. C. *Cultural, social, and programmatic considerations for the design and implementation of an Asian-American training program.* Paper presented to the Western Psychological Association, Los Angeles, April 1981.
3. Lopez, S. *Chicanos and quality of mental health care: A new direction for research.* Paper presented at the annual conference of the Society for Advancement of Chicanos and Native Americans in Science, Albuquerque, November 1980.
4. Livingston, M. M. *An analogue investigation of sex related bias in clinical judgment.* Unpublished doctoral dissertation, University of Alabama, 1981.
5. DeHardt, D. C., & Lerman, H. *Evaluating sex bias in psychotherapy research: A prime example of paradigm I thinking.* Unpublished manuscript, Los Angeles, 1981.
6. Schwartz, J. M. Psychiatrists' treatment decisions as a function of patient race and sex. In N. Haan (Chair), *Clinician value and client sex, race, and social-class effects on clinical decisions.* Symposium presented at the meeting of the American Psychological Association, New Orleans, 1974.

References

Abramowitz, S. I. Splitting data from theory on the black patient-white therapist relationship. *American Psychologist,* 1978, 957–958.

Acosta, F. X., Evans, L. A., Yamamoto, J., & Wilcox, S. A. Helping minority and low-income psychotherapy patients "Tell it like it is." *Journal of Biocommunication,* 1980, *7* (3), 13–19.

Adebimpe, V. R. Overview: White norms and psychiatric diagnosis of black patients. *American Journal of Psychiatry,* 1981, *138* (3), 279–285.

Alper, T. G. The relationship between role orientation and achievement motivation in college women. *Journal of Personality,* 1973, *41,* 9–31.

American Psychological Association (APA). Report of the task force on sex bias and sex role stereotyping in psychotherapeutic practice. *American Psychologist,* 1975, *30,* 1169–1175.

American Psychological Association (APA). Task force on sex bias and sex role stereotyping in psychotherapeutic practice: Guidelines for therapy with women. *American Psychologist,* 1978, *33,* 1122–1123.

Ananth, J. Psychopathology in Indian females. *Social Science and Medicine,* 1978, *12b,* 177–178.

Beere, C. A. *Women and women's issues: A Handbook of tests and measures.* San Francisco: Jossey-Bass, 1979.

Bem, S. L. The measurement of psychological androgyny. *Journal of Consulting and Clinical Psychology,* 1974, 47, 155–162.

Bem, S. L., & Bem, D. J. Case study of a nonconscious ideology: Training the woman to know her place. In D. J. Bem (Ed.), *Beliefs, attitudes and human affairs.* Belmont, Calif.: Brooks/Cole, 1970.

Berzins, J. I. Therapist-patient matching. In A. S. Gurman & A. M. Razin (Eds.), *Effective psychotherapy: A handbook of research.* New York: Pergamon Press, 1977.

Blake, W. The influence of race on diagnosis. *Smith College Studies in Social Work,* 1973, *43,* 184–192.

Bloombaum, M., Yamamoto, J., & James, Q. Cultural stereotyping among psychotherapists. *Journal of Consulting and Clinical Psychology,* 1968, *32*(1), 99.

Brodsky, A. M. A decade of feminist influence on psychotherapy. *Psychology of Women Quarterly,* 1980, *4*(3), 331–344.

Brodsky, A. M., & Hare-Mustin, R., (Eds.). *Women and psychotherapy: An assessment of research and practice.* New York: Guilford Press, 1980.

Broverman, I. K., Broverman, D. M., Clarkson, F. E., Rosenkrantz, P. S., & Vogel, S. R. Sex-role stereotypes and clinical judgments of mental health. *Journal of Consulting and Clinical Psychology,* 1970, *34,* 1–7.

Carter, J. H., & Haizlip, T. M. Race and its relevance to transference. *American Journal of Orthopsychiatry,* 1972, *42,* 865–871.

Chambless, D., & Goldstein, A. Anxieties: Agoraphobia and hysteria. In A. M. Brodsky & R. Hare-Mustin (Eds.), *Women and psychotherapy.* New York: Guilford Press, 1980.

Chesler, P. *Women and madness.* New York: Doubleday, 1972.

Davidson, C. V., & Abramowitz, S. I. Sex bias in clinical judgment: Later empirical returns. *Psychology of Women Quarterly,* 1980, *4*(3), 377–395.

Del Castillo, J. C. The influence of language upon symptomatology in foreign born patients. *American Journal of Psychiatry,* 1970, *127*(2), 242–244.

Epstein, C. F. Positive effects of the mutiple negative: Explaining the success of black professional women. *American Journal of Sociology,* 1973, *78,* 912–935.

Finney, J. C. Judgments of ethnic groups. *Journal of Psychology,* 1968, *68,* 321–328.

Fry, P. S., Kropf, G., & Coe, K. J. Effects of counselor and client racial similarity on the counselor's response patterns and skills. *Journal of Counseling Psychology,* 1980, *27* (2), 130–137.

Garfield, S. L., & Bergin, A. E. (Eds.). *Handbook of psychotherapy and behavior change: An empirical analysis* (2nd ed.). New York: Wiley, 1978.

Goldensohn, S. S. Psychotherapy for the economically disadvantaged: Contributions from the social sciences. *Journal of the American Academy of Psychoanalysis,* 1981, *9*(2), 291–302.

Grand, S., Marcos, L. R., Greedman, N., & Barroso, F. Relation of psychopathology and bilingualism to kinesic aspects on interview behavior in schizophrenia. *Journal of Abnormal Psychology,* 1977, *85*(5), 492–500.

Heitler, J. B. Preparation of lower-class patients for expressive group psychotherapy. *Journal of Consulting and Clinical Psychology,* 1973, *41*(2), 251–260.

Herschberger, R. *Adam's rib.* New York: Harper & Row, 1970.

Horner, M. Achievement-related conflicts in women. *Journal of Social Issues,* 1972, *28,* (2), 157–175.

Hyde, J. S., & Rosenberg, B. G. *Half the human experience: The psychology of women* (2nd ed.). New York: D. C. Heath, 1980.

Hynan, M. T. On the advantages of assuming that the techniques of psychotherapy are ineffective. *Psychotherapy: Theory, research and practice,* 1981, *18*(1), 11–13.

Jefferies, D. Counseling for the strengths of the black woman. *The Counseling Psychologist,* 1976, *6*(2), 20–22.

Jones, A., & Seagull, A. A. Dimensions of the relationship between the black client and the white therapist: A theoretical overview. *American Psychologist,* 1977, *32,* 850–855.

Jones, E. Social class and psychotherapy: A critical review of research. *Psychiatry,* 1974, *37*(4), 307–320.

Kulka, R. A., Veroff, J., & Douvan, E. Social class and the use of professional help for personal problems, 1957 & 1976. *Journal of Health and Social Behavior,* 1979, *20,* 2–17.

Lerner, B. *Therapy in the ghetto.* Baltimore: Johns Hopkins Press, 1972.

Livingood, J. M. (Ed.). *National institute of mental health task force on homosexuality: Final report and background papers* (DHEW-ADM-76-357). Rockville, Md.: National Institute of Mental Health, 1976.

Lopez, S. Clinical stereotypes of the Mexican-American. In J. Martinez (Ed.), *Chicano psychology.* New York: Academic Press, 1977.

Lopez, S. Mexican American usage of mental health facilities: Underutilization reconsidered. In A. Baron (Ed.), *Explorations in Chicano psychology.* New York: Praeger Press, in press.

Marcos, L. R., & Alpert, M. Strategies and risks in psychotherapy with bilingual patients: The phenomenon of language independence. *American Journal of Psychiatry,* 1976, *133* (11), 1275–1278.

Marcella, A. J., Sanborn, K. O., Kameoka, V., Shizuru, L., & Brennan, J. Cross-validation of self-report depression among normal populations of Japanese, Chinese and Caucasian ancestry. *Journal of Clinical Psychology,* 1975, *31*(2), 281–287.

Mayo, J. A. The significance of sociocultural variables in the psychiatric treatment of black out-patients. *Comprehensive Psychiatry,* 1974, *15*(6), 471–482.

Meltzoff, J., & Kornreich, M. *Research in psychotherapy.* New York: Atherton Press, 1970.

Melville, M. B. Selective acculturation of female Mexican migrants. In Melville, M. B. (Ed.), *Twice a minority: Mexican American women.* St. Louis: C. V. Mosby, 1980, 155–163.

Midlarsky, E. Women, psychopathology, and psychotherapy: A partially annotated bibliography. *JSAS Catalog of Selected Documents in Psychology,* 1977, *7,* 41–42.

Morales, A. Distinguishing psychodynamic factors from cultural factors in the treatment of the Spanish-speaking patient. In N. N. Wagner & M. J. Haug (Eds.), *Chicanos: Social and psychological perspectives.* St. Louis: C. V. Mosby, 1971.

Morin, S. F. Heterosexual bias in psychological research on lesbianism and male homosexuality. *American Psychologist,* 1977, *32*(8), 629–637.

Morin, S. F., & Charles, K. A. Heterosexual bias in psychotherapy. In J. Murray & P. R. Abramson (Eds.), *The handbook of bias in psychotherapy.* Los Angeles: University of California Press, in press.

Morishima, J. K., Sue, S., Teng, L. N., Zane, N. W. S., & Cram, J. R. *The handbook of Asian-American/Pacific Islander mental health* (Vol. 1). Rockville, Md.: National Institute of Mental Health, 1979.

Olmedo, E. L., & Parron, D. L. Mental health of minority women: Some special issues. *Professional Psychology,* 1981, *12*(1), 103–111.

Orlinsky, D. E., & Howard, K. I. The relation of process to outcome in psychotherapy. In S. L. Garfield & A. E. Bergin (Eds.), *Handbook of psychotherapy and behavior change: An empirical analysis.* New York: Wiley, 1978.

Orlinsky, D. E., & Howard, K. I. Gender and psychotherapeutic outcome. In A. M. Brodsky & R. Hare-Mustin (Eds.), *Psychotherapy and women: An assessment of research and practice.* New York: Guilford Press, 1980.

Parloff, M. B., Waskow, I. E., & Wolfe, B. E. Research on therapist variables in relation to process and outcome. In S. L. Garfield & A. E. Bergin (Eds.), *Handbook of psychotherapy and behavior change: An empirical analysis.* New York: Wiley, 1978.

Rabkin, J. G. Therapists' attitudes toward mental illness and health. In A. S. Gurman & A. M. Razin (Eds.), *Effective psychotherapy: A handbook of research.* New York: Pergamon Press, 1977.

Rosenthal, R. *Experimenter effects in behavior research.* New York: Appleton-Century-Crofts, 1966.

Sabin, J. E. Translating despair. *American Journal of Psychiatry,* 1975, *132* (2), 197–199.

Sattler, J. M. The effects of therapist-client racial similarity. In A. S. Gurman & A. M. Razin (Eds.), *Effective psychotherapy: A handbook of research.* New York: Pergamon Press, 1977.

Schlesinger, B., & James, G. M. Psychiatry and poverty: A selected review of the literature. *Canadian Medical Association Journal 18,* 1969, *101*(8), 76–83.

Schubert, D. S. P., & Miller, S. I. Differences between the lower social classes: Some new trends. *American Journal of Orthopsychiatry,* 1980, *50(4),* 712–716.

Seiden, A. M. Overview: Research on the psychology of women. I. Gender differences and sexual and reproductive life. *American Journal of Psychiatry,* 1976, *133*(9), 995–1007.

Sherman, J. Therapist attitudes and sex-role stereotyping. In A. M. Brodsky & R. Hare-Mustin (Eds.), *Women and psychotherapy.* New York: Guilford Press, 1980.

Siegel, J. M. A brief review of the effects of race in clinical service interactions. *American Journal of Orthopsychiatry,* 1974, *44*(4), 555–562.

Sloane, R. B., Staples, F. R., Cristol, A. H., Yorkston, N. J., & Whipple, K. Patient characteristics and outcome in psychotherapy and behavior therapy. *Journal of Consulting and Clinical Psychology,* 1976, *44*(3), 330–339.

Smith, M. L. Sex bias in counseling and psychotherapy. *Psychological Bulletin,* 1980, *87*(2), 392–407.

Stearns, B. C., Penner, L. A., & Kimmel, E. Sexism among psychotherapists: A case not yet proven. *Journal of Consulting and Clinical Psychology,* 1980, *48,* 548–550.

Stein, L. S., Green, B. L., & Stone, W. N. Therapist attitudes as influenced by A-B therapist type, patient diagnosis, and social class. *Journal of Consulting and Clinical Psychology,* 1972, *39*(2), 301–307.

Stricker, G. Implications of research for psychotherapeutic treatment of women. *American Psychologist,* 1977, *32*(1), 14–22.

Strupp, H. H., & Bloxom, A. L. Preparing lower-class patients for group psychotherapy: Development and evaluation of a role-induction film. *Journal of Consulting and Clinical Psychology,* 1973, *41,* 373–384.

Sue, D. W. (Ed.). *Counseling the culturally different: Theory and practice.* New York: Wiley, in press.

Tonaka, P. H., Oyama, T., & Osgood, C. E. Cross-cultural and cross-concept study of the generality of semantic spaces. *Journal of Verbal Learning and Verbal Behavior,* 1963, *2,* 392–405.

Tsung, X. L., Tardiff, T., Donetz, G., & Goresky, W. Ethnicity and patterns of help-seeking. *Culture, Medicine and Psychiatry.* 1978, *2,* 3–13.

Weiss, B. L., & Kupfer, D. J. The black patient and research in a community mental health center: Where have all the subjects gone? *American Journal of Psychiatry,* 1974, *131* (4), 415–418.

Weissman, M. Depression. In A. M. Brodsky & R. Hare-Mustin (Eds.), *Women and psychotherapy.* New York: Guilford Press, 1980.

Weisstein, N. Kinder, kuche, kirche as scientific law: Psychology constructs the female. *Motive,* 1969, *29,* 6–7.

Wolowitz, H. M. Hysterical character and feminine identity. In J. M. Bardwick (Ed.), *Readings on the psychology of women.* New York: Harper & Row, 1972.

Worell, J. Sex roles and psychological well-being: Perspectives on methodology. *Journal of Consulting and Clinical Psychology,* 1978, *46*(4), 777–791.

Wyatt, G. E., Powell, G. J., & Bass, B. The survey of Afro-American behavior: Its development and use in research. In G. E. Wyatt, G. J. Powell, & B. Bass (Eds.), *The Afro-American family: Assessment, treatment and research issues.* New York: Grune-Stratton, 1981.

Yamamoto, J. Research priorities in Asian-American mental health delivery. *American Journal of Psychiatry,* 1978, *135*(4), 457–458.

Yamamoto, J., Dixon, F., & Bloombaum, M. White therapists and negro patients. *Journal of the National Medical Association,* 1972, *64*(4), 312–316.

Yamamoto, J., & Goin, M. K. On the treatment of the poor. *American Journal of Psychiatry,* 1965, *122,* 267–271.

Yamamoto, J., James, Q. C., & Palley, N. Cultural problems in psychiatric therapy. *Archives of General Psychiatry,* 1968, *19,* 45–49.

Zukerman, E. *Changing direction in the treatment of women: A mental health bibliography.* Rockville, Md.: National Institute of Mental Health, 1979.

ALAN E. KAZDIN

METHODOLOGY OF PSYCHOTHERAPY OUTCOME RESEARCH: RECENT DEVELOPMENTS AND REMAINING LIMITATIONS

ALAN E. KAZDIN

Alan E. Kazdin is a professor of child psychiatry at the University of Pittsburgh School of Medicine and is also the program and research director at the Children's Psychiatric Intensive Care Service, Western Psychiatric Institute and Clinic. Having obtained his doctorate from Northwestern University in 1970, he served on the faculty of the Pennsylvania State University before coming to the University of Pittsburgh.

Kazdin is the author of over 180 journal articles and book chapters. He has written or edited 15 books, including *Behavior Modification in Applied Settings* (1975), *History of Behavior Modification* (1978), and *Research Design in Clinical Psychology* (1980). He has been on the review board of 18 journals, and he is presently the editor of *Behavior Therapy*.

Kazdin has been a fellow at the Center for Advanced Study in the Behavioral Sciences and the president of the Association for Advancement of Behavior Therapy. He is a fellow of the American Psychological Association and a member of numerous professional and honorary organizations. His current research focuses on the assessment and treatment of childhood psychopathology, especially depression and conduct disorder.

ALAN E. KAZDIN

METHODOLOGY OF PSYCHOTHERAPY OUTCOME RESEARCH: RECENT DEVELOPMENTS AND REMAINING LIMITATIONS

The effectiveness of alternative psychotherapy techniques continues as a major area of research in clinical psychology and psychiatry. Identification of effective treatments is a high professional and research priority for several reasons. To begin with, estimates of the number of persons in the population at large in the United States who experience psychiatric dysfunction and problems of living and who might benefit from treatment have been as high as 15 to 25 percent (President's Commission on Mental Health, 1978). The untoward social, economic, and personal repercussions that mental health problems present are extensive (Kiesler, 1979). Although psychotherapy might not alleviate all mental health problems, certainly the availability of effective techniques would have a large pool of consumers who might benefit directly.

Apart from the need for services, professional interest in the multiple questions of psychotherapy outcome is high (e.g., Agras, Kazdin, & Wilson, 1979; Garfield, 1981; VandenBos, 1980). Efforts to unravel the underlying bases of clinical disorders and the mechanisms of therapeutic change and to evaluate the effects and relative efficacy of alternative treatments continue. The need to develop the scientific bases of psychotherapy is widely recognized.

Completion of this paper was supported by a Research Scientist Development Award (K02 MH00353) from the National Institute of Mental Health.

Perhaps the most recent impetus for the scrutiny of therapy outcome in the United States comes from the Congressional interest in the cost of psychological services (Marshall, 1980). Because of the reimbursement for psychotherapy as part of national health-care policy proposals, Congress has a keen interest in determining whether demonstrably effective techniques exist and whether the benefits warrant the costs (Kiesler, 1979; Parloff, 1979). The need for clear answers to questions about treatment effects is great; however, the answers are not likely to come quickly, and simple answers are not likely to come at all. The ways in which research questions are often formulated, the ways in which answers are sought, and the difficulties in conducting research in clinical settings create enormous obstacles to finding the answers.

The present paper discusses characteristics, issues, and methods of current outcome research. Notwithstanding clear methodological advances in outcome research methods, fundamental problems remain for answering the pressing questions about treatments and their effects. Exemplary outcome studies are highlighted to convey the limitations of current methods in identifying techniques that can be implemented effectively in clinical practice. To meet the demands for knowledge about treatments and their effective implementation, additional research strategies are needed. A major portion of this paper identifies the limits of existing strategies and proffers new strategies to extend the potential yield of psychotherapy outcome research.[1]

Evaluation of Psychotherapy: Issues and Debates

That many unresolved issues and sources of ambiguity exist in psychotherapy research is an obvious understatement. Commonly discussed issues and ambiguities pertain to the substantive findings or to what can be said about the effects of various treatments. Yet confusion at the level of substantive findings reflects ambiguity about fundamental issues of ways to investigate and to evaluate the psychotherapies. Several issues that contribute to the ambiguities can be identified.

First, the focus on different therapy orientations or schools has impeded therapy evaluation. The need to categorize techniques for purposes of communications is understandable because of the extremely large number of available therapy techniques (Herink, 1980). The categorization of techniques usually is based on common theoretical orien-

[1] The reference throughout the paper to "psychotherapy" is to psychosocial treatments generally rather than to a particular conceptual orientation or treatment technique. Thus diverse forms of psychotherapy, unless otherwise distinguished by name, are encompassed by the discussion.

tations (e.g., psychodynamic, behavioral, and cognitive therapies) or on common characteristics regarding the format in which treatment is administered (e.g., brief, group, and intensive therapies). In particular, the categorization of techniques on the bases of conceptual orientations has clouded discussions of treatment effects. For example, the contemporary interest in contrasting or combining psychodynamic and behavior therapy reflects the unfortunate consequence of delineating treatments by orientation. Yet comparisons at the level of general orientations of treatments are problematic because, within each orientation, multiple techniques exist. The conceptual diversity and empirical status of constituent techniques within a particular approach may vary to such an extent as to make discussions of the effects of global orientations meaningless. Much greater precision is needed in discussing, evaluating, and investigating techniques. General discussions of treatments designed to examine whether psychotherapy, behavior therapy, cognitive therapy, or other general categories "work" only obfuscate the genuine questions about the effects of particular techniques.

A second issue that partially clouds treatment evaluation is what the most appropriate measures of therapy outcome are. The usual criteria consist of patient improvements on one or a few measures considered to reflect the dysfunction or problem of adjustment more generally. Yet multiple criteria have been proposed that make simple conclusions about the effects of treatment difficult to reach. For example, some authors have suggested the importance of considering measures that reflect the separate vantage points of society, the patient, and mental health professionals (Strupp & Hadley, 1977). Measures that represent these different perspectives may vary greatly in attesting to the effects of particular treatments. Other authors have suggested several different measures that might be used to evaluate therapeutic change, including the clinical significance of the changes, the proportion of persons completing treatment who attain this level, the durability of change, and the extent to which most persons are affected (Kazdin & Wilson, 1978a). With increased concerns over the costs of therapy, certainly criteria that combine costs and benefits are also quite relevant.

When the range of outcome measures is extended beyond simple pretreatment to posttreatment changes on particular measures, a major point becomes clear. The different criteria that might legitimately be used to evaluate treatment do not necessarily lead to the same conclusions about treatment efficacy. For example, the treatment that produces the greatest change for all patients as a whole (average within-group change) might not be the treatment that produces a clinically significant change for the largest number (a change of a particular magnitude). Or the treatment that produces the greatest change at posttreatment may not be the one that produces the greatest change by the time of follow-up. In general, multiple criteria have been proposed to evaluate therapy outcome. Yet conclusions about treatment efficacy continue to be restricted to a narrow range of outcome criteria.

A third issue is the lack of consensus on the appropriate methods of evaluating multiple outcome studies to reach conclusions about treatment efficacy. Traditionally the method of deciding the current state of the art for particular treatment techniques or sets of techniques has been to complete a review of the literature. Indeed, this method of evaluating treatment continues to enjoy wide acceptance.[2] The difficulty with reviews of the literature are obvious. We have learned all too well that essentially the same literature can be reviewed with vastly discrepant conclusions. Reviews frequently generate their own debates; they are rarely regarded as impartial accounts because of basic disagreements about methodological standards that are to be invoked or overlooked and the resultant conclusions that are drawn. Basic disagreements exist about the studies that are appropriate to include in many reviews. Attempts have been made to quantify the weight of the evidence by keeping a box score count across studies to tally which treatments work better than others (e.g., Ledwidge, 1978; Luborsky, Singer, & Luborsky, 1975). Present variations of such procedures, however, seem to exacerbate, through oversimplification, the problems that ordinary reviews commit (Kazdin & Wilson, 1978b).

The recent emergence of meta-analysis has greatly augmented the hopes for an objective way of evaluating multiple outcome studies (Smith & Glass, 1977). Meta-analysis examines effect sizes produced in individual investigations and draws conclusions across a large number of studies for a particular treatment. The attractive feature of meta-analysis is the capacity to reach conclusions from large numbers of studies that otherwise would be difficult to synthesize. Also, the analysis has the virtues of increased sophistication and respectability through the use of quantitative methods. Although meta-analysis has been seized upon in the evaluation literature, it has been subject to several criticisms (e.g., Eysenck, 1978; Gallo, 1978; Rachman & Wilson, 1980; Sechrest, West, Phillips, Redner, & Yeaton, 1979). Meta-analysis is by no means universally accepted as an appropriate method of evaluating outcome research.

[2] Individual areas of treatment have become so specialized and reviews so extensive that many handbooks have appeared which provide reviews of multiple techniques (e.g., Bellack, Hersen, & Kazdin, in press; Garfield & Bergin, 1978; Gurman & Kniskern, 1981; Turner, Calhoun, & Adams, 1981).

In general, the criteria for evaluating treatment and the methods of evaluating individual studies and aggregates of studies are hardly agreed upon. Other basic issues also make the task of evaluating treatment difficult. These issues include the continued paucity of research that examines long-term follow-up, focuses on clinical samples, or replicates research findings. The purpose here is to convey only that fundamental difficulties in obtaining clear evaluations of psychotherapy remain. To emphasize the difficulties might convey wrongly that advances have not been made or that treatment research has not begun to provide the answers we need. Actually, the purpose of this paper is to present major advances and to make suggestions for new types of research to accelerate the current rate of progress.

Recent Trends in Outcome Research

Treatment research has evolved remarkably in the last several years. The theoretical diversity and the presence of several unresolved issues, as highlighted above, have stimulated many advances in the search for answers to questions about psychotherapies and their effects. The specification of treatment, the multifaceted nature of therapeutic change, and the range of outcome questions studied point to salient advances in psychotherapy research and the manner in which it is conducted.

Treatment Specification

Advances. Psychotherapy techniques typically have been couched in theoretical terms that specify the bases for the development of the problem and the manner in which the treatment operates to produce change. Theory specification has been an important part of treatment development because of the research generated to improve what is known about behavior.

Apart from theory specification, there is an increased appreciation for treatment specification. Techniques that are grounded theoretically are not necessarily well specified procedurally. Increased specification of treatment is needed to ensure that techniques can be replicated in research and clinical practice. The specification of treatment procedures can be seen in the recent appearance of treatment manuals that usually develop as part of research protocols. A large number of treatment techniques have been detailed in manual form.[3] The purpose of the manuals is to provide explicit and often detailed guidelines for the way therapy is to be conducted, not to eliminate the need for additional training of therapists.

Specification of treatments in manual form is an important advance in psychotherapy research for several reasons. First, treatment manuals facilitate replication of treatments across settings. A treatment manual indicates the structure and content of individual sessions. Perhaps not all of the facets of treatment can be codified in manual form, but the manual at least attempts to detail the sequence and implementation of major procedures.

Second, when procedures are well specified, more analytic research to evaluate their relevance to therapeutic change is possible. Theory can convey the mechanisms and components of treatment that are likely to be important; however, the theory eventually must be translated into procedures that can be varied for purposes of research. In principle, treatment manuals allow for specification of procedures that can be analyzed in research.

Third, because manuals provide a way to codify treatment, they can be frequently updated and thus can document progress and improvements through ongoing revision. The benefits of experience with a treatment can be reflected explicitly in further refinements of the manual.

Limitations. Although the move toward treatment specification is excellent, there are some limitations as well. To begin with, not all psychosocial techniques are equally specifiable in manual form. Techniques that encompass directive and concrete procedures are more readily placed into manual form. Consequently, many behavior therapy techniques have been especially conducive to codification. Other techniques such as psychodynamically oriented psychotherapy, gestalt therapy, and experiential treatments may be more difficult to specify. To be sure, these latter treatments encompass specific techniques but are procedurally more nebulous. Many treatments identify *processes* rather than particular procedures as critical therapeutic ingredients. It may be

[3] For examples, treatment manuals are available for social learning treatment of children with conduct problems (Patterson, Reid, Jones, & Conger, 1975); social skills training and cognitive therapy of depressed patients (Beck, Rush, Shaw, & Emery, 1979; Bellack, Hersen, & Himmelhoch, 1980); token economy, milieu therapy, and social skills training for psychiatric patients (Beidel, Bellack, Turner, Hersen, & Luber, 1981; Paul & Lentz, 1977); and many others. In addition to the above published manuals, there exists a large informal network of unpublished manuals that investigators share as part of their research. Apart from manuals designed for researchers and therapists, the increased specification of treatment is also reflected in the appearance of self-help manuals for parents, teachers, clients, and patients with various problems (e.g., Glasgow & Rosen, 1979). The present discussion is restricted to reference of treatment manuals designed for professionals and especially for research purposes.

important to examine and to specify processes, the ways processes develop, and the therapist's role in their emergence in treatment. Without improved attempts to specify processes, many treatments are likely to be ignored for research purposes. The differential capacity of treatments to be specified may serve as an inadvertent screening criterion for what researchers study.

The specification of treatments in manual form has the potential of moving research away from some of the complexities of individual treatment techniques. Even among treatments that are more readily specifiable, selected processes or important components of treatments that are procedurally elusive may be overlooked. Researchers may seize upon the more specifiable components as if they constitute the core influences of treatment. For example, within selected behavioral treatments, nonspecific treatment factors and features of the therapeutic relationship are not well specified. Since evidence suggests that these factors often influence outcome (e.g., Alexander, Barton, Schiavo, & Parsons, 1976; Ford, 1978), they may be essential to specify.

The increased specification of therapies is an excellent development with important implications for theory, research, and practice. The attempt to specify treatments in manual form, however, may move researchers away from the complex treatments and multifaceted variables of client-therapist interaction. The move away from such factors might be desirable if evidence indicated that only concrete procedures account for therapeutic change. Since the evidence does not clearly argue for procedures alone as mediators of change, the move toward specification needs to focus on several other facets of treatments.

Assessment

Advances. A number of advances have been made in the assessment of therapeutic change. The advances reflect the acknowledgment and the investigation of the multifaceted nature of personality and behavior changes that follow therapy (Kazdin, in press). Currently considerable attention has been devoted to the assessment of multiple facets of clinical problems. Perhaps the area that most obviously reflects this approach is the treatment of anxiety-based disorders. Changes in anxiety are usually evaluated in measures of self-report, overt performance, and psychophysiological responses. The use of multiple channels of assessment is extremely important, because measures respond differently to a given treatment.

The multiple channels of assessment have led to the recognition of complex interresponse relationships. For example, the specificity of performance to particular measures or conditions of assessment is increasingly acknowledged. Assessment of clinical change may be restricted to the stimulus conditions in which assessment is administered, to the particular measures that persons complete, and to the particular responses that are sampled (Kazdin, 1979b). The specificity of performance has been actively discussed in personality research for many years (see Endler & Magnusson, 1976; Mischel, 1968); however, the implications have not had wide impact on therapy outcome assessment. Situational and response specificity are of special importance because of their implications for conclusions about the efficacy or relative efficacy of alternative techniques. The claims about treatment effects need to be qualified by the circumstances of assessment. General claims about the superiority of one technique over another are difficult to make without a clear statement of the precise measures and measurement conditions.

Apart from response and situational specificity, other complexities have emerged from the study of multiple response assessment that can influence the conclusions reached about therapy outcome. Multiple measures of a particular construct (for example, anxiety) may vary together over the course of outcome or may vary independently or inversely, processes referred to as *synchrony* and *desynchrony*, respectively (Hodgson & Rachman, 1974; Rachman & Hodgson, 1974). Thus the correspondence and convergence of measures of a particular construct have become important measures in their own right.

The relationships among entirely different responses that are not part of a single construct have also received attention in the study of treatment outcome. Therapeutic changes in a particular area of overt performance can systematically produce changes in other, seemingly unrelated areas of performance, a phenomenon that has been termed *response covariation* (Kazdin, in press; Wahler, Berland, & Coe, 1979; Wahler & Fox, 1980b). Behaviors apparently are organized in clusters so that impact on particular behaviors may lead to changes in other behaviors. Some of the concomitant changes might be viewed as desirable (adaptive or appropriate) while others may be viewed as undesirable (maladaptive or inappropriate). Only the simultaneous investigation of cognitive processes, personality measures, and overt performance within and across constructs would reveal the complex interplay of changes following treatment.

The empirical relationships among responses assessed as part of therapy outcome have increased the complexity of outcome questions. The effectiveness of a particular technique or the relative effectiveness of alternative techniques may look very different depending on the measures that are used. The evaluation of outcome is not resolved merely by looking at change on a particular measure or set of measures after treatment. The answers to important outcome questions depend upon the conceptualization underlying the selection of dependent measures. Insofar as therapy produces change, the changes are likely to be multifaceted, to vary over time, and to affect diverse areas of performance. Until basic assessment issues regarding the complexities and nature of therapeutic change are resolved, few answers regarding traditional therapy outcome questions seem possible. However, recognition of the complexities of outcome is a distinct methodological advance in psychotherapy research. The process of change in clinical problems is manifold, and simple conclusions about changes on simplistic outcome measures cannot begin to represent the nature of treatment effects.

Limitations. An important issue in therapy is identifying initially what should be assessed and treated. Therapy research has taken both extremes of the issue. On the one hand, therapy traditionally has attempted to alter general characteristics (e.g., disorders, general adjustment, and underlying personality) of the clients. In such investigations, outcome measures tend to be global clinical ratings of adjustment. On the other hand, treatments have focused on concrete overt behaviors. In such investigations, the outcome measures tend to be specific behaviors that are observed and are considered to reflect the problem directly. Certainly the movement in recent years has been toward increased specificity of assessment and treatment.

A difficulty for outcome research at these extremes is the basis for selecting particular measures. In some areas, assessment may be obviously relevant in terms of its focus on a clinical problem. For example, for conduct problem and oppositional children, samples of aggressive and noncompliance behavior are often observed directly (e.g., Wahler & Fox, 1980a). The basis of the focus and selection of the measures may be relatively clear. Even here, however, unless a wide range of situations is sampled, the conclusions about treatment effects may be restricted to a narrow range of conditions. For other areas, the bases of selecting the focus of treatment and the assessment procedures are often unclear.

An illustration of the problem is the area of social skills training which has received attention in research with diverse populations (see Bellack & Hersen, 1979; Singleton, Spurgeon, & Stammer, 1980). The importance of developing interpersonal behavior is widely acknowledged because of the relationship between social behavior (e.g., social interaction, participation in social activities, popularity, and social competence) and psychopathology (Kazdin, 1979c; Phillips, 1978). Scrutiny of many treatment investigations, however, reveals that social skills refer to such measures as eye contact, voice volume, speech duration, facial expressions, and body movements. The focus on molecular behaviors may not encompass the deficits or debilitating problems of the particular clinical population included in treatment. Also, the changes in behavior may not be genuinely relevant to social interaction measured in more molar units, such as quality of interaction with peers, fellow employees, relatives, or other persons in the community. Although many benefits accrue from specificity of assessment, greater work is needed within particular areas of treatment research to ensure that the concrete behaviors included in training and assessment affect directly those problems that pertain to the dysfunction of the client or patient.

Range of Outcome Questions

Advances. A major characteristic of outcome research has been expansion of the range of research questions addressed (Kiesler, 1981). The two basic questions that typically have guided outcome research are whether a particular treatment is effective for persons with a given problem and whether one particular technique is better than another for that problem. These questions are associated with specific treatment evaluation strategies (Kazdin, 1980). The treatment package strategy attempts to evaluate whether a particular technique produces greater change than no treatment at all. No attempt is made to analyze facets of treatment that may contribute to change. The comparative strategy contrasts two (or more) competing treatments to determine which one produces greater (or greatest) change. Although these strategies are of obvious importance, they exclude a spectrum of intervening questions.

Attention to the range of alternative treatment evaluation strategies and to the scope of outcome questions that are posed has broadened (Kazdin, 1980). For example, psychotherapy research has increasingly focused on dismantling existing treatments. Dismantling research analyzes components of a given treatment to show the elements necessary or sufficient to produce change and to discover whether specific components produce additive or interactive effects.

Other therapy research has focused on constructing different treatments. With a constructive treatment strategy, the investigator usually begins with a basic treatment component that is relatively narrow or circumscribed and adds various ingredients. As research continues, the accretion of procedures, techniques, or variables can lead to increasingly effective techniques. Research has also explored parameters of individual treatments to discover how to maximize therapeutic change with a given technique. Variables usually are evaluated along quantitative dimensions, such as duration of presentation of various stimuli or amount of extratherapy practice. Of course, individual techniques specify the parameters that for theoretical or practical reasons may improve outcome.

The different strategies pose different questions about treatment. The strategies do not attempt merely to identify the technique variation most effective for a particualr problem, although identification in itself is an important goal. The strategies provide important tests of theoretical propositions about the mechanisms through which treatment techniques achieve their effects. For example, if a particular therapy is based upon the view that some components are essential, a dismantling strategy may be useful to test whether treatment is impeded by subtracting a supposedly essential ingredient. The dismantling strategy has played an important role in evaluating systematic desensitization in which special ingredients (e.g., the presentation of relaxation to compete with anxiety, the hierarchical presentation of anxiety-provoking stimuli, and the pairing of relaxation with anxiety-provoking stimuli) were once thought to be essential to therapeutic change. Several dismantling studies have shown these ingredients to be nonessential for therapeutic change (see Kazdin & Wilcoxon, 1976; Wilkins, 1971). The findings have had important implications for the theoretical explanation about the mechanisms of change by ruling out interpretations relying upon these ingredients.

Limitations. Although attention to the range of outcome questions addressed in recent years has increased, so has the range of available questions that can be asked. Because psychotherapy is an expanding universe of techniques, the research questions that can be asked are increasing at a rapid and ever-expanding rate. For example, when one considers the commonly investigated question about the relative effectiveness of alternative techniques for a particular clinical problem, one is faced with over 250 different therapy techniques that have been enumerated (Herink, 1980). Although all the available techniques might not be applicable to a particular problem, a sufficient number exists to keep researchers who are interested in comparative research occupied for some time.

Also, the comparative treatment strategy is only one type of investigation that might be conducted. If a constructive strategy, in which selected procedures or entire treatments are combined to build increasingly effective treatments, is explored, the specific questions that can be asked and the requisite investigations increase geometrically. As each of the other treatment evaluation strategies are considered (e.g., dismantling, parametric, and client-therapist variation strategies), the questions to be addressed by research are astronomical.

The problem is exacerbated by the putative question that is supposed to guide psychotherapy research, namely, "What kinds of changes are produced by what kinds of treatments, for what kinds of patients, by what kinds of therapists, and under what kinds of conditions?" (e.g., Parloff, Wolfe, Hadley, & Waskow, 1978; Paul, 1969). If one takes this question seriously, the task of research, given the existing range of techniques, could not be achieved. Of course, the problems stem not only from the range of techniques, the clinical problems, and the therapy evaluation strategies. Many basic issues about assessment and design that dictate how to address outcome questions appropriately are also far from resolved. Hence there is no singular or universally agreed-upon assessment battery or design strategy that could, in any definitive fashion, put to rest particular questions about therapy.

The prospect of addressing the questions of therapy in a piecemeal fashion is not very attractive. To advance beyond empirical evaluations of permutations of alternative techniques, researchers need clearer theoretical work to identify mechanisms of therapeutic change. The existence of multiple techniques for a problem must generate theoretical propositions that can be tested—not necessarily in the context of clinical research. The propositions would suggest basic processes that may account for particular treatment effects.

One area that is a likely candidate for theoretical work and programmatic research spanning many different techniques is that of the so-called nonspecific treatment factors, i.e., those components perhaps accounting for change that are common to many treatments. Although many nonspecific factors have been carefully elaborated (e.g., Frank, 1973) and subjected to much discussion (e.g., Bootzin & Lick, 1979; Kazdin, 1979a; Wilkins, 1979), relatively little sound theory followed by actual research exists in fact. Advances in understanding nonspecific factors, the ways these factors produce change, and the ways they combine to maximize treatment effects await elaboration. A general line of work, such as (but not restricted to) evaluation of nonspecific treatment factors, might help identify processes that bring coherence to the multiplicity of treatment techniques.

Recent attempts have been made to identify mechanisms of therapeutic change that transcend individual techniques. The work on self-efficacy theory (Bandura, 1977) as a possible account of how treatment effects are achieved illustrates the search for common mechanisms across treatments. The approach of research has been to evaluate self-efficacy in relation to behavior changes under highly controlled laboratory conditions (e.g., Bandura & Adams, 1977; Bandura, Adams, & Beyer, 1977). The search for mechanisms and processes of change in laboratory work continues to be needed to provide the conceptual foundations from which the different treatments and treatment parameters can be viewed.

The Spectrum of Psychotherapy Research

Many methods of research for investigating psychotherapy are in active use. Three methods of evaluating treatment outcome include case studies, analogue research, and clinical trials. These methods reflect the spectrum of research and convey current advances, conceptualizations, and limitations of outcome research more generally.

The Case Study

The case study has played a central role in the evaluation of alternative psychotherapy techniques. Typically, case studies have consisted of anecdotal reports of a client's problem and the ways treatment effected its amelioration. Classic case descriptions (e.g., Anna O., Little Hans, Little Albert, and Peter) have had remarkable impact because they have been considered to reveal important information about the nature of personality and psychopathology, the development of maladaptive behavior, the process of therapeutic change, and the efficacy of particular treatment approaches. Cases invariably have provided a rich source of information for hypotheses about disordered behavior and therapeutic change.

Despite its heuristic value, the case study usually is considered to be inadequate as a basis for drawing valid inferences. The uncontrolled case study has a limited capacity to identify factors responsible for therapeutic change. Although the delivery of treatment may be associated with therapeutic change, the basis of the change cannot be readily determined. Even if treatment were responsible for change, several alternative interpretations of the results might be readily proposed (see Cook & Campbell, 1979; Kazdin, 1980).

The case study has been discounted as a potential source of scientifically validated information because plausible rival explanations of the results (e.g., threats to internal validity) cannot be ruled out. The rejection of the case study as a means for empirical research is unfortunate for several reasons. To begin with, treatment ordinarily is administered at the level of individual cases in various clinical settings. In this context of individual treatment as practiced, many innovative and clinically relevant hypotheses emerge. Also, clinical treatment provides one of the most demanding situations in which treatment efficacy can be tested. The complexity of the problems that individuals present, the relationship that emerges between the therapist and patient, and the nature of the change resulting from therapy may be most meaningfully evaluated at the level of the individual case. The study of groups of clients and average change from pretreatment to posttreatment, commonly examined in research, may distort the pattern of changes evident in individual clients (see Barlow, 1981; Strupp & Hadley, 1979). Thus evaluation of individual cases may provide the most relevant information about treatment effects.

The failure to use the case study as the basis for empirical investigation is unfortunate also because it fosters the professional hiatus between research and practice. Professionals who provide direct treatment services or engage in clinical practice are infrequently involved in conducting research, and vice versa (see Garfield & Kurtz, 1976). Consequently, research usually is conducted in academic settings, whereas treatment is usually conducted in clinical settings not associated with research departments (Parloff, 1979). The types of patients and of clinical problems and the variations of treatments examined in research often depart from routine treatment conditions. Hence much of the outcome research appears to be or in fact is irrelevant to practitioners.

The hiatus between research and practice may exist in part because of the absence of research methodology that can be feasibly applied in clinical settings. The control over assessment and treatment administration, recruitment of homogeneous patients, standardization, delay, or withholding of treatment are not viable options in most clinical settings. Consequently, clinical work at the level of the individual case has remained uncontrolled because of the lack of viable alternatives.

Recent Developments. Recently movements have been made toward advocating the investigation of individual cases as a research method. One recommendation has been to reconceptualize the uncontrolled case study as an experiment and to bring to bear multiple sources of information to increase the strength of the inferences that can be drawn (see Kazdin, 1981). The logic of experimentation can be followed in an uncontrolled case study to controvert particular sources of ambiguity. The purpose of experimentation is to make alternative explanations of the results as implausible as possible. At the end of an experimental investigation, the effects of treatment should be the most plausible and parsimonious interpretation of the results. Case studies can also rule out alternative explanations that might compete with inferences about the impact of treatment.

The major additions required of the case study to make various threats to internal validity implausible include using objective measures (e.g., self-report inventories, ratings, and direct observation), assessing performance at a few points before, during, and after treatment, and obtaining information from research on other cases or from data for the given case about the stability of the problem. Also, the accumulation of a few cases and the evaluation of the pattern change during treatment can be used to draw valid inferences from uncontrolled case studies. With relatively minor changes in the ways therapists assess individual cases, a quantum leap can be made in the informational yield. The assessment data and the other information the clinician can bring to bear on the case can address specific concerns that ordinarily arise in case studies.

Apart from the valid inference approach highlighted above, several authors have advocated the use of single-case experimental designs to evaluate treatment cases (e.g., Hersen & Barlow, 1976; Kazdin, 1982; Kratochwill, 1978). The designs consist of different ways of arranging the ways and the times the treatment is presented to the client to make implausible threats to internal validity. The designs are true experiments, and they greatly surpass the strength of the inferences that can be drawn in relation to controlled case studies.

In the more commonly used single-case designs, treatment may be presented at some times and withdrawn at other times (ABAB design), or treatment may focus on one area of performance (e.g., a particular problem or performance in a particular setting) and be extended to other areas of performance at different times (multiple-baseline design). Many designs are available, and their widespread use in clinical research has attested to their methodological strength in demonstrating causal relations (cf. Hersen & Barlow, 1976; Kazdin, 1982).

Single-case experimental designs have been advocated as a method suitable for clinical practice (Hayes, 1981); however, the designs make some rather stringent demands on the clinical investigator that may interfere with the usual service delivery priorities of treatment. The requirements for assessing performance continuously, for arranging treatments to evaluate their impact experimentally, and for procuring the resources needed to ensure objectivity of the measures are likely to restrict the use of the designs. Also, the designs have been used heavily in cases where the clinical problems can be readily translated into specific target behaviors that can be observed directly. The multifaceted nature of clinical problems and the unavailability of direct behavioral referents, either in principle or in practice, introduce special problems for the designs. However, the important point to convey here is that single-case experimental designs represent a methodology for experimentation with individual clients. Even though the demands the designs place on treatment may restrict their widespread use by practicing clinicians, certainly the methodology is much more feasible than between-group methodology for ordinary clinical practice.

Analogue Research

Although recommendations to conduct research with the single case have recently increased, the bulk of the outcome research continues to use between-group research designs. Typically research is conducted under highly controlled experimental conditions. Selection of homogenous subjects, random assignment, administration of narrowly focused and standardized treatment, and several other features are highly controlled to meet the rigors of experimentation. Investigations of this sort have frequently been referred to as *analogue research* because they tend only to resemble in varying degrees the clinical situation to which the results might be generalized. Conditions of treatment are purposely altered to provide greater control over the experimental arrangement and to evaluate a wider range of treatment questions than clinical situations normally afford.

Analogue research has proliferated especially in behavior therapy. So-called analogue studies have several characteristics (Borkovec & Rachman, 1979; Kazdin, 1978). First, the problem that is treated usually departs from the typical problems seen in inpatient or outpatient treatment. The target problems (e.g., fears, social skills deficits) usually are less severe and more circumscribed than those problems patients bring to treatment. The problems in analogue research and clinical treatment may differ along quantitative or qualitative dimensions or both, depending on the problem area.

Second, the persons who receive treatment in analogue research usually differ from persons seen in clinical settings. Typically, college students and volunteers serve as subjects. They are recruited quite differently from the procedures that bring clinical patients to treatment. In analogue research, subjects are actively solicited; course credit or money often are offered as incentives for participation. Apart from the type and severity of target problems that such recruitment procedures are likely to yield, the resulting sample is likely to vary in subject and demographic variables from persons usually seen in clinics.

Third, and related to the above, the motivations and expectancies of persons seen in analogue research are likely to vary from those who seek treatments in outpatient settings. In clinical settings, persons usually seek treatment for relief from a particular problem that may have reached a crisis point. Patients are likely to expect to benefit from the results and to hope for improvements before and during treatment (Frank, 1973). In contrast, subjects in analogue research may not be interested in treatment or in cures for their problems. The expectancies of persons who receive the intervention may be quite different in analogue and clinical research.

Fourth, the therapists who serve in analogue studies usually differ from professional clinicians. Typically, graduate or undergraduate students serve as therapists in analogue research and differ considerably in subject and demographic variables and clinical experience from those who ordinarily provide treatment. The differences may also extend to the credibility of the therapist as a provider of treatment and to the expectations for improvement that therapists generate in the client.

Fifth, the manner of delivering treatment varies greatly from analogue research to clinical settings. In analogue research, treatments often are highly specified and even placed in manual form so that a script can be followed. The treatments tend to be standardized so that all persons in a particular treatment condition or group receive the identical treatment with little or no individualization. Many features of treatment, such as duration of individual sessions, number of sessions, and statements that can be made by the therapist, usually allowed to vary in clinical settings, are often meticulously controlled in analogue research. Moreover, treatment may be administered in a relatively pure form in analogue research because it is applied to a circumscribed problem. Because clinical patients usually bring multifaceted problems to treatment, techniques are often combined and included as part of a multifaceted intervention.

Advantages and Limitations. Analogue research has as its major advantage the capacity to surmount many of the methodological, practical, and ethical issues associated with conducting research in clinical settings. For example, it is difficult to obtain a sufficient number of patients who share similar clinical problems so that homogeneous groups can be formed, to assign patients randomly to conditions, to obtain therapists who are interested in following a protocol rather than conducting their own form of treatment (e.g., "what works"), and so on. The limited experimental control allowed in many clinical settings restricts the type of questions that can be asked in clinical outcome studies. A few questions about treatment require withholding treatment from some persons and administering nonspecific treatment control procedures to others (Kazdin, 1980). Control conditions raise obvious ethical problems when one considers persons who require and who have requested immediate intervention because of their distress.

The priority of analogue research is the experimental question rather than treatment delivery. Thus conditions in analogue research can be arranged in ways that usually would not be feasible in clinical settings. Because of obstacles in clinical research, much of what is known about therapeutic processes and behavior changes is learned from analogue studies. Analogue research provides opportunities to evaluate mechanisms of therapeutic change and to dismantle treatment by looking at basic elements and their contribution to outcome. The ability to control multiple conditions of the experiment and, consequently, to minimize variability in the data permits analogue research to evaluate questions that would otherwise be difficult to study.

Analogue research, however, bears not only benefits but also potential costs. The obvious concern with analogue research is the extent to which the results can be generalized to the clinical setting. Since analogue studies depart in varying degrees from the clinical situation, perhaps the applicability and generality of the results depart commensurately. Generality of results from analogue studies to clinical situations probably is a complex function of the several variables, including the treatment technique, the clinical problem, the characteristics of the patients, and the therapist. Thus the fact that treatment research is conducted under well-controlled analogue conditions does not automatically delimit the results. Although the generality of so-called analogue studies can be examined empirically, relatively little evidence is available to address the issue.

Clinical Trials

Clinical trials refer generally to outcome investigations conducted in clinical settings. In relation to analogue research, the characteristics of clinical trials usually are easily discerned. Instead of students or volunteers, patients who actively seek treatment are included in clinical studies; instead of graduate students, professional therapists and clinicians provide treatment; instead of treatment of relatively mild, subclinical and circumscribed problems, relatively severe or multifaceted clinical disorders are treated. In general, in a clinical trial, treatment is tested under conditions where it would ordinarily be applied.

In addition to allowing direct evaluation of treatment in the clinical situation, clinical trials meet the methodological desiderata of controlled research. Thus, depending on the precise research question, random assignment, double-blind procedures, and placebo controls are used. Because the research is conducted in a clinical setting, methodological compromises and sacrifices often have to be made to meet practical, administrative, and, of course, ethical demands. For example, withholding treatment is especially difficult with a clearly identified clinical problem for a patient in distress. Yet the obstacles can be overcome in varying degrees to address the important questions of extending research to clinical settings.

Clinical trials can vary markedly along a variety of dimensions and in their resemblance to the clinical situation where treatment is ordinarily practiced. In clinical trials, as in analogue research, many features of treatment delivery may be altered to permit evaluation of the intervention. The research exigencies may make the situation slightly different from the clinical situation. Thus, in some clinical trials, the most severely disturbed or impaired patients may be excluded. For example, hypertensive or depressed patients whose dysfunctions are severe may be intentionally excluded from the protocol and placed under immediate care if available treatments with known efficacy exist. Similarly, screening criteria of patients for clinical trials often select patients who have circumscribed or well-delineated dysfunctions rather than diffuse and multiple disorders. In any case, patients included in clinical trials are not always the same as those seen in routine treatment.

Clinical trials are conducted under varying conditions that closely resemble clinical settings, but the conditions are not necessarily identical. In the extreme cases, analogue research and clinical trials can be readily distinguished. As analogue research includes dimensions that approach clinical work or as clinical trials include dimensions that move more toward nonclinic characteristics, however, the distinction may become blurred, if meaningful at all.

There is general agreement that clinical trials represent somewhat of a final achievement or end point in outcome research in terms of the evolution of evaluation strategies (Parloff, 1979). Positive leads from case studies, uncontrolled trials, and analogue studies can culminate in a clinical demonstration. Once a controlled clinical trial attests to the efficacy of treatment, the research process has achieved a major accomplishment. The evidence is considered to attest to the effectiveness of treatment when applied clinically. Special characteristics of controlled clinical trials, however, may greatly delimit the generality of findings from situations where treatment techniques are evaluated experimentally to clinical practice.

General Comments

Case studies, analogue research, and clinical trials represent the kinds of demonstrations that are used to evaluate psychotherapy. These types of research represent an evolutionary methodology in terms of their place in establishing the efficacy of a technique. Initial demonstrations in case studies may provide suggestive evidence for a technique, particularly if some attempt is made to evaluate the intervention. Indeed, a single-case experiment may demonstrate unambiguously that treatment led to change. Analogue research is especially well suited to analyze facets of treatment and to evaluate the underlying mechanism responsible for change, the parameters that influence treatment efficacy, and similar questions requiring careful experimental control.

Clinical trials are especially well suited for examining the effectiveness of alternative techniques under conditions that approximate routine clinical care. The complexities and priorities of the treatment settings make evaluation of subtle questions about particular treatments difficult. Hence theory testing, dissection of treatment, and evaluation of subtle treatment parameters that may alter outcome are usually reserved for analogue research.

Difficulties arise when the results from a particular type of demonstration are interpreted beyond the boundaries of what the study can reasonably accomplish. For example, objections to analogue research are infrequent when particular studies focus on evaluation of the theoretical bases of treatment or on parameters that may influence outcome. Yet when explicit claims are made that the results of analogue research represent the effects likely to be obtained with clinical populations, objections are likely to arise. The clinical utility of treatment is addressed better by a clinical trial where the main thrust of the demonstration is to test the treatment under such conditions.

The purpose of discussing the spectrum of research is two-fold. First, the different types of research raise major issues current in psychotherapy research and reflect new developments. Second, and more important, the spectrum of current research inadequately addresses the questions of critical importance for psychotherapy evaluation. To this latter point I wish to devote the remainder of the paper.

The Hiatus Between Clinical Research and Practice

As noted earlier, clinical trials represent a test of treatments under conditions that closely resemble those evident in clinical settings. The clinical trial is somewhat of an endpoint in the evolutionary step of treatment evaluation. If clinical trials show that psychosocial treatments produce change with a clinical population, the treatment results are generally viewed as demonstrations about the clinical utility of treatment. Yet findings obtained for particular treatments evaluated in clinical trials may not represent the results likely to be obtained in clinical practice. Special characteristics of clinical trials may contribute to the efficacy of treatment. Once the techniques are extended to practice, these characteristics, described below, may be omitted. Consequently, the techniques may not achieve the effects attained in research.

To illustrate the bases for questioning the relevance of clinical research to clinical practice, three major clinical outcome studies are evaluated. The investigations encompass several techniques applied to diverse clinical populations and include the studies by Paul and Lentz (1977), who evaluated social learning and milieu therapies with psychiatric inpatients; by Rush, Beck, Kovacs, and Hollon (1977), who compared cognitive therapy and pharmacotherapy with depressed outpatients; and by Sloane, Staples, Cristol, Yorkston, and Whipple (1975), who evaluated behavior therapy and psychotherapy for outpatients with neurotic or personality disorders. These investigations represent landmark studies for several reasons, including the focus on clinically relevant problems, the comparison of competing treatments, and the evaluation of treatments under conditions more or less typical of clinical care.

Social-Learning Treatment of Psychiatric Patients

Paul and Lentz (1977) compared social-learning and milieu therapies with routine hospital care for chronic psychiatric patients. The investigation included comprehensive assessment procedures to evaluate patient and staff changes over the course of treatment and control over procedures that might have threatened the internal validity of the study. In general, several methodological characteristics were excellent, especially under the circumstances of tremendous administrative and sociopolitical obstacles (see Liberman, 1980).

The social-learning program was based primarily on a token economy where patients received incentives for a variety of adaptive behaviors on the ward (e.g., attending activities, self-care activities, and social interaction). Milieu therapy consisted of organizing the unit so that residents were considered to be responsible for much of their own affairs. Staff expectancies for improvement, patient involvement, and group pressure were major sources of patient motivation. The routine hospital care condition consisted of a traditional state hospital program with patients distributed across several different wards.

The results indicated that both social-learning and milieu programs were effective in improving patients on a large number of measures, including direct behavioral assessment, in the hospital and on measures obtained up to several years after patient release. The social-learning program was consistently more effective on measures in the hospital, discharge of patients, and status in the community over the course of follow-up.[4] In general, the program demonstrated the remarkably potent effects of a token economy in improving chronic psychiatric patients.

Several features of the Paul and Lentz study, apart from the content of the treatments, probably contributed to the success of the program. The features are relevant for evaluating whether the program could be conducted as effectively in other treatment settings. First, the training of the staff to implement the treatments was extensive. Nonprofessional clinical staff received academic training that consisted of carefully planned instruction in the different procedures, using detailed treatment manuals as a guide. Training included opportunities for role-playing, modeling, rehearsal, and feedback. The academic training was followed with on-the-job training in which individual staff observed supervisory staff as models, received supervised practice for their own interactions with patients, and were checked before working independently.

Second, monitoring of treatment was extensive to ensure that the programs were administered as planned. Daily and moment-to-moment data were gathered on staff-patient interaction. Supervisory staff monitored the resulting data daily and provided positive feedback to staff for flawless performance or corrective feedback for departures from the desired procedures. The project included a contingent of professional observers who monitored staff and patients over the entire course of the program. Patient behavior was observed in every waking hour. Constant patient assessment and evaluation of the patient data provided a further check on execution of the program.

Third, the program included several personnel in roles that departed from the usual inpatient program. Among the positions were several interns who helped implement and evaluate the program, persons to monitor staff-patient interaction, professional observers, Ph.D.-level staff to supervise the research, and so on. The mere presence of separate research and clinical staff and Ph.D.-level research supervisors to monitor the day-to-day program was a special feature to ensure proper implementation of the treatments. The goal-directed nature of the project and the evaluation of all persons, including observers, in relation to the overall objective provided an accountability for staff that might be critical to successful implementation of treatment.

Finally, the treatment procedures were relatively complex, as would be expected with techniques that focus on difficult clinical problems. The fact that the treatments were written in manual form certainly

[4] The descriptions of the Paul and Lentz (1977), the Rush et al. (1977), and the Sloane et al. (1975) studies are not intended to summarize the procedures or the results fully. The original sources should be consulted. The purpose of citing these examples is to convey the points they make about the generality of clinical research.

should facilitate extension of the program to other settings. Clinical researchers familiar with therapy manuals, however, will realize that manuals do not specify all of the exigencies that arise in treatment. Indeed, in the Paul and Lentz (1977) study, constant updating of procedures was handled through memoranda to clarify implementation of practices, to answer questions, and so on. Both the recording of subtle day-to-day details and the resources to have knowledgeable personnel were special program features that helped ensure treatment was conducted as intended.

Characteristics such as those mentioned above might be viewed as admirable methodological features and left at that. Yet the meticulous data collection and monitoring system may have major bearing on the clinical impact of treatment and the generality of the results to other clinical settings. The results suggest that a social-learning program can lead to dramatic inhospital and extrahospital changes and can effectively return chronic patients to the community. The demonstration was completed in a clinical setting with seriously disturbed patients. Yet is it reasonable to expect that the results represent the likely effects of such programs in most clinical settings with a similar population? Of course, a definitive answer cannot be provided, but I will argue that the likely answer is no.

One of the major problems of treatment or program evaluation is ensuring the integrity of treatment, i.e., that treatment is carried out as intended (Sechrest et al., 1979). Outcome investigations must evaluate implementation of the treatments carefully to ensure that the procedures are followed. From a methodological standpoint, integrity of treatment is required to provide a veridical test of the techniques and to specify procedures to allow replication. From a clinical standpoint, checks on the integrity of treatment may help ensure the correct execution of treatment. The complex assessment procedures to monitor treatment may be partially reactive for staff and may contribute to adherence to the treatment protocol. It remains an open question whether the results obtained by Paul and Lentz (1977) could be obtained elsewhere without adoption of the excellent features of the program related to training, monitoring, and evaluating. Perhaps the requirements of maintaining the integrity of treatment could not be met in clinical settings for various reasons, including the lack of resources for observing and monitoring daily execution of the treatment by staff and the administrative issues surrounding the control of treatment for purposes of evaluation.

It is important to make no mistake about the evaluation of the Paul and Lentz (1977) investigation. The present comments are not intended in any way to demean the demonstration. Indeed, in many ways the study stands as a model for clinical research. However, many of those excellent features that make it a landmark study threaten to reduce the generality of its results. It would be naive to assume that the investigation demonstrated the effects of a social-learning program per se. The treatment cannot be separated from the extremely elaborate monitoring system that may have partially ensured or contributed to its efficacy.

Cognitive Therapy for Depressed Outpatients

Another example is the study by Beck and his colleagues who compared cognitive therapy and pharmacotherapy to treat unipolar depressed outpatients (Beck, Rush, Shaw, & Emery, 1979; Rush et al., 1977). The investigation is significant because it represents the first controlled study to demonstrate the superiority of psychosocial treatment over pharmacotherapy. In the investigation cognitive therapy was based upon a conceptual model developed over several years by Beck (1976). The therapy focused on the negative cognitive distortions considered to be central to depression. Over the course of treatment, the therapist used a variety of methods to confront the assumptions and cognitive processes that underlay the depressive affect and symptoms. Opportunities were provided to the patient to re-evaluate and correct misconceptions and maladaptive assumptions about experience. The pharmacotherapy in the study consisted of the administration of imipramine, an antidepressant medication.

Both treatments showed significant decreases in depressive symptoms as reflected on self-report measures, observer evaluations, and therapist ratings. Cognitive therapy produced greater changes on self-report and clinical ratings. Follow-up at 3, 6, and 12 months showed that cognitive therapy patients continued to evince greater changes than pharmacotherapy patients (cf. Kovacs, Rush, Beck, & Hollon, 1981; Rush et al., 1977).

A few features of the Rush et al. (1977) study may be critical prerequisites for the success of cognitive therapy and may have implications for extension of this technique to clinical practice. The training of the therapists and the implementation of treatment warrant special scrutiny. Eighteen therapists participated, including psychiatric residents, pre- and postdoctoral clinical psychology trainees, and psychiatrists. Although training was not formally conducted for the entire period, the residents received relevant didactic and instructional experiences as part of training for up to a three-year period. Similarly, the psychology trainees brought considerable background in the general approach before they began training. The extent of the relevant training experiences is not clear because the study was completed prior to a formally developed training program; however, the residents and clinical psychology trainees had extended relevant training experiences associated with treatment and its administration (Beck, Note 1). For participation in the study, all therapists completed at least one supervised case of cognitive therapy. Thus there was also formal clinical training as well.

Along with training, therapists were provided with a detailed treatment manual (Beck, Rush, & Kovacs, Note 2) to convey how the procedures were to be implemented. During the execution of the Rush et al. (1977) study, therapists were supervised on a weekly basis by three clinicians experienced in cognitive therapy. Supervision consisted of one hour per week on a one-to-one basis with the supervisor along with a weekly case conference (Beck, Note 1). Tape recordings of sessions were also checked periodically to evaluate adherence to the treatment protocol.

Overall, the details of the Rush et al. (1977) investigation indicate that therapists were carefully trained and closely supervised to ensure proper execution of treatment. The training and close supervision may be prerequisites to attain effective results. Since completion of the study, more information about the training experiences required for effective delivery of cognitive therapy for depressed patients is available. Beck et al. (1979) have noted that formal training from several months up to two years at a center for cognitive therapy may be essential. Even a three-month intensive crash course, including supervision of treatment of two to three depressed patients, led to less than 25% of the therapists meeting even minimal criteria for competency. Beck et al. (1979) have claimed that cognitive therapy cannot be applied effectively without detailed knowledge of the cognitive model of psychopathology and the theoretical basis of cognitive therapy. Formal training for a protracted period involving didactic instruction and continued clinical supervision are viewed as essential. The pitfalls of conducting treatment without sufficient training and the misuse or misconstruing of specific techniques in certain areas have been described in some detail (Beck et al., 1979).

Beck and his associates deserve credit for examining training requirements essential for the effective application of cognitive therapy. And the monitoring and ongoing supervision of therapists during the Rush et al. (1977) study may represent critical features of the investigation. As with the Paul and Lentz (1977) study, it is appropriate to question whether cognitive therapy, when executed without the therapist-training and research-monitoring procedures, would attain the promising results demonstrated in this study. Replications of the findings in other individual investigations (e.g., Blackburn, Bishop, Glen, Whalley, & Christie, in press; Shaw, 1977) or eventual replications in a large-scale, multi-site, collaborative investigation (e.g., Waskow, 1981) might indicate that persons could be trained in other research settings. Such replications, however, would not address the issue because of the hiatus between research and practice. The different conditions under which treatment is administered would still remain.

Behavior Therapy for Outpatient Treatment

The final illustration of the special characteristic of clinical trials is the investigation by Sloane et al. (1975), also a landmark study in outcome research. This study compared behavior therapy, analytically oriented psychotherapy, and a minimal contact condition for outpatients primarily diagnosed as being neurotic and having personality disorders. Behavior therapy was based upon techniques such as relaxation training, desensitization, and assertive training; analytically oriented psychotherapy focused upon interpretive procedures that were generally nondirective. During the four-month treatment interval, minimal contact patients received telephone contact; later they were assigned to treatment. The results for target symptoms and general areas of functioning indicated that behavior therapy and psychotherapy were no different from each other in efficacy but both were different from the minimal contact group which made little or no change during the no-treatment interval. Over the course of a one-year follow-up, the gains were generally maintained in the active treatment groups.

A few important design features of the investigation may have contributed to the lack of differences between behavior therapy and psychotherapy including the use of heterogeneous subjects, the reliance upon global ratings for many of the measures, and other points (Kazdin & Wilson, 1978b). For present purposes, however, it is important to mention issues that relate to generalizing information from this demonstration to clinical practice.

Sloane et al. (1975) selected three therapists from each conceptual view encompassed by behavior therapy and psychotherapy. Therapists treated patients only in the treatments with which they were experienced. Rather than structuring treatment and narrowly limiting the techniques that could be used, Sloane et al. were interested in studying treatment as ordinarily practiced. Thus, within each treatment condition, therapists were allowed to use "whatever therapeutic techniques they felt to be most appropriate" (p. 81).

General guidelines were provided so that behavior therapy and psychotherapy would be somewhat distinct. For example, the three behavior therapists were encouraged to provide advice, to use relaxation, desensitization, or assertive training as needed, and to avoid interpretations of dreams or symptoms and resistances. Conversely, psychotherapists were encouraged to avoid the use of advice and specific behavioral procedures and encouraged to interpret dreams, symptoms, and resistances and to focus on childhood memories.

Providing only general guidelines and allowing flexibility in the specific techniques are features of the study that take into account clinical realities of how treatment is actually practiced. Patients bring multiple problems to treatment and are treated by therapists who are usually committed to a particular orientation and who apply multiple procedures as needed to achieve changes. Thus, in terms of clinical research, the Sloane et al. study has been regarded by many as exemplary (e.g., Bergin & Lambert, 1978; Marmor, 1975; Strupp, Hadley, & Gomes-Schwartz, 1977).

The demonstration was completed in a clinical setting, by experienced psychotherapists, and with genuine patients. Hence one might expect the results to be highly generalizable to the clinical situation. Yet, for several reasons, the study provides little information that can be generalized to the clinical situation. The initial concern is that the therapies were not well specified and probably could not be replicated. The individual therapists were left on their own to introduce and combine techniques as they saw fit. This independence has methodological as well as clinical implications. First, the greater the leeway allowed, probably the greater the within-therapist variability (i.e., statistical error). The higher the within-therapist variability, of course, the less likely that differences between the two treatments could be detected. Second, the less well specified each of the treatments, the greater the likelihood that the treatments would overlap in substance. For example, behavior therapists were encouraged to use direct advice and to promote direct action; psychotherapists were encouraged to give advice infrequently and only indirectly. Thus therapists for the different treatments in many cases could use the same general techniques but in differing amounts. The net effect would be a diffusion of treatments (Cook & Campbell, 1979), that is, an overlap of the conditions that could lead to the failure to find differences.

From the standpoint of the relevance of the findings for clinical practice, the study has more serious faults. Essentially, one can ask, "What *were* the treatments?" If one of the treatments produced spectacular effects, would we know what was done? And, consequently, could the treatment be replicated in other studies or disseminated to practitioners? The study does not make clear what was done.

Some therapists were said to practice behavior therapy, but there is no technique used in treatment properly called "behavior therapy."

There *are* many different techniques embraced by that term. These techniques are so different from each other that there is little value for research purposes in viewing them as a singular modality of treatment. Even in the Sloane et al. study, the range of techniques included in behavior therapy was large, encompassing carbon dioxide inhalation, medication, and electric shock, not to mention more commonly used procedures such as desensitization and assertive training. The study did not actually investigate a particular technique but rather contrasted two general orientations as carried out by three respective proponents. There is little in the way of concrete information that might be replicated or extended to clinical settings.

In general, the study was conducted under many of the conditions of clinical practice. But the yield, for reasons of the design and the implementation of the treatment, is difficult to discern in terms of developing techniques for clinical practice. Concrete guidelines for what therapists should do with what kinds of patients are not available from the study.

General Comments

The above investigations represent three important clinical studies of several different techniques. The studies were selected as examples in part because of their significance as clinical investigations. Also, extensive information is available from each study either because it was published in book form (Paul & Lentz, 1977; Sloane et al., 1975) or the original article was followed by publication of a text to detail the larger project of which the study was a part (Beck et al., 1979). Hence more information about procedural details is available than is typically the case from journal articles alone.

The studies were highlighted to point to important characteristics of well-controlled clinical trials. Specifically, in clinical trials, investigators often train therapists to special levels of competence, monitor therapist execution of treatment and patient progress over the course of treatment, and supervise treatment sessions closely to ensure the integrity of treatment. The features included in an investigation to monitor and to ensure the correct execution of treatment are quite desirable from the standpoint of research; however, the generality of the results may be restricted to execution of the procedures with the same degree of close supervision and monitoring. Application of the technique without the level of training, of supervision, and of feedback to therapists may yield results that do not mimic those evident in research. In short, in the case of psychosocial techniques, clinical trials do not necessarily provide information about procedures that will be effective in clinical practice. This statement does not negate the value of clinical trials. It is still critical to determine whether treatments implemented with clinical populations can achieve important changes. Something more is needed, however, once techniques have passed the important and necessary test that clinical trials provide.

In terms of external validity of the results, the hiatus from clinical research to clinical practice can be as large as that from analogue research to clinical research. Clinical research and practice differ in many ways. The main point emphasized in the present discussion, however, pertains to the administration of treatment. Procedures utilized to maintain the integrity of treatment in research may not only contribute to the design of the study but may also serve as a necessary medium for achieving therapeutic change with the techniques under investigation. Use of treatment without care to ensure the integrity of treatment may yield results quite different from those evident in research. Thus the generality of findings from clinical research may need to be tested further to determine whether the procedures can be effectively implemented in clinical practice. One means of testing the generality of findings from clinical research is discussed below.

Clinical Replication

Generalizing from Research to Practice

Clinical trials may introduce into the situation special characteristics that depart from most clinical situations where treatment is delivered. The degree of experimental control, of specification of treatment, and of monitoring of treatment administration that characterize research departs from the circumstances of clinical practice. And this is how research should be. The purpose of experimental research is to show what *can* happen under certain well-specified conditions. A separate issue, of obvious importance in clinical research, is whether in fact this is what *does* happen under similar circumstances outside of the context of research.

The training of staff or therapists and the specifying and monitoring of treatment essential for research were illustrated in the Paul and Lentz (1977) and Rush et al. (1977) studies. Yet this level of control, while needed for sound research, raises questions about the generality of the results. The control over treatment administration is not a disadvantage. In the extreme, leaving treatment unspecified can lead to results about unclear procedures that might not be replicable, as illustrated perhaps on the Sloane et al. (1975) study. In general, once a treatment technique has been shown to be effective in a carefully controlled clinical trial, whether the procedures will produce such effects in situations where treatment is less well regulated and monitored is still an open question.

Linking Research and Practice

The generality of results from clinical research to routine treatment administration in clinical practice is a potential problem because of the large hiatus in how treatments are implemented, monitored, and evaluated in these separate contexts. The hiatus can be reduced by increasing the resemblance of clinical research to the conditions of clinical practice. This increased resemblance can be accomplished by altering procedures of clinical practice so they include the conditions of research or by introducing into research more of the characteristics of routine clinical practice. Although the point here is to propose the latter solution to increase the clinical relevance of research, there may be merit in considering the former as well.

Typically, the ways in which treatments are implemented in clinical research and practice differ markedly along several dimensions, including the extent to which therapists are trained to prespecified levels of competence in the techniques they use; treatment is conducted in pure form without combining multiple components of other techniques; treatment is (or can be) specified in manual form to permit consistent use across therapists and patients; therapists are monitored, supervised, and provided with feedback for adherence to the treatment; and patient change is systematically assessed during treatment to evaluate progress. These characteristics help sustain the integrity of treatment and determine whether the desired responses on the part of therapists and patients are attained. Perhaps one solution to the hiatus between clinical research and practice is to alter how clinical practice is conducted. In principle, clinical practice could routinely include procedures to train and retrain therapists to levels of competence in specified treatment techniques shown to be effective in clinical trials. Therapist adherence to treatment manuals might be monitored, and corrective feedback could be provided. And procedures for assessing both therapist execution of treatment and patient responsiveness might be used further to check on practitioners.

Although much might be said in favor of increasing the rigor of clinical practice either through professional regulation or legislation, large-scale changes in treatment delivery are not likely to be feasible.

The monitoring and the evaluation of treatment implementation discussed here consist of close supervision on a daily or weekly basis rather than the somewhat more general licensure or certification requirements that may imply professional competence to practice. Feasibility is only one of the issues that might preclude large-scale monitoring of treatment delivery in clinical settings. Whether the changes in clinical practice that such monitoring would produce are desirable or necessarily in the best interests of patients, practitioners, or the profession is a matter readily subject to debate.

A second alternative may be more feasible to reduce the hiatus between clinical research and practice and to determine if clinical research findings apply to treatment conducted in practice. Once a treatment has been shown to be effective in clinical trials, a field test of treatment can be provided. The field test, referred to here as a *clinical replication,* involves a distinct methodological extension from controlled clinical research. A clinical replication consists of introducing treatment into clinical settings without the controls and monitoring systems characteristic of controlled clinical trials. Obviously, some assessment and evaluation are needed to examine the extent to which treatment effects occur; however, a clinical replication refers to the evaluation of treatment while the methodology for experimental evaluation is purposely loosened.

The purpose of a clinical replication must be seen in the context of other research strategies required to evaluate therapy outcome. Typically, analogue research and clinical trials are devoted to a wide range of outcome questions such as whether a particular treatment is responsible for change, what the relative efficacy of alternative techniques is, and for which types of patients and clinical problems is treatment most effective (see Kazdin, 1980). The questions require meeting the methodological demands raised by such notions as internal, statistical conclusion, construct, and external validity (Cook & Campbell, 1979). Clinical trials examine whether treatment effects can be extended to relevant domains of clinical settings, for example, applications with genuine patients; however, even a clinical trial does not address the issue of the dissemination of treatment to clinical settings where research demands typically are not invoked.

Once clinical trials have shown that treatment is effective, the techniques could be extended in a clinical replication to selected clinics or hospitals that routinely see patients for whom the technique may be applicable. Treatment could be introduced to the therapists using training procedures likely to permit wide circulation, perhaps including workshops, brief courses for continuing education credits, and films to convey treatment procedures. Treatment manuals which convey the general guidelines for treatment and delineate the features of treatment that need to be carefully followed could be provided for the therapists. Adherence to the treatment procedures could be monitored loosely, perhaps even partially self-monitored through therapist self-report at the end of each treatment case or session. Extraneous sources of monitoring, assessment, and feedback might not meet the demands of clinical settings or practitioners and could be intentionally omitted.

A crucial facet of a clinical replication is evaluation of patient response to treatment. The purpose is to evaluate whether the effects attained in clinical practice reach or approximate the level of change found for similar patients in clinical research. The clinical replication would not need to include no-treatment, waiting-list, or analogous-control groups that have been evaluated in research. Evaluation of treatment effects might rely on comparing treated patients with the groups evaluated previously in clinical research. Assessment of patient response to treatment could be completed within clinical settings in several ways, such as self-report measures, interviews, clinical ratings, and informant ratings, some of which already may be used in routine intake procedures. Alternatively, assessment might be conducted by persons outside of the clinical setting so that special resources unavailable to clinical settings or to individual practitioners would not be required.

In general, the characteristics of a clinical replication permit evaluation of patient responsiveness to treatment under conditions that purposely deviate from the rigors of experimentation. The purpose is not to evaluate the internal validity of treatment effects because such demonstrations will have been achieved before the technique is extended to a clinical replication. Rather, the purpose is to assess whether treatments that have been shown to produce specific effects under well-controlled conditions of experimentation (clinical research) can achieve similar ends when the controls are relaxed (clinical practice).

Limitations of Clinical Replication

A clinical replication is designed to address the question of generality of findings from research to practice. Even though clinical replication is proposed as a solution of sorts, it raises its own potential problems. To begin, a clinical replication is not totally devoid of the accoutrements of research. To assess whether treatment can be transplanted from research to practice requires evaluation of some sort. Yet in clinical replication the priorities of treatment administration and service delivery can be maintained. Hence clinical replication represents a critical step between the usual clinical trial and generally unmonitored treatment delivery. The step is important in evaluating whether treatment of demonstrated efficacy can realistically achieve therapeutic effects outside of carefully controlled situations.

Another concern about clinical replication is its dubious methodological status in terms of research design. Researchers might consider the clinical replication as an evaluation method devoid of experimental controls and, consequently, totally limited in the conclusions that can be drawn. Alternatively, practitioners might view the procedure as an attempt of researchers to superimpose artificial constraints on clinical practice. In fact, clinical replication is proposed to address issues of interest to both researchers and practitioners.

For researchers, clinical replication raises important questions about the variables that contribute to treatment efficacy, the vulnerability to degradation of alternative treatments when widely disseminated, and the methods of therapist training. For practitioners, clinical replication permits evaluation of clinical practice as part of a larger research effort to identify techniques of immediate benefit to patients seen in treatment. Restraints characteristic of highly controlled research are relaxed intentionally to evaluate whether treatment under conditions of ordinary practice can produce the desired changes. As discussed here, clinical replication is more of technological than of theoretical significance and, hence, focuses on the genuine problems of producing changes in patients in clinical practice. However, technological problems of extending treatments effectively are likely to generate important insights about the nature of treatments, the limits of practice, and so on.

A clinical replication represents a methodological step further along on a continuum beginning with highly controlled analogue research and passing through clinical trials. Clinical replication, as a step beyond clinical trials, does not answer causal questions about treatment nor meticulously analyze the components of particular techniques according to different treatment evaluation strategies (Kazdin, 1980). Rather, the clinical replication addresses the generality of findings regarding a treatment technique from research to practice.

General Comments

The demonstration of effective psychosocial techniques in analogue research or even in clinical trials may remain of academic interest if these techniques cannot be applied with similar effects in clinical settings. The demands placed upon the therapists in clinical settings, the absence of resources for monitoring treatment, and the overall lack of accountability for adherence to a specified treatment regimen may degrade the effects of treatment once the treatment is not part of well-monitored research.

The variables essential for effective administration of those few psychosocial treatment techniques with reasonable outcome evidence are not known. When techniques are shown to be effective in well-controlled analogue or clinical research, asking whether the technique could be executed effectively in routine clinical practice is still reasonable. The execution of the procedure and the therapist adherence to the techniques may be pivotal for effective outcome. Thus, to complete the process of treatment evaluation, demonstrations are needed to evaluate whether a particular technique can achieve outcome effects that approximate the effects demonstrated in controlled clinical research.

Conclusions

Fundamental issues about therapy outcome continue to be debated. Issues highlighted briefly include the conceptualization of alternative treatments, the criteria for therapy evaluation, and the methods of evaluating existing research. In recent years major advances have been made relating to the specification of treatments, the more comprehensive assessment of clinical disorders, and the range of questions asked about therapy. Also, the types of investigations that are conducted, including single-case studies, analogue research, and clinical trials, provide a broad-based attack on the basic scientific questions about therapeutic change and the clinical effectiveness of treatment.

Even with existing advances, answers to questions about treatments and their effects remain relatively elusive. Indeed, increased sophistication in the methods of investigating therapy has led researchers to eschew the simple questions about treatments and their effects. The difficulties in answering questions about therapy are often attributed to the complexities of the subject matter. The delineation of clinical disorders, the assessment of their change over time, the appropriate focus of treatment, and the dynamic nature of patient-therapist interaction illustrate some of the complexities. Because of the number of variables that cannot easily be controlled, assessed, or narrowly conceptualized, the likelihood that progress will be slow is widely accepted. The repeated call for more research suggests that the field is on the right road but that the journey will be longer than originally thought.

Few doubt that more research following current models will result in some progress. However, it is appropriate to raise basic questions about the conceptualizations and the models of existing research methods and their likely yield. The progression of therapy research for particular clinical disorders or clinical techniques is not clearly mapped in the work of individual investigators or in the field as a whole. As an illustration, tremendous progress has been made in the treatment of anxiety-based disorders. A progression of research can be culled from existing case studies, to explore the techniques, and from existing analogue research, to explore theory and technique development. Also, clinical trials show that treatments elaborated in analogue research can produce change in clinical patients. Both analogue research and clinical trials continue because fundamental questions about the bases of treatment and the limits of effectiveness remain. Little attention, however, has been given to the next step for treatments of anxiety-based disorders, namely, evaluating whether existing techniques can be extended widely and effectively to clinical practice where the treatments are needed. More research alone will not address this question; rather, a different type of research is needed.

For the many areas of treatment where progress has not been as great as for anxiety-based disorders, the priorities for the type of research need to be made explicit. The present paper has suggested an evolutionary model that encompasses different strategies for the development and dissemination of research. The model consists of an overall plan involving basic research, controlled trials under clinic conditions, and clinical replications to extend treatment to practice. An evolutionary progression must be followed, not necessarily in a rigid sequence, but in a systematic fashion so that research on basic questions about treatment has as an end the effective application of treatment in therapeutic practice.

Reference Notes

1. Beck, A. T. Personal communication, April 16, 1981.
2. Beck, A. T., Rush, A. J., & Kovacs, M. *Individual treatment manual for cognitive/behavioral psychotherapy of depression.* University of Pennsylvania School of Medicine, 1975.

References

Agras, W. S., Kazdin, A. E., & Wilson, G. T. *Behavior therapy: Toward an applied clinical science.* San Francisco: W. H. Freeman, 1979.

Alexander, J. F., Barton, C., Schiavo, R. S., & Parsons, B. V. Systems-behavioral intervention with families of delinquents: Therapist characteristics, family behavior, and outcome. *Journal of Consulting and Clinical Psychology,* 1976, *44,* 656–664.

Bandura, A. Self-efficacy: Toward a unifying theory of behavioral change. *Psychological Review,* 1977, *84,* 191–215.

Bandura, A., & Adams, N. E. Analysis of self-efficacy theory of behavioral change. *Cognitive Therapy and Research,* 1977, *1,* 287–310.

Bandura, A., Adams, N. E., & Beyer, J. Cognitive processes mediating behavioral change. *Journal of Personality and Social Psychology,* 1977, *35,* 125–139.

Barlow, D. H. On the relation of clinical research to clinical practice: Current issues, new directions. *Journal of Consulting and Clinical Psychology,* 1981, *49,* 147–155.

Beck, A. T. *Cognitive therapy and emotional disorders.* New York: International Universities Press, 1976.

Beck, A. T., Rush, A. J., Shaw, B. F., & Emery, G. *Cognitive therapy for depression.* New York: Guilford, 1979.

Beidel, D. C., Bellack, A. S., Turner, S. M., Hersen, M., & Luber, R. F. Social skills training for chronic psychiatric patients: A treatment manual. *JSAS Catalog of Selected Documents in Psychology,* 1981, *11,* 36.

Bellack, A. S., & Hersen, M. (Eds.). *Research and practice in social skills training.* New York: Plenum, 1979.

Bellack, A. S., Hersen, M., & Himmelhoch, J. M. Social skills training for depression: A treatment manual. *JSAS Catalog of Selected Documents in Psychology,* 1980, *10,* 92.

Bellack, A. S., Hersen, M., & Kazdin, A. E. *International handbook of behavior modification and therapy.* New York: Plenum, in press.

Bergin, A. E., & Lambert, M. J. The evaluation of therapeutic outcomes. In S. L. Garfield & A. E. Bergin (Eds.), *Handbook of psychotherapy and behavior change: An empirical analysis* (2nd ed.). New York: Wiley, 1978.

Blackburn, I. M., Bishop, S., Glen, A. I. M., Whalley, L. J., & Christie, J. E. The efficacy of cognitive therapy in depression: A treatment trial using cognitive therapy and pharmacotherapy, each alone and in combination. *British Journal of Psychiatry,* in press.

Bootzin, R. R., & Lick, J. R. Expectancies in therapy research: Interpretive artifact or mediating mechanism? *Journal of Consulting and Clinical Psychology,* 1979, *47,* 852–855.

Borkovec, T., & Rachman, S. The utility of analogue research. *Behaviour Research and Therapy,* 1979, *17,* 253–261.

Cook, T. D., & Campbell, D. T. (Eds.). *Quasi-experimentation: Design and analysis issues for field settings.* Chicago: Rand-McNally, 1979.

Endler, N. S., & Magnusson, D. Toward an interactional psychology of personality. *Psychological Bulletin,* 1976, *83,* 956–975.

Eysenck, H. J. An exercise in mega-silliness. *American Psychologist,* 1978, *33,* 517.

Ford, J. D. Therapeutic relationship in behavior therapy: An empirical analysis. *Journal of Consulting and Clinical Psychology,* 1978, *46,* 1302–1314.

Frank, J. D. *Persuasion and healing: A comparative study of psychotherapy* (2nd ed.). Baltimore: Johns Hopkins University Press, 1973.

Gallo, P. S., Jr. Meta-analysis—A mixed meta-phor? *American Psychologist,* 1978, *33,* 515–516.

Garfield, S. L. Psychotherapy: A 40-year appraisal. *American Psychologist,* 1981, *36,* 174–183.

Garfield, S. L., & Bergin, A. E. (Eds.). *Handbook of psychotherapy and behavior change: An empirical analysis* (2nd ed.). New York: Wiley, 1978.

Garfield, S. L., & Kurtz, R. Clinical psychologists in the 1970s. *American Psychologist,* 1976, *31,* 1–9.

Glasgow, R. E., & Rosen, G. M. Self-help behavior therapy manuals: Recent developments and clinical usage. *Clinical Behavior Therapy Review,* 1979, *1,* 1–20.

Gurman, A. S., & Kniskern, D. P. (Eds.). *Handbook of family therapy.* New York: Brunner/Mazel, 1981.

Hayes, S. C. Single case experimental design and empirical clinical practice. *Journal of Consulting and Clinical Psychology,* 1981, *49,* 193–211.

Herink, R. (Ed.), *The psychotherapy handbook.* New York: New American Library, 1980.

Hersen, M., & Barlow, D. H. *Single case experimental designs: Strategies for studying behavior change.* New York: Pergamon, 1976.

Hodgson, R., & Rachman, S. II. Desynchrony in measures of fear. *Behaviour Research and Therapy,* 1974, *12,* 319–326.

Kazdin, A. E. Evaluating the generality of findings in analogue therapy research. *Journal of Consulting and Clinical Psychology,* 1978, *46,* 673–686.

Kazdin, A. E. Nonspecific treatment factors in psychotherapy outcome research. *Journal of Consulting and Clinical Psychology,* 1979, *47,* 846–851. (a)

Kazdin, A. E. Situational specificity: The two-edged sword of behavioral assessment. *Behavioral Assessment,* 1979, *1,* 57–75. (b)

Kazdin, A. E. Sociopsychological factors in psychopathology. In A. S. Bellack & M. Hersen (Eds.), *Research and practice in social skills training.* New York: Plenum, 1979. (c)

Kazdin, A. E. *Research design in clinical psychology.* New York: Harper & Row, 1980.

Kazdin, A. E. Drawing valid inferences from case studies. *Journal of Consulting and Clinical Psychology,* 1981, *49,* 183–192.

Kazdin, A. E. *Single-case research designs: Methods for clinical and applied settings.* New York: Oxford University Press, 1982.

Kazdin, A. E. Symptom substitution, generalization, and response covariation: Implications for psychotherapy outcome. *Psychological Bulletin,* in press.

Kazdin, A. E., & Wilcoxon, L. A. Systematic desensitization and nonspecific treatment effects: A methodological evaluation. *Psychological Bulletin,* 1976, *83,* 729–758.

Kazdin, A. E., & Wilson, G. T. Criteria for evaluating psychotherapy. *Archives of General Psychiatry,* 1978, *35,* 407–416. (a)

Kazdin, A. E., & Wilson, G. T. *Evaluation of behavior therapy: Issues, evidence, and research strategies.* Cambridge, Mass.: Ballinger, 1978. (b)

Kiesler, C. A. Mental health policy as a field of inquiry for psychology. *American Psychologist,* 1979, *35,* 1066–1080.

Kiesler, D. J. Empirical clinical psychology: Myth or reality? *Journal of Consulting and Clinical Psychology,* 1981, *49,* 212–215.

Kovacs, M., Rush, A. J., Beck, A. T., & Hollon, S. D. Depressed outpatients treated with cognitive therapy or pharmacotherapy. *Archives of General Psychiatry,* 1981, *38,* 33–39.

Kratochwill, T. R. (Ed.). *Single-subject research: Strategies for evaluating change.* New York: Academic Press, 1978.

Ledwidge, B. Cognitive behavior modification: A step in the wrong direction? *Psychological Bulletin,* 1978, *85,* 353–375.

Liberman, R. P. A review of Paul and Lentz's *Psychosocial treatment for chronic mental patients: Milieu versus social-learning programs. Journal of Applied Behavior Analysis,* 1980, *13,* 367–371.

Luborsky, L., Singer, B., & Luborsky, L. Comparative studies of psychotherapies: Is it true that "everyone has won and all must have prizes"? *Archives of General Psychiatry,* 1975, *32,* 995–1008.

Marmor, J. Foreword. In R. B. Sloane et al., *Psychotherapy versus behavior therapy.* Cambridge, Mass.: Harvard University Press, 1975.

Marshall, E. Psychotherapy works, but for whom? *Science,* 1980, *207,* 506–508.

Mischel, W. *Personality and assessment.* New York: Wiley, 1968.

Parloff, M. B. Can psychotherapy research guide the policymaker?: A little knowledge may be a dangerous thing. *American Psychologist,* 1979, *34,* 296–306.

Parloff, M. B., Wolfe, B., Hadley, S., & Waskow, I. E. *Assessment of psychosocial treatment of mental disorders: Current status and prospects.* Report by NIMH Working Group, Advisory Committee on Mental Health, Institute of Medicine, National Academy of Sciences, February 1978.

Patterson, G. R., Reid, J. B., Jones, R. R., & Conger, R. E. *A social learning approach to family intervention* (Vol. 1). Eugene, Oregon: Castalia, 1975.

Paul, G. Behavior modification research: Design and tactics. In C. M. Franks (Ed.), *Behavior therapy: Appraisal and status.* New York: McGraw-Hill, 1969.

Paul, G. L., & Lentz, R. J. *Psychosocial treatment of chronic mental patients: Milieu versus social-learning programs.* Cambridge, Mass.: Harvard University Press, 1977.

Phillips, E. L. *The social skills basis of psychopathology: Alternatives to abnormal psychology.* New York: Grune & Stratton, 1978.

President's Commission on Mental Health. *Report to the President* (Vols. 1–4). Washington, D.C.: U.S. Government Printing Office, 1978.

Rachman, S., & Hodgson, R. I. Synchrony and desynchrony in fear and avoidance. *Behaviour Research and Therapy,* 1974, *12,* 311–318.

Rachman, S. J., & Wilson, G. T. *The effects of psychotherapy.* New York: Pergamon, 1980.

Rush, A. J., Beck, A. T., Kovacs, M., & Hollon, S. Comparative efficacy of cognitive therapy and pharmacotherapy in the treatment of depressed outpatients. *Cognitive Therapy and Research,* 1977, *1,* 17–37.

Sechrest, L., West, S. G., Phillips, M. A., Redner, R., & Yeaton, W. Some neglected problems in evaluation research: Strength and integrity of treatments. In L. Sechrest, S. G. West, M. A. Phillips, R. Redner, & W. Yeaton (Eds.), *Evaluation studies: Review annual* (Vol. 4). Beverly Hills: Sage, 1979.

Shaw, B. F. Comparison of cognitive therapy and behavior therapy in the treatment of depression. *Journal of Consulting and Clinical Psychology,* 1977, *45,* 543–551.

Singleton, W. T., Spurgeon, P., & Stammer, R. B. (Eds.). *The analysis of social skill.* New York: Plenum, 1980.

Sloane, R. B., Staples, F. R., Cristol, A. H., Yorkston, N. J., & Whipple, K. *Psychotherapy versus behavior therapy.* Cambridge, Mass.: Harvard University Press, 1975.

Smith, M. L., & Glass, G. V. Meta-analysis of psychotherapy outcome studies. *American Psychologist,* 1977, *32,* 752–760.

Strupp, H. H., & Hadley, S. W. A tripartite model of mental health and therapeutic outcomes. *American Psychologist,* 1977, *32,* 187–196.

Strupp, H. H., & Hadley, S. W. Specific vs. nonspecific factors in psychotherapy. *Archives of General Psychiatry,* 1979, *36,* 1125–1137.

Strupp, H. H., Hadley, S. W., & Gomes-Schwartz, B. *Psychotherapy for better or worse: The problem of negative effects.* New York: Jason Aronson, 1977.

Turner, S., Calhoun, K., & Adams, H. (Eds.). *Handbook of clinical behavior therapy.* New York: Wiley, 1981.

VandenBos, G. R. (Ed.). *Psychotherapy: Practice, research, policy.* Beverly Hills, California: Sage, 1980.

Wahler, R. B., Berland, R. M., & Coe, T. D. Generalization processes in child behavior change. In B. B. Lahey & A. E. Kazdin (Eds.), *Advances in clinical child psychology* (Vol. 2). New York: Plenum, 1979.

Wahler, R. G., & Fox, J. J. Response structure in deviant child–parent relationships: Implications for family therapy. Paper presented to the Nebraska Symposium on Motivation, University of Nebraska, Lincoln, October, 1980. (a)

Wahler, R. G., & Fox, J. J. III. Solitary toy play and time out: A family treatment package for children with aggressive and oppositional behavior. *Journal of Applied Behavior Analysis,* 1980, *13,* 23–39. (b)

Waskow, I. E. On the relevance of clinical trials: Rewards of collaborative outcome research. Paper presented at the Temple University Conference, Psychotherapy Outcome: Current Status and Future Directions, Philadelphia, March, 1981.

Wilkins, W. Desensitization: Social and cognitive factors underlying the effectiveness of Wolpe's procedure. *Psychological Bulletin,* 1971, *76,* 311–317.

Wilkins, W. Expectancies in therapy research: Discriminating among heterogeneous nonspecifics. *Journal of Consulting and Clinical Psychology,* 1979, *47,* 837–845.